THE
BIBLE
STUDY

ALSO BY ZACH WINDAHL

The Bible Study

The Bible Study: Youth Edition

The Bible Study for Kids

Memory Verse Cards

The New Testament Made Easy

See the Good

See the Good Journal

The Best Season Planner

Launch with God

SUNDAY.

THE
BIBLE
STUDY

A ONE-YEAR STUDY OF THE ENTIRE BIBLE
AND HOW IT RELATES TO YOU

ZACH WINDAHL

BETHANYHOUSE

a division of Baker Publishing Group
Minneapolis, Minnesota

© 2017, 2024 by Zach Windahl

Published by Bethany House Publishers
Minneapolis, Minnesota
BethanyHouse.com

Bethany House Publishers is a division of
Baker Publishing Group, Grand Rapids, Michigan

Printed in China

Library of Congress Cataloging-in-Publication Data
Names: Windahl, Zach, author.
Title: The Bible study : a one-year study of the entire Bible and how it relates to you / Zach Windahl.
Description: Minneapolis, Minnesota : Bethany House, a division of Baker Publishing Group, [2024]
Identifiers: LCCN 2024004328 | ISBN 9780764243097 (cloth) | ISBN 9781493446704 (epub)
Subjects: LCSH: Bible—Study and teaching. | Devotional calendars.
Classification: LCC BS600.3 .W54 2024 | DDC 220.6—dc23/eng/20240213
LC record available at https://lccn.loc.gov/2024004328

This book contains original material as well as excerpts from *The Bible Study: Part One: Old Testament* by Zach Windahl, published by The Brand Sunday, 2017; *The Bible Study: Part Two: New Testament* by Zach Windahl, published by The Brand Sunday, 2017; *Sunday School: The Basics* by Zach Windahl, published by The Brand Sunday, 2020; and *The Bible Study: Youth Edition* by Zach Windahl, published by The Brand Sunday, 2019.

Baker Publishing Group publications use paper produced from sustainable forestry practices and post-consumer waste whenever possible.

24 25 26 27 28 29 30   7 6 5 4 3 2 1

CONTENTS

Introduction

I know that God aligned our paths on purpose, and I couldn't be more excited about what He is going to do in your life during this year-long journey together through the Bible.

My prayer is not only for you to have a better understanding of the Word, but that you will also find a better sense of meaning for your life and really understand the heart of our Father. He loves you SO much. It's amazing.

Before we dive into Genesis, I wanted to share a little bit about my journey and how I got here. Who knows, you and I might even have some things in common. We're in this thing called life together. Let's go!

A SEARCH FOR MEANING

Identity.

It's what makes you . . . you.

For many of us, it takes years to figure out who we are and what we want to be. For some it comes easily; for others it takes a lifetime.

We have society, parents, teachers, friends, siblings, girlfriends, boyfriends all telling us how we should live and act. Why is it so easy for them to see it, but so difficult for us to figure it out?

I spent years trying to be the person everyone else wanted me to be. Growing up, people would constantly tell me that I was going to be famous someday and that I should do this or that with my life. It all came from the fact that I was an entrepreneur from an early age and had a pretty unhealthy work ethic to back it. But it didn't matter how unhealthy that work ethic was because I was going to be *famous* someday and be among the elite. Or at least that's what I was told.

So my head grew.

And grew. And grew.

I believed the hype and did all that I could to live it.

You see, I'm a product of my society. I'm a bachelor's degree-graduate who had $70k in student debt from a Christian university that did anything but spark my interest in God—it actually pushed me further away. Little did I know that the darkness inside me at the time didn't like the Light inside the other students. Funny how that happens. So after graduating, I had quite a bad taste in my mouth.

But I kept talking the talk. I wrote two Christian books my senior year but didn't have the nerve to promote them as I should have since I didn't even believe what was coming out of my mouth. I went on to run a clothing line and recording studio with some friends, which I left after a few years. I worked on other entrepreneurial projects after that, but the hard work I was putting into them was not lining up with the success (or lack thereof). Everything that I touched began to fail.

I was "good" though. Or at least that's what I told myself.

In reality, I had no direction for where to go from there. I remember sitting in my car outside of Starbucks talking to my friend Geoff about it. I had never felt so lost in my life. If you know me, you know I always have a plan. But this time I didn't. I was at the bottom. Broken and lost. I had spent the last several years focusing on myself and trying to become the best person I could be. But, to tell you the truth, I'm weak when I try to live life on my own. From the outside, everything looked great, but the inside was a whole different story. I was lacking something. My pride was fully intact, but my heart desired more.

I started to contemplate what all of this was about. I grew up considering myself a Christian, but I had no idea what that truly meant. I hadn't been following God's call at all. I still believed in Him; I just wasn't pursuing Him. I hadn't been to church in over a year for the simple reason that I couldn't stand the majority of Christians I met because I didn't

trust them. They all seemed fake to me. So I sat there thinking.

Is life really all about going to college, getting a job, getting married, having kids, buying new things, and then (hopefully) one day retiring so I can enjoy life?

Really? That's it?

I felt like there should be so much more.

So I spent time looking at religion. Every religion outside of Christianity takes their faith so seriously, it's wild. And then there's us. Many Christians have no idea what the Bible actually says, and a ton of so-called Christian ideals are pretty skewed from the truth. I was fed up.

So I read the Bible. Front to back. In ninety days.

I was blown away by how different the Bible is from how it's presented in a large portion of America. Nothing was lining up. I was confused.

So I went on my own "Search for Meaning" journey. I quit my job and moved to a little beach town on the Sunshine Coast of Australia for nine months to study the Bible for twelve hours per day. That's a pretty big leap, if you ask me. And at twenty-seven years old, it may not have been the wisest of decisions, but I wouldn't change it for anything.

FINDING A FIRM FOUNDATION

My whole reason for this journey was to build a firm foundation in my faith. One that could not be crumbled by society. And that's exactly what I got. Plus more.

And that's my hope for you: that you are able to build a firm foundation in your faith over the next year.

Understanding the Word is one of the most important things you can do.

It doesn't matter what you have done in the past. What matters is now.

God loves you so much and is so delighted that you want to spend time getting to know Him through Scripture.

▶ With all that said, what are you hoping to get out of this study?

Basics of Christianity

Before we get started, we need to build the foundation of our faith. The following seven pillars are the starting point for understanding the Bible and growing in your relationship with God, whether you recently accepted Jesus as your Savior or have been practicing Christianity your entire life.

God the Father and what it means to be a child of God.

Jesus Christ and how He saved you and me.

The Holy Spirit and the power we are given.

The Bible and the story of humanity as a whole.

Prayer and how we communicate with God.

Grace and the favor that is placed upon us.

Community and the importance of doing life with others.

GOD THE FATHER

Also known as Lord God, YHWH, Abba, Elohim, Jehovah, Ancient of Days, Most High, El-Shaddai, Adonai

Who Is God the Father?

First things first. To understand who God is, you need to understand that He consists of three equal persons: God the Father, God the Son, and God the Holy Spirit. This is called the *Trinity*. There is nothing in our reality that we can compare it to, which makes understanding the three-part nature of God fairly difficult. Many theologians have tried to break it down into analogies, such as water, ice, and mist, or all the pieces of an egg: shell, yolk, and egg white. All of which have their own purpose separately as well as their purpose together. Our God, the one true God, is Three in One.

The initial person of the Trinity is God the Father. We see God the Father predominantly in the first section of the Bible, called the Old Testament, where we begin to understand the nature of God. We see Him as holy, faithful, just, and all-knowing, and as a protector, friend, provider; He is a true father figure to His children, pouring out unconditional love on them.

What Does That Mean for Me?

God the Father loves His Son, Jesus, more than anything in the world. Since we have accepted Jesus into our lives and we are now viewed through the lens of Jesus (which we will look at next), God the Father loves us in exactly the same way, as one of His own children. So we are called "children of God" (1 John 3:1). This is the best news ever. No matter what your relationship with your earthly father is, God calls you His child and wants to love you even better.

Not only is God now our eternal Father figure, but all sorts of blessings come along with that. We are loved, provided for, and protected. Scripture says that we are co-heirs (Romans 8:17), new creations (2 Corinthians 5:17), and holy priests (1 Peter 2:5). There is nothing we can do to run away from the love of the Father. It's eternal and unconditional. All we have to do is accept it.

JESUS CHRIST

Also known as Christ, Savior, Messiah, Son of God, Son of Man, Emmanuel, the Word, Redeemer

Who Is Jesus Christ?

The second person of the Trinity is God the Son, Jesus Christ. To understand the importance of Jesus, you need to have a big-picture understanding of the whole story.

In the beginning, God created two people: Adam and Eve. He placed them in an area called the Garden of Eden, which they were to cultivate. In the Garden, Adam and Eve had a perfect relationship with God. One day a serpent came on the scene and convinced them to go against God's plan (God always gives us the choice to obey His Word or not to). . . . Adam and Eve sinned. In Christianity, this event is called the *Fall of Man*, and that one decision changed the course of humanity because it put a barrier between man and God. As a response, God said that one day He would provide a Son through Eve who would crush the serpent's head and the serpent would bite his heel. This may be confusing but stick with me.

Fast-forward in the first book of the Bible, Genesis, we meet a gentleman named Abraham. God said that through Abraham there would be the birth of a new nation, God's chosen people. One of Abraham's sons was named Judah, and God promised that the Savior would come through the line of Judah. A while later, God explains things even more and says that the Savior will be from the line of King David. At this time in history, God's presence resided in the temple (for the most part), and very few people could have a personal relationship with God, as Adam and Eve did before the Fall of Man.

In the second section of the Bible, called the New Testament, we are introduced to a man named Jesus. This is the Messiah, the Savior, the Chosen One whom the people have been waiting for since the Fall. Jesus was there to redeem humanity. He was 100 percent man and 100 percent God.

Jesus was born of a virgin, lived a sinless life, and was crucified for the sins of mankind. The shedding of His sinless blood was necessary to pay for all our sins. So now, if we have accepted Jesus into our heart, when God the Father looks at you and me, He sees His Son, Jesus, spotless and redeemed. Jesus rose from the dead on the third day and ascended to the right hand of the Father in heaven, and will one day return for His "bride," the church, and will restore earth to its original intent forever.

What Does That Mean for Me?

This is incredible news for us because by believing in Jesus alone and turning from our sins, we are saved from God's wrath and given eternal life. We don't have to perform for God to bless us. He loves us as we are.

THE HOLY SPIRIT

Also known as Holy Ghost, Helper, Comforter, Intercessor, Spirit of God, Spirit of Truth, Dove, Presence of God

Who Is the Holy Spirit?

The third person of the Trinity is the Holy Spirit, God's presence and power on earth today. We first see the Holy Spirit hovering over the chaos at the beginning of the Bible before anything or anyone was created. Then we begin to see the Spirit come upon different people throughout the Old Testament, enabling them to do great and wondrous things. In the New Testament, when Jesus was baptized, the Holy Spirit descended from heaven and rested upon Him in the form of a dove. The Spirit remained with Jesus for the rest of His life, which allowed Him to produce good fruit and perform miracles, such as healing the sick, prophesying, and raising people from the dead.

When Jesus left the earth, the Spirit descended upon all his disciples, empowering them to also perform miracles and lead others to Jesus. The Spirit is still present today, alive and active, moving in ways that our minds can't even comprehend.

What Does That Mean for Me?

Just as the Holy Spirit descended upon the disciples back then, He descends upon those of us who believe today and empowers us to do things we can't do on our own. He is our Helper, Teacher, Guide to truth, and He encourages us to share our faith. He gives us spiritual gifts, produces godly characteristics within, and even uses us in supernatural ways to share God's love with others. The more time you spend in God's presence, the more He will use you in incredible ways.

THE BIBLE

Also known as the Word, Word of God, Holy Book, Scripture, Canon, Sword, the Good Book

What Is the Bible?

To put it simply, the Bible is God's Word. It tells the story of God's love for humanity. The Bible is accurate, authoritative, inspired by the Holy Spirit, and applicable to our everyday lives.

The layout of the Bible is a collection of sixty-six books, split into two sections called the Old Testament and the New Testament. The Old Testament contains thirty-nine books that tell the history of God's chosen people, Israel, and the struggles they went through when choosing to do life with and without God's help. The New Testament contains twenty-seven books that describe the life of Jesus and the early church. Even though there are two major sections of the Bible, the overarching theme of the story is God's desire for humanity to know Him, love Him, and trust Him. The Bible ends by telling us about a day in the future when Jesus will return and restore everything.

Why Should I Study the Bible?

The Bible is the most important book you could ever read and study. The more time you spend in it, the more God will speak to you through His Word. Its purpose is to teach you, correct you, and develop you into the person God made you to be. It answers questions, brings clarity, teaches us about God, and shows us that He has a plan for us. The key will be to not get overwhelmed by such a big book. It might not all make sense at first, but keep diving in and your life will be changed for the better.

PRAYER

Also known as Intercession, Invocation, Devotion, Communication, Conversation, Direct Access

What Is Prayer?

Prayer is conversation with God. To put it as simply as possible, prayer is when you talk to God. And you can tell Him everything. He isn't afraid of your thoughts or your situation. Since He is all-knowing, nothing will shock Him. Nothing is too big or too small to pray about because God wants to be involved in every part of your life. You can ask for help, guidance, clarity, forgiveness, wisdom, or just share about how grateful you are. Prayer doesn't have to be long and drawn out. It can be short and sweet if you'd like it to be. All God wants is for you to talk to Him with an open heart and be transparent with your thoughts and feelings.

Why Should I Pray?

Not only is the ability to pray a miracle in itself because you are able to talk directly to the God of the universe, but prayer also changes your life in many other ways too.

Prayer gives us strength.

Prayer leads to breakthroughs.

Prayer makes us more like Jesus.

It builds our relationship with God.

It provides restoration.

It brings forgiveness.

God speaks back to us when we speak to Him.

GRACE

Also known as Favor, Acceptance, Purpose, Kindness, Blessing, Compassion, Mercy

What Is Grace?

Grace is the unmerited favor of God upon our lives. It's what saves us. There is nothing we can do to earn God's grace. It's a free gift from Him.

Why Is Grace Important?

To understand God's grace, think back to before you accepted Jesus into your heart. As a sinner, guilty of breaking God's laws and deserving of death, the only way to redeem your soul was through Jesus.

Enter grace.

When we trust in Jesus to save us, God by His grace forgives us of our sins and transforms us into new creations completely—the old is gone, the new has come. And although we still sin and make mistakes, grace also equips us to walk out the plans God has for our lives. We don't deserve grace, but God gives it to us anyway because He loves us unconditionally.

COMMUNITY

Also known as Body, Church, Gathering of Saints, Bride of Christ, Assembling of Believers

What Is Community?

Christian community is special. There's nothing like it when it's done well. Christian community refers to a group of people who have been united through faith in Jesus. It's the church, whether big or small. Community functions to support people in their faith journey and to grow together. It's a safe place for people to be taught, encouraged, and corrected in their faith.

Why Should I Be Part of a Church Community?

Every Christian should be part of a church community because the Christian faith was not meant to be lived alone. Life is meant to be done with others. And getting plugged into a solid Christian community will only push you further along in your relationship with God. A healthy community will help you when you are down, build you up, be a shoulder to cry on, celebrate alongside you, and answer your questions about God.

Once you pick a church community in your area that you want to be a part of, there are multiple ways you can get involved. You can serve on a team, attend a small group, take a next-steps class, or just begin by having meals with other people in the community. If you don't know where to start, ask a church staff member and they can help point you in the right direction.

Salvation

By now you should have a good understanding of the basics and what it means to walk out a Christian lifestyle. If you have not already done so, the next step on your faith journey is to begin a personal relationship with God whereby you will be saved from the consequences of your sins. This is called salvation.

As Christians, we are saved by grace through faith in Jesus Christ. Jesus died and rose again to pay the price for our sins. Salvation doesn't come from our good deeds or by doing anything special; it's a free gift from God because He loves us so much. We need to turn away from our sins, believe that Jesus Christ is God's Son and our Savior, and submit to Him as Lord of our lives. By doing so, we receive salvation and eternal life. How awesome is that!

If this is something you want for your life, repeat this prayer:

Jesus, I believe that you are the Son of God and Savior of the world. I believe that you died for my sins and rose from the dead. I believe that through your sacrifice, I am a new person. Forgive me for my sin and fill me with your Spirit. Today, I choose to follow you for the rest of my life as Lord of my life. Amen.

NEXT STEPS

- Tell another Christian that you accepted Jesus into your life.
- Find a local church community to get plugged into.
- Try to read the Bible and spend time in prayer for at least ten to fifteen minutes every day.
- Get baptized.

Big-Picture Story of the Bible

One of the most important things you can do for your faith is have a big-picture understanding of the Bible as a whole. Then, as you're diving deeper, you'll have a big-picture understanding of each book to always bring it back to the full story that's taking place: the story of God's love for His people.

In one sentence, the main theme of Scripture is that God created something beautiful, humanity chose to go against His plan, and the rest of the story is about God chasing after His people, of which we see a full restoration at the end.

Paradise → disobedience →
restoration → paradise again

To start things off, in the beginning of the Bible we see that there is chaos all over the earth, and out of that chaos God begins to create order through light and land and life. He creates an area called the Garden of Eden, which is a place of perfection. He was present, and everything inside the Garden was performing as originally intended. God created a man named Adam and a woman named Eve. They were ordered to create a family and cultivate the Garden. They were to fill the earth and live in perfect relationship with God.

But one day a serpent came on the scene and convinced them to go against God's plan. God always gives us a choice—to obey His Word or not to. To choose good or evil. And Adam and Eve chose evil. They sinned.

In Christianity, this event is called the *Fall of Man*, and that single decision changed the course of humanity because it put a barrier between man and God. As a response, God said that one day He would create through Eve a Son who would redeem all of humanity in the eyes of God.

Fast-forward in the story and we meet a man named Abraham. God said that through Abraham He was going to birth a new nation, God's chosen people, covered in God's blessings. And it was through his family that God was going to bring restoration to the world. The family grows and grows, and the people end up in slavery in Egypt. God uses a man named Moses to set them free from slavery through a series of miracles.

The people wander through the desert for a while, and God gives them what is called the Law. It's basically a rulebook on how to live a holy life that is pleasing to God. By following the Law, the Israelites stood out among their neighbors and represented a new, countercultural way to live.

We see God's people, the Israelites, arrive at an area called the Promised Land, "a land flowing with milk and honey" (Joshua 5:6). It was supposed to be amazing, but the people continued to disobey God and chose evil instead.

In the rest of the Old Testament, which is the first section of the Bible, we see the story line going up and down and up and down. The people chose good and then evil, then good, then evil. It's a pattern that reflects their wanting to do things on their own instead of following what they have been told is right.

The Israelites end up in exile again, this time under the new world power called Babylon. We're then introduced to a bunch of prophets who speak to the people on behalf of God, saying that if they turn from evil He will deliver them through a Messiah, a Savior. But that person didn't show up right away. It was quite a while before He did, actually. God went silent for four hundred years. It's not that He wasn't moving, He just wasn't speaking to His people.

In the first four books of the New Testament, the Gospels, we meet Jesus, and He teaches us how to bring the kingdom of God into our everyday life.

The authorities didn't like Jesus, though, and didn't believe He was truly the Son of God, so they killed Him. But little did they know that the shedding of His sinless blood was necessary because on the cross He bore the sins of all of humanity to cancel out our debt. So now, if we accept Jesus into our heart, when God the Father looks at you and me, He sees His Son, Jesus, spotless and redeemed.

Jesus then rose from the dead on the third day. This is the most significant moment in all of history, and our lives will never be the same because of it. Jesus defeated the power of sin and death, saving us, and allowing us to have a future alongside Him. Because of this, we become new creations spiritually.

The Bible's story ends with full restoration of the earth itself; all the evil we allowed to consume it will be destroyed.

So that's the big-picture story of the Bible. Once you know that, you are able to see how each story throughout the Bible plays into the big picture and, ultimately, what part you have to play in it all.

THE

BIBLE
STUDY

How to Use *The Bible Study*

The Bible Study is a year-long journey through the Word of God. We will hold your hand as you read from Genesis through Revelation. All you need is this workbook and a Bible. The content is suitable for any believer. No matter the length or depth of your relationship with Jesus, it's for you.

Every week you will be studying one to four books of the Bible, depending on their size. Don't worry, I spaced them out so it's manageable.

WEEKLY BREAKDOWN

1 In this workbook, read the first page about each biblical book you'll be studying in order to get the basics of what you are about to dive into (e.g., author, date, key verse).

2 Read the selected book(s) of the Bible at your own pace, ranging from one to four hours of reading time.

3 Then you will spend roughly an hour answering the questions from the workbook, digging a little deeper into the text and learning how to apply the books to your life.

That's it! That's all I've got for you. Enjoy your first book!

—Z

PS: Just like you, I want to know the truth, so I spend a lot of my time soaking in the Word of God and researching views of scholarly believers around the world. I love studying, really. It brings me to life. With that said, this study is a compilation of material I have gathered over the last few years and simplified it to help better your understanding of the text (and mine). I am by no means an expert or a scholar. I just love helping people further their faith in Jesus Christ, our Lord and Savior.

Option A

Weekly Study Plan

For those who prefer a flexible reading plan every week.

☐ Weeks 1 & 2: Genesis

☐ Weeks 3 & 4: Exodus

☐ Week 5: Leviticus

☐ Week 6: Numbers

☐ Week 7: Deuteronomy

☐ Week 8: Joshua

☐ Week 9: Judges & Ruth

☐ Week 10: 1 Samuel

☐ Week 11: 2 Samuel

☐ Week 12: 1 Kings

☐ Week 13: 2 Kings

☐ Week 14: 1 & 2 Chronicles

☐ Week 15: Ezra & Nehemiah

☐ Week 16: Esther

☐ Week 17: Job

☐ Week 18: Psalms & Proverbs Overview

☐ Week 19: Ecclesiastes

☐ Week 20: Song of Songs

☐ Weeks 21 & 22: Isaiah

☐ Weeks 23 & 24: Jeremiah & Lamentations

☐ Week 25: Ezekiel

☐ Week 26: Daniel

☐ Week 27: Hosea & Joel

☐ Week 28: Amos & Obadiah

☐ Week 29: Jonah & Micah

☐ Week 30: Nahum & Habakkuk

☐ Week 31: Zephaniah & Haggai

☐ Week 32: Zechariah & Malachi

☐ Week 33: BREAK

☐ Week 34: Matthew

☐ Week 35: Mark

☐ Week 36: Luke

☐ Week 37: John

☐ Week 38: Acts

☐ Week 39: Romans

☐ Week 40: 1 Corinthians

☐ Week 41: 2 Corinthians

☐ Week 42: Galatians

☐ Week 43: Ephesians

☐ Week 44: Philippians & Colossians

☐ Week 45: 1 & 2 Thessalonians

☐ Week 46: 1 & 2 Timothy

☐ Week 47: Titus & Philemon

☐ Week 48: Hebrews

☐ Week 49: James

☐ Week 50: 1 & 2 Peter

☐ Week 51: 1, 2, 3 John & Jude

☐ Week 52: Revelation

Option B

Daily Study Plan

This is for those who need a little more structure every day.

- ☐ Day 1: Genesis 1–3
- ☐ Day 2: Genesis 4–6
- ☐ Day 3: Genesis 7–9
- ☐ Day 4: Genesis 10–12
- ☐ Day 5: Genesis 13–15
- ☐ Day 6: Genesis 16–18
- ☐ Day 7: Genesis 19–21
- ☐ Day 8: Genesis 22–24
- ☐ Day 9: Genesis 25–27
- ☐ Day 10: Genesis 28–30
- ☐ Day 11: Genesis 31–33
- ☐ Day 12: Genesis 34–36
- ☐ Day 13: Genesis 37–39
- ☐ Day 14: Genesis 40–42
- ☐ Day 15: Genesis 43–45
- ☐ Day 16: Genesis 46–48
- ☐ Day 17: Genesis 49–50
- ☐ Day 18: Exodus 1–3
- ☐ Day 19: Exodus 4–6
- ☐ Day 20: Exodus 7–9
- ☐ Day 21: Exodus 10–12
- ☐ Day 22: Exodus 13–15

- ☐ Day 23: Exodus 16–18
- ☐ Day 24: Exodus 19–21
- ☐ Day 25: Exodus 22–24
- ☐ Day 26: Exodus 25–27
- ☐ Day 27: Exodus 28–30
- ☐ Day 28: Exodus 31–33
- ☐ Day 29: Exodus 34–36
- ☐ Day 30: Exodus 37–40
- ☐ Day 31: Leviticus 1–3
- ☐ Day 32: Leviticus 4–6
- ☐ Day 33: Leviticus 7–9
- ☐ Day 34: Leviticus 10–12
- ☐ Day 35: Leviticus 13–15
- ☐ Day 36: Leviticus 16–18
- ☐ Day 37: Leviticus 19–21
- ☐ Day 38: Leviticus 22–24
- ☐ Day 39: Leviticus 25–27
- ☐ Day 40: Numbers 1–3
- ☐ Day 41: Numbers 4–6
- ☐ Day 42: Numbers 7–9
- ☐ Day 43: Numbers 10–12
- ☐ Day 44: Numbers 13–15

- ☐ Day 45: Numbers 16–18
- ☐ Day 46: Numbers 19–21
- ☐ Day 47: Numbers 22–24
- ☐ Day 48: Numbers 25–27
- ☐ Day 49: Numbers 28–30
- ☐ Day 50: Numbers 31–33
- ☐ Day 51: Numbers 34–36
- ☐ Day 52: Deuteronomy 1–3
- ☐ Day 53: Deuteronomy 4–6
- ☐ Day 54: Deuteronomy 7–9
- ☐ Day 55: Deuteronomy 10–12
- ☐ Day 56: Deuteronomy 13–15
- ☐ Day 57: Deuteronomy 16–18
- ☐ Day 58: Deuteronomy 19–21
- ☐ Day 59: Deuteronomy 22–24
- ☐ Day 60: Deuteronomy 25–27
- ☐ Day 61: Deuteronomy 28–30
- ☐ Day 62: Deuteronomy 31–34
- ☐ Day 63: Joshua 1–3
- ☐ Day 64: Joshua 4–6
- ☐ Day 65: Joshua 7–9
- ☐ Day 66: Joshua 10–12

- ☐ Day 67: Joshua 13–15
- ☐ Day 68: Joshua 16–18
- ☐ Day 69: Joshua 19–21
- ☐ Day 70: Joshua 22–24
- ☐ Day 71: Judges 1–3
- ☐ Day 72: Judges 4–6
- ☐ Day 73: Judges 7–9
- ☐ Day 74: Judges 10–12
- ☐ Day 75: Judges 13–15
- ☐ Day 76: Judges 16–18
- ☐ Day 77: Judges 19–21
- ☐ Day 78: Ruth 1–2
- ☐ Day 79: Ruth 3–4
- ☐ Day 80: 1 Samuel 1–3
- ☐ Day 81: 1 Samuel 4–6
- ☐ Day 82: 1 Samuel 7–9
- ☐ Day 83: 1 Samuel 10–12
- ☐ Day 84: 1 Samuel 13–15
- ☐ Day 85: 1 Samuel 16–18
- ☐ Day 86: 1 Samuel 19–21
- ☐ Day 87: 1 Samuel 22–24
- ☐ Day 88: 1 Samuel 25–27
- ☐ Day 89: 1 Samuel 28–31
- ☐ Day 90: 2 Samuel 1–3
- ☐ Day 91: 2 Samuel 4–6
- ☐ Day 92: 2 Samuel 7–9
- ☐ Day 93: 2 Samuel 10–12
- ☐ Day 94: 2 Samuel 13–15
- ☐ Day 95: 2 Samuel 16–18

- ☐ Day 96: 2 Samuel 19–21
- ☐ Day 97: 2 Samuel 22–24
- ☐ Day 98: 1 Kings 1–2
- ☐ Day 99: 1 Kings 3–4
- ☐ Day 100: 1 Kings 5–6
- ☐ Day 101: 1 Kings 7–8
- ☐ Day 102: 1 Kings 9–10
- ☐ Day 103: 1 Kings 11–12
- ☐ Day 104: 1 Kings 13–14
- ☐ Day 105: 1 Kings 15–16
- ☐ Day 106: 1 Kings 17–18
- ☐ Day 107: 1 Kings 19–20
- ☐ Day 108: 1 Kings 21–22
- ☐ Day 109: 2 Kings 1–2
- ☐ Day 110: 2 Kings 3–4
- ☐ Day 111: 2 Kings 5–6
- ☐ Day 112: 2 Kings 7–8
- ☐ Day 113: 2 Kings 9–10
- ☐ Day 114: 2 Kings 11–12
- ☐ Day 115: 2 Kings 13–14
- ☐ Day 116: 2 Kings 15–16
- ☐ Day 117: 2 Kings 17–18
- ☐ Day 118: 2 Kings 19–20
- ☐ Day 119: 2 Kings 21–22
- ☐ Day 120: 2 Kings 23–25
- ☐ Day 121: 1 Chronicles 1–3
- ☐ Day 122: 1 Chronicles 4–6
- ☐ Day 123: 1 Chronicles 7–9
- ☐ Day 124: 1 Chronicles 10–12

- ☐ Day 125: 1 Chronicles 13–15
- ☐ Day 126: 1 Chronicles 16–18
- ☐ Day 127: 1 Chronicles 19–21
- ☐ Day 128: 1 Chronicles 22–24
- ☐ Day 129: 1 Chronicles 25–27
- ☐ Day 130: 1 Chronicles 28–29
- ☐ Day 131: 2 Chronicles 1–3
- ☐ Day 132: 2 Chronicles 4–6
- ☐ Day 133: 2 Chronicles 7–9
- ☐ Day 134: 2 Chronicles 10–12
- ☐ Day 135: 2 Chronicles 13–15
- ☐ Day 136: 2 Chronicles 16–18
- ☐ Day 137: 2 Chronicles 19–21
- ☐ Day 138: 2 Chronicles 22–24
- ☐ Day 139: 2 Chronicles 25–27
- ☐ Day 140: 2 Chronicles 28–30
- ☐ Day 141: 2 Chronicles 31–33
- ☐ Day 142: 2 Chronicles 34–36
- ☐ Day 143: Ezra 1–3
- ☐ Day 144: Ezra 4–7
- ☐ Day 145: Ezra 8–10
- ☐ Day 146: Nehemiah 1–3
- ☐ Day 147: Nehemiah 4–5
- ☐ Day 148: Nehemiah 6–8
- ☐ Day 149: Nehemiah 9–11
- ☐ Day 150: Nehemiah 12–13
- ☐ Day 151: Esther 1–3
- ☐ Day 152: Esther 4–6
- ☐ Day 153: Esther 7–10

- ☐ Day 154: Job 1–5
- ☐ Day 155: Job 6–10
- ☐ Day 156: Job 11–15
- ☐ Day 157: Job 16–20
- ☐ Day 158: Job 21–25
- ☐ Day 159: Job 26–30
- ☐ Day 160: Job 31–35
- ☐ Day 161: Job 36–40
- ☐ Day 162: Job 41–42
- ☐ Day 163: Psalms 1–6
- ☐ Day 164: Psalms 7–12
- ☐ Day 165: Psalms 13–18
- ☐ Day 166: Psalms 19–24
- ☐ Day 167: Psalms 25–30
- ☐ Day 168: Psalms 31–36
- ☐ Day 169: Psalms 37–42
- ☐ Day 170: Psalms 43–48
- ☐ Day 171: Psalms 49–54
- ☐ Day 172: Psalms 55–60
- ☐ Day 173: Psalms 61–66
- ☐ Day 174: Psalms 67–72
- ☐ Day 175: Psalms 73–78
- ☐ Day 176: Psalms 79–84
- ☐ Day 177: Psalms 85–90
- ☐ Day 178: Psalms 91–96
- ☐ Day 179: Psalms 97–102
- ☐ Day 180: Psalms 103–108
- ☐ Day 181: Psalms 109–114
- ☐ Day 182: Psalms 115–120

- ☐ Day 183: Psalms 121–126
- ☐ Day 184: Psalms 127–132
- ☐ Day 185: Psalms 133–138
- ☐ Day 186: Psalms 139–144
- ☐ Day 187: Psalms 145–150
- ☐ Day 188: Proverbs 1–4
- ☐ Day 189: Proverbs 5–8
- ☐ Day 190: Proverbs 9–12
- ☐ Day 191: Proverbs 13–16
- ☐ Day 192: Proverbs 17–20
- ☐ Day 193: Proverbs 21–24
- ☐ Day 194: Proverbs 25–28
- ☐ Day 195: Proverbs 29–31
- ☐ Day 196: Ecclesiastes 1–4
- ☐ Day 197: Ecclesiastes 5–8
- ☐ Day 198: Ecclesiastes 9–12
- ☐ Day 199: Song of Songs 1–4
- ☐ Day 200: Song of Songs 5–8
- ☐ Day 201: Isaiah 1–3
- ☐ Day 202: Isaiah 4–6
- ☐ Day 203: Isaiah 7–9
- ☐ Day 204: Isaiah 10–12
- ☐ Day 205: Isaiah 13–15
- ☐ Day 206: Isaiah 16–18
- ☐ Day 207: Isaiah 19–21
- ☐ Day 208: Isaiah 22–24
- ☐ Day 209: Isaiah 25–27
- ☐ Day 210: Isaiah 28–30
- ☐ Day 211: Isaiah 31–33

- ☐ Day 212: Isaiah 34–36
- ☐ Day 213: Isaiah 37–39
- ☐ Day 214: Isaiah 40–42
- ☐ Day 215: Isaiah 43–45
- ☐ Day 216: Isaiah 46–48
- ☐ Day 217: Isaiah 49–51
- ☐ Day 218: Isaiah 52–54
- ☐ Day 219: Isaiah 55–57
- ☐ Day 220: Isaiah 58–61
- ☐ Day 221: Isaiah 62–64
- ☐ Day 222: Isaiah 65–66
- ☐ Day 223: Jeremiah 1–3
- ☐ Day 224: Jeremiah 4–6
- ☐ Day 225: Jeremiah 7–9
- ☐ Day 226: Jeremiah 10–12
- ☐ Day 227: Jeremiah 13–15
- ☐ Day 228: Jeremiah 16–18
- ☐ Day 229: Jeremiah 19–21
- ☐ Day 230: Jeremiah 22–24
- ☐ Day 231: Jeremiah 25–27
- ☐ Day 232: Jeremiah 28–30
- ☐ Day 233: Jeremiah 31–33
- ☐ Day 234: Jeremiah 34–36
- ☐ Day 235: Jeremiah 37–39
- ☐ Day 236: Jeremiah 40–42
- ☐ Day 237: Jeremiah 43–45
- ☐ Day 238: Jeremiah 46–48
- ☐ Day 239: Jeremiah 49–52
- ☐ Day 240: Lamentations 1–2

☐ Day 241: Lamentations 3–5   ☐ Day 270: Obadiah, Jonah   ☐ Day 299: Mark 15–16

☐ Day 242: Ezekiel 1–3   ☐ Day 271: Micah   ☐ Day 300: Luke 1–2

☐ Day 243: Ezekiel 4–6   ☐ Day 272: Nahum, Habakkuk   ☐ Day 301: Luke 3–4

☐ Day 244: Ezekiel 7–9   ☐ Day 273: Zephaniah, Haggai   ☐ Day 302: Luke 5–6

☐ Day 245: Ezekiel 10–12   ☐ Day 274: Zechariah 1–5   ☐ Day 303: Luke 7–8

☐ Day 246: Ezekiel 13–15   ☐ Day 275: Zechariah 6–10   ☐ Day 304: Luke 9–10

☐ Day 247: Ezekiel 16–18   ☐ Day 276: Zechariah 11–14   ☐ Day 305: Luke 11–12

☐ Day 248: Ezekiel 19–21   ☐ Day 277: Malachi   ☐ Day 306: Luke 13–14

☐ Day 249: Ezekiel 22–24   ☐ Day 278: Matthew 1–2   ☐ Day 307: Luke 15–16

☐ Day 250: Ezekiel 25–27   ☐ Day 279: Matthew 3–4   ☐ Day 308: Luke 17–18

☐ Day 251: Ezekiel 28–30   ☐ Day 280: Matthew 5–6   ☐ Day 309: Luke 19–20

☐ Day 252: Ezekiel 31–33   ☐ Day 281: Matthew 7–8   ☐ Day 310: Luke 21–22

☐ Day 253: Ezekiel 34–36   ☐ Day 282: Matthew 9–10   ☐ Day 311: Luke 23–24

☐ Day 254: Ezekiel 37–39   ☐ Day 283: Matthew 11–12   ☐ Day 312: John 1–2

☐ Day 255: Ezekiel 40–42   ☐ Day 284: Matthew 13–14   ☐ Day 313: John 3–4

☐ Day 256: Ezekiel 43–45   ☐ Day 285: Matthew 15–16   ☐ Day 314: John 5–6

☐ Day 257: Ezekiel 46–48   ☐ Day 286: Matthew 17–18   ☐ Day 315: John 7–8

☐ Day 258: Daniel 1–2   ☐ Day 287: Matthew 19–20   ☐ Day 316: John 9–10

☐ Day 259: Daniel 3–4   ☐ Day 288: Matthew 21–22   ☐ Day 317: John 11–12

☐ Day 260: Daniel 5–6   ☐ Day 289: Matthew 23–24   ☐ Day 318: John 13–14

☐ Day 261: Daniel 7–8   ☐ Day 290: Matthew 25–26   ☐ Day 319: John 15–16

☐ Day 262: Daniel 9–10   ☐ Day 291: Matthew 27–28   ☐ Day 320: John 17–18

☐ Day 263: Daniel 11–12   ☐ Day 292: Mark 1–2   ☐ Day 321: John 19–21

☐ Day 264: Hosea 1–5   ☐ Day 293: Mark 3–4   ☐ Day 322: Acts 1–3

☐ Day 265: Hosea 6–10   ☐ Day 294: Mark 5–6   ☐ Day 323: Acts 4–6

☐ Day 266: Hosea 11–14   ☐ Day 295: Mark 7–8   ☐ Day 324: Acts 7–9

☐ Day 267: Joel   ☐ Day 296: Mark 9–10   ☐ Day 325: Acts 10–12

☐ Day 268: Amos 1–4   ☐ Day 297: Mark 11–12   ☐ Day 326: Acts 13–15

☐ Day 269: Amos 5–9   ☐ Day 298: Mark 13–14   ☐ Day 327: Acts 16–18

- ☐ Day 328: Acts 19–21
- ☐ Day 329: Acts 22–24
- ☐ Day 330: Acts 25–28
- ☐ Day 331: Romans 1–3
- ☐ Day 332: Romans 4–6
- ☐ Day 333: Romans 7–9
- ☐ Day 334: Romans 10–12
- ☐ Day 335: Romans 13–16
- ☐ Day 336: 1 Corinthians 1–3
- ☐ Day 337: 1 Corinthians 4–6
- ☐ Day 338: 1 Corinthians 7–9
- ☐ Day 339: 1 Corinthians 10–12
- ☐ Day 340: 1 Corinthians 13–16
- ☐ Day 341: 2 Corinthians 1–4

- ☐ Day 342: 2 Corinthians 5–8
- ☐ Day 343: 2 Corinthians 9–13
- ☐ Day 344: Galatians
- ☐ Day 345: Ephesians
- ☐ Day 346: Philippians
- ☐ Day 347: Colossians
- ☐ Day 348: 1 Thessalonians, 2 Thessalonians
- ☐ Day 349: 1 Timothy 1–6
- ☐ Day 350: 2 Timothy 1–4
- ☐ Day 351: Titus, Philemon
- ☐ Day 352: Hebrews 1–4
- ☐ Day 353: Hebrews 5–8
- ☐ Day 354: Hebrews 9–13

- ☐ Day 355: James
- ☐ Day 356: 1 Peter
- ☐ Day 357: 2 Peter
- ☐ Day 358: 1 John
- ☐ Day 359: 2 John, 3 John, Jude
- ☐ Day 360: Revelation 1–4
- ☐ Day 361: Revelation 5–8
- ☐ Day 362: Revelation 9–12
- ☐ Day 363: Revelation 13–16
- ☐ Day 364: Revelation 17–20
- ☐ Day 365: Revelation 21–22

OLD TESTAMENT

Genesis—Malachi

Pentateuch	Historical	Wisdom	Prophetic
Genesis	Joshua	Job	Isaiah
Exodus	Judges	Psalms	Jeremiah
Leviticus	Ruth	Proverbs	Lamentations
Numbers	1 Samuel	Ecclesiastes	Ezekiel
Deuteronomy	2 Samuel	Song of Songs	Daniel
	1 Kings		Hosea
	2 Kings		Joel
	1 Chronicles		Amos
	2 Chronicles		Obadiah
	Ezra		Jonah
	Nehemiah		Micah
	Esther		Nahum
			Habakkuk
			Zephaniah
			Haggai
			Zechariah
			Malachi

GENESIS

AUTHOR
Genesis and the rest of the Pentateuch (the first five books of the Bible), as a whole, were written by Moses.

DATE
Genesis was written between the Exodus out of Egypt in 1446 BC and the conquest into the Promised Land in 1406 BC. First Kings 6:1 gives us insight into those dates by stating that Solomon began to build the temple 480 years after the Exodus; we know Solomon began his reign in 970 BC, and it was the fourth year of his reign, putting the Exodus at 1446 BC.

AUDIENCE
Genesis was written to God's chosen people, the Israelites. They were in slavery for 400 years, so their entire history had been wiped out and they were force-fed Egyptian history instead.

REASON
Moses teaches them their heritage and redirects their view of who God really is.

THEME
Creation, the flood, the patriarchs, and God's plan of redemption.

KEY VERSES
"I will make you into a great nation, and I will bless you; I will make your name great, and you will be a blessing. I will bless those who bless you, and whoever curses you I will curse; and all peoples on earth will be blessed through you" (Genesis 12:2–3 NIV).

SECTIONS
Creation (ch. 1–2), the Fall (ch. 3–5), the flood (ch. 6–10), Abraham (ch. 11–20), Isaac (ch. 21–26), Jacob (ch. 27–36), Joseph (ch. 37–50).

KEY WORDS / PHRASES
Covenant, bless, sin, God said

STORY OVERVIEW

Genesis is the starting point for all of humanity. This book is required reading to understand the rest of the Bible. It introduces characters and topics that depict our entire history.

Genesis is the first part of a five-part section of the Bible called the Pentateuch (which is Greek for "five books") or you might have heard it referred to as the Torah, meaning "Instructions," in Hebrew. The Torah is the basis for all of Judaism and is many times considered to be "the Law" in the New Testament. The Law was Jewish people's go-to guide—their life manual.

The book of Genesis starts off at the very beginning of time. Before the stars, the sea, and even the human race. But in the beginning, God was present. He was there, and His Spirit was hovering over the waters.

Then, God began to speak things into existence.

He was bringing order to chaos. Speaking life.

On day one He created light and separated it from the darkness.

Day two He created an expanse between the waters above and waters below, creating heavens above.

Day three He split the land from the water and created vegetation.

Day four He created the sun, moon, and stars.

Day five He created fish and birds.

Day six He created all kinds of animals plus this is when He created humanity.

And on day seven He rested. So He worked for six days and rested on the seventh.

After each day, God saw that everything He had created was good, but when He created man on the sixth day, He saw that it was "very good," (Genesis 1:31).

So now we have Adam and Eve in the Garden of Eden, and God gave them dominion over the earth and all that was in it. According to the Word, everything up until this point in time was GOOD. It was like heaven on earth, and there was no sickness or death. God was in their midst and in relation with Adam and Eve.

Enter: the Fall.

Satan deceived Adam and Eve so that they relied on his word instead of the Word of the Father. If they had realized their identity or obeyed God and walked in truth away from Satan's lie, everything would still be good today. In order to cover the shame of Adam and Eve, blood was shed on their behalf, and God clothed them with animal skin.

GOD NEVER

BREAKS HIS PROMISE

Then we fast-forward hundreds of years, bringing us to the classic Sunday school story of Noah's ark, when things had become really bad on earth. Nobody was following God except for a man named Noah. So God asked Noah to build a massive boat, the ark, and to fill it with his family and one pair of every animal. Then God made it rain for a very long time, flooding the entire earth to wipe out all of the wickedness.

Even though all the wicked men were wiped out in the flood, sin itself was still present. As we see, Noah plants a vineyard, gets drunk, and curses his grandson.

God makes a promise with Noah that He will never wipe out humanity again. Now that there was a fresh slate, God focused His attention on a man named Abram, who is later renamed Abraham.

Abraham had to live his life from a place of great faith. Remember, he didn't have the Bible or fellowship or even other testimonies. He was it, the first of God's truly chosen people that He was going to build a great nation from.

Abraham was old, and his wife, Sarah, thought it was crazy when God said they were going to have children. But then came Ishmael and Isaac. And from Isaac we see Jacob and Esau. And Jacob ends up having twelve sons with four women; God will refer to them later as the "twelve tribes of Israel" (Genesis 49:28). Those twelve sons/tribes will play a major part in the future of God's people throughout the rest of the Bible. Keep an eye out for them.

We are then introduced to Jacob's son Joseph. Joseph is very important to the story of Israel because his life experience shows how all twelve tribes ended up in Egypt and were blessed.

From the outside, his life didn't look like it started out as blessed when his brothers decided to sell him into slavery in Egypt. After his arrival in Egypt, Joseph is falsely accused of a crime and thrown into prison until God uses Joseph to interpret dreams for Pharaoh.

After the first dream was interpreted by Joseph, Pharaoh recognized God's hand on Joseph's life; Pharaoh himself was known as a god in the eyes of the Egyptians.

Note that this is one of the many times God gives wisdom to His people.

Pharaoh was so blown away by this miraculous act that he basically made Joseph the prime minister of the world—and it was unheard of for a non-Egyptian to get close to that position.

Along came a famine in Egypt, which God had prepared Joseph for. This famine drove Joseph's brothers into Egypt to look for grain, but everyone back home thought Joseph was either dead or a slave. When Joseph's brothers show up, he makes sure that they have had a change of heart before giving them anything.

They didn't deserve to be blessed by Joseph either way, but Joseph had a divine perspective and knew that everything had happened the way it did so his family would be protected from the famine. All his relatives (about seventy of them) ended up moving to Egypt so Joseph could take care of them. And the rest was history until Moses decided to pick the

THE TWELVE TRIBES OF ISRAEL

story back up 400 years later in the book of Exodus, which we'll see next.

In each story within Genesis, you see God being a God of second chances. A God who takes people who have messed up and ultimately uses their life for good.

I believe that God can and will use everything for a reason. Good or bad . . . as long as you let Him. The fact that God gives us the ability to choose to love Him also allows for evil to step in and distort our lives. Satan is very real and very interested in pulling you away from God in any way he can. But the good news is that God wins in the end! Nothing can overpower Him, so He can use everything that happens to you for His glory.

God is a GOOD God. A GOOD Father. He's so talented, He can take any sort of junk, and mold it into something beautiful. Genesis does an amazing job modeling that.

So no matter what you've done in the past, God is a God of second chances. You are never too far away from Him to let Him work into your life and change things for the better.

He loves you and truly does care about you. ■

▶ What did God create/do on each day of Creation? (Genesis 1:1–2:3)

Day One:

Day Two:

Day Three:

Day Four:

Day Five:

Day Six:

Day Seven:

▶ Why do you think God created all of this in the first place?

▶ Moses states that man was made in God's image. What do you think that means?

▶ Why do you think God rested on the seventh day?

▶ What curse toward women came out of the Fall? Toward men?
(Genesis 3:15–19)

▶ What was the sign or symbol of the Noahic Covenant? What did God promise?

▶ What do you think Abram's reason for following God was?

▶ Similar to the story of Jacob and Esau, can you think of a time when you settled for immediate enjoyment over future blessings? Why?

▶ Which sons did each woman have with Jacob?

Leah (Genesis 29:32–35; 30:17–20):

Zilpah (Genesis 30:10–13):

Rachel (Genesis 30:22–24; 35:16–18):

Bilhah (Genesis 30:5–7):

▶ Why do you think Potiphar confined Joseph with Pharaoh's prisoners instead of with the general prison population? (Genesis 39)

▶ As we saw God do with Joseph, what has God done in your life that you didn't realize was for a greater purpose until later?

▶ Out of all the blessings Jacob gave his sons, who received the top blessing? Why do you think that is? (Hint: Matthew 1:3–16)

EXODUS

AUTHOR
The first five books of the Bible, the Torah, were written as a whole by Moses and are also known by the Greek word *Pentateuch*, which means five books.

DATE
Moses wrote the book of Exodus sometime during the forty years of wandering the wilderness of Sinai in between the Israelite exodus out of Egypt in 1446 BC and the conquest into the Promised Land in 1406 BC.

AUDIENCE
Exodus was written to God's chosen people, the Israelites, who were beginning to form a nation after being enslaved for 400 years. They had lost much of their sense of identity at this point and their mindset was more or less Egyptian by influence.

REASON
Moses wrote this book to create a historical record of their escape from Egypt and the giving of the Law.

THEME
Deliverance from slavery and the creation of a nation.

KEY VERSES
"I am the Lord your God, who brought you out of the land of Egypt, out of the house of slavery. You shall have no other gods before me" (Exodus 20:2–3).

SECTIONS
The early life of Moses (ch. 1–4), the plagues and Exodus (ch. 5–15), the Red Sea and giving of the Law (ch. 16–24), the tabernacle (ch. 25–40).

KEY WORDS
Slaves, deliver, covenant, Law, tabernacle, holy

STORY OVERVIEW

The first half of Exodus is all about God setting the Israelites free from slavery, while the second half is about how they were to live now that they were free. There is a direct correlation to the New Testament here. God sets us free from our sin and then gives us direction on how to live by properly serving Him.

As we saw near the end of the book of Genesis, a group of seventy people from the line of Jacob went into Egypt to be saved from a worldwide famine; Exodus picks up 400 years later, and we see that what was originally great for them had turned into something terrible: slavery.

A new Pharaoh entered the scene after Joseph died and he didn't agree with the blessing of the Hebrews. He wasn't dealing with a group of seventy people anymore either. The Hebrews had multiplied. By the time of their release, they had grown into a group of 600,000 men, with women and children it is estimated to be about 2.5 million people total. That seems like a massive multiplication when you first look at it, but we must remember that a lot can happen over 400 years.

Chapters 2 and 3 of Exodus cover a broad span of Moses's life. Eighty years, actually—from his birth and being raised by Pharaoh's daughter to his fleeing into the wilderness and becoming a shepherd for forty years.

The reason behind Moses's fleeing was that Moses was an Israelite who was born in an era when all the baby boys his age were being slaughtered, but miraculously his life was spared. He was placed in a basket and put into the river, then discovered by Pharaoh's daughter and raised in Egyptian royalty.

Moses then goes on to understand the persecution of his own people as an adult and kills an Egyptian over the abuse of another Israelite. So he ran from Egypt. He wanted to get as far away as possible so he wouldn't get in trouble.

He ended up in Midian and had begun to build a new life as a shepherd there, which is modern-day Saudi Arabia. Remember, Moses was out in the wilderness for forty years, so he no longer had ties with the Israelites when God shows up in the burning bush and tells Moses His plans. Moses immediately puts up a defense about why he isn't the right one for the job. He makes excuses. God had prepared him for the task of leading the people in a way that he never would have expected, by learning how to shepherd sheep first.

And not only did God prepare Moses and his brother Aaron with signs and wonders to prove the power of their God, but He called them both to obedience by telling them to approach Pharaoh himself, the leader of the political world, essentially.

So they set out with God on their side. And instead of being amazed at the wonders of God, Pharaoh hardened his heart and ended up increasing the workload of the Hebrews on top of not letting them go. Pharaoh even had a group of magicians who could call on dark powers and do many of the same things that the God of the Hebrews was doing.

Moses and Aaron spent some time going back and forth with Pharaoh and his magicians, performing different signs accompanied with the command of letting God's people go.

Egyptian culture was polytheistic, which meant that they had a god for everything, and they would worship that god in order to have an increase in their blessing. Our God is so creative in His mockery. Each one of the plagues (ten in total) that He placed on Pharaoh and the Egyptians, was an attack upon one of their gods. It was as if He was saying, "I am God the Almighty. See, I have power over every one of your gods."

But Pharaoh's heart was hardened after each of the ten plagues. The first seven times, he chose to harden it himself, while God hardened it for him the final three. That's because God allows us to choose our own destiny and may even help us get there.

During the final plague, the death of the firstborn, God commands the Hebrews to sacrifice a lamb and spread the blood over their doorposts. As God gave the angel of death free reign over the firstborn, he was commanded to pass over the houses that were covered by the blood. This final plague ends up costing a hardened Pharaoh the life of his firstborn son, and he finally allows the Israelites to leave Egypt.

But that decision didn't last long. Out of Pharaoh's bitterness, he and his soldiers decided to chase after the Israelites to capture them again. God decided to use Moses to part the Red Sea, moving a whole nation of 2.5 million people through the sea on dry land, to help them escape from the Egyptians.

Then came the time of the wilderness.

As the Israelites were wandering through the wilderness trying to get to the Promised Land, God fed them with manna and quenched their thirst with the outpouring of water from two different rocks. Just as Jesus today is our Bread of Life and Living Water, God sustained the Israelites way back then.

It's important to note that the forty years of wandering through the wilderness by the Israelites was never God's plan. His plan for His people was that they would receive their Promised Land. However, because the first generation of Israelites who were delivered from Egypt complained and disobeyed, God allowed them to wander.

And forty years is how long it took for the first generation to die out. God had promised that none of them would see the land because of their disobedience, but even in their wandering, He remained faithful to His people.

God always knew exactly what the Israelites needed in order to live a whole and holy life. BUT it was their responsibility to accept it. The same is true for us today. We are responsible to accept God's direction and correction so that we are blessed with an abundant life.

In many instances of my life, I thought I knew what was best for me, but it turned out that God had a completely different plan. I feel that becomes more and more common as people grow in their faith.

SPLIT THE SEA

AND THEY
PASSED OVER ON
DRY GROUND

One way God tried to help the Israelites follow His plan to become more holy was to give them the Ten Commandments and, later on, the Law. Before Christ, the only way you could be counted as holy and blameless in front of God was by following the Law to the letter. There was zero room for error. God knew what was best for them. So, in reality, the Law was a way of protecting them.

Jesus later sums up the Ten Commandments as a whole in Luke 10:27: "Love the Lord your God with all your heart and with all your soul and with all your strength and with all your mind, and your neighbor as yourself."

After Moses received the Ten Commandments, God provided him with instructions on how to build the tabernacle so that He could dwell among the people. The instructions were extremely precise because it is impossible for pure holiness, God, and sin to exist at the same time. Therefore, the priests and the tabernacle were held to God's standard and nothing less.

Once the tabernacle was built, God's glory filled it. The pillars of cloud and fire were with God's people as they wandered through the wilderness for forty years.

God was finally dwelling among His people, but differently than He had with Adam and Eve.

Today, God's presence no longer resides in one place. As much as that may sound like a bummer, it's actually one of the biggest blessings that we have. Because of the New Covenant, the New Testament states seven different times that we are now the temple of God. That means the Lord's presence is now inside all of us instead of in one location. It is wherever we are.

The book of Exodus is crucial for understanding the history we have acquired through our adoption into God's holy nation. ▪

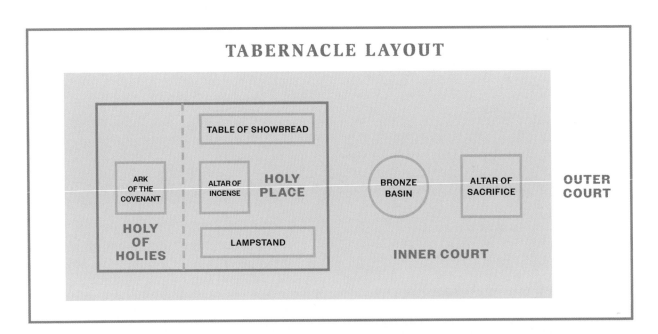

TABERNACLE LAYOUT

TABLE OF SHOWBREAD

ARK OF THE COVENANT

ALTAR OF INCENSE

HOLY PLACE

BRONZE BASIN

ALTAR OF SACRIFICE

OUTER COURT

HOLY OF HOLIES

LAMPSTAND

INNER COURT

▶ Why do you think God allowed the Israelites to be enslaved for so long?

▶ How did Moses's upbringing have a positive impact on the Israelites?

▶ What leadership traits did Moses acquire during his time in the wilderness as a shepherd?

▶ What excuses did Moses offer when God called him to lead the Israelites out of Egypt? (Exodus 3:11; 4:1, 10)

▶ Has God ever called you to fulfill a task that you weren't qualified for? What happened?

▶ Looking back, how did God prepare you for what He has currently called you to do (whether that's ministry, being a mother, your job, discipleship, etc.)?

▶ After reading about Passover, how is Jesus our Passover Lamb?
(1 Corinthians 5:7)?

▶ What are the Ten Commandments?

1.

2.

3.

4.

5.

6.

7.

8.

9.

10.

▶ How can teachings of Exodus be applied to your current walk with the
Lord?

THE

LAW

LEVITICUS

AUTHOR

The author of Leviticus, along with the rest of the Pentateuch, is traditionally attributed to Moses.

DATE

We know that the Law was given to Moses at Mount Sinai in 1446 BC, but there is a possibility that it wasn't written down until just before his death forty years later.

AUDIENCE

Leviticus was written to the Levites but was used among all the Israelites afterward. They had just been set free from Egyptian bondage when these laws were introduced.

REASON

Moses had to provide the Levites with a handbook about God's view on holiness and the standards they needed to live up to.

THEME

Holiness and purification.

KEY VERSE

"You must be holy because I, the LORD, am holy. I have set you apart from all other people to be my very own" (Leviticus 20:26 NLT).

SECTIONS

Approaching holiness (ch. 1–10), becoming holy (ch. 11–27).

KEY WORDS

Law, offering, atonement, holy, sacrifice

STORY OVERVIEW

Most Christians who choose to read the Bible all the way through tend to skip over Leviticus because it seems to be boring and irrelevant for a New Testament believer today.

Many people feel that it is just a bunch of rules and regulations that contradict our understanding of Scripture, now that we are no longer under a legalistic type of faith. So things *must* be different now. And they are.

The question we must ask ourselves is: *Why* did God give the Israelites all these rules to follow in the first place? What was the *point*?

From the beginning of the world it was God's desire to live among His creation. His people. In communion. But His holiness demanded holiness, and once mankind fell into their sinful nature they could no longer be counted as holy.

Now that the Israelites were out of bondage, God wanted to live among them again, but that required holiness on both sides. Enter: the Law. As long as the priests and Levites lived up to God's standard of holiness, He would live among them in the Ark of the Covenant. Hence, being in communion again.

The Hebrew word for holy means to be set apart. God also looks at holiness as a lifestyle that has to be taken seriously. The lifestyle the Israelites had adopted over the previous 400 years was Egyptian and did not represent God at all. In the future, they would take over the Promised Land, where the Canaanites were even worse than the Egyptians, so God was giving them a way to remain in His will instead of falling for the desires of the world.

The rules God was giving them were not meant to restrict them from enjoying life, as so many people would think. God was actually giving them standards to uphold in order to remain healthy spiritually, mentally, and physically and to be protected from outside influence. He was looking out for their best interests even though they didn't realize it.

Not only did God have His mind set on the current situation of the Israelites, but He also gave them the Law for future generations to follow, even after they acquired the Promised Land. The Law was to be used as a handbook on how to live until the Messiah came. The Law is not just the Ten Commandments that we saw while studying Exodus either. Leviticus shows us that there are actually 613 rules and regulations for how to live right by God, and the Israelites were commanded to follow them all to a T. This meant that if you had broken one rule, you had broken them all in God's eyes. Holiness was a way of life that demanded perfection. And it was impossible to attain without a Savior.

There are also punishments in Leviticus for breaking the rules. If you are anything like me, you have broken dozens of them and should be given the death penalty time and time again.

One crucial strategy that will help us in studying the rest of the Bible is to have an understanding of the offerings and feasts that God commanded His people to celebrate. As we look at them, note what each of them means for us today.

THE OFFERINGS

Burnt Offerings

Burnt offerings are the most common offerings in Scripture. They are voluntary offerings for the Lord, most commonly used for cleansing and purification. They portray a complete devotion and dedication to life with God.

Grain Offering

The grain offering is the only offering that doesn't require the shedding of blood. Grain offerings were required in all burnt offerings, but also were used as solo burnt offerings for the poor. It gave them an opportunity to show the Lord how they really felt about Him and to praise Him for provision.

Peace Offering

Peace offerings were used for fellowship with God to display peace among them and offer thanksgiving for who God is and what He has done. It displayed a true act of worship and admiration for the Lord.

Guilt Offering

The guilt offering was conducted when an individual attacked or disrespected another person or their property. Amends were made between the two and an extra one-fifth was included on top of the offering. Atonement was given through the shedding of blood and forgiveness between the people.

Sin Offering

Unlike the four above, this is the first offering that is not voluntary. It was required of every single person. Period. It was done to make atonement for sins that were committed out of ignorance, unintentional sins. The sin offering gives us a picture of Christ becoming sin for us.

THE SEVEN FEASTS

1. Passover

Passover begins the entire festival year on the fourteenth day of the first month, which is April on our calendar. It represents the deliverance from bondage in Egypt, based on the miracles that God performed through Moses. Passover signifies the beginning of new life and promised protection in the future. The term itself meant to be protected or delivered from something, in this case the angel of death. The Feast of Passover is fulfilled in the New Testament as we see the believer in Christ being delivered from slavery (aka the bondage of sin). We move from death surrounding us to the presence of God protecting us and offering eternal life. Jesus is our Passover Lamb and our salvation! He protects us from darkness and delivers us from evil. We move from death to eternal life. Dark to light.

2. Feast of Unleavened Bread

The Feast of Unleavened Bread begins the day after the Passover meal and lasts for the following seven days. Many people combine Passover with the Feast of Unleavened Bread and celebrate it as an eight-day festival. When the Israelites left Egypt, they didn't have enough time to let their bread rise, so this feast is meant to be in remembrance of their departure from Egypt. We also see yeast as a symbol of sin throughout the Bible. In the New Testament, Jesus says He is the true "bread of life" (John 6:35).

3. Feast of Firstfruits

The Feast of Firstfruits takes place on the day after the Sabbath of the Feast of Unleavened bread. The purpose of this feast is to thank God for the fertility of the land that He provided to the Israelites. For the believer, the resurrection of Jesus shows that He is the "firstfruits" of the righteous. His resurrection took place on this very day. It was a new beginning and a new year. In the Western world we call this celebration Easter, or Resurrection Sunday.

4. Feast of Weeks

The Feast of Weeks is also known as Pentecost, or Shavu'ot in Hebrew. It is celebrated as a remembrance of God giving the law to Moses fifty days after the Sabbath following Passover. As shown in Acts 2, on the day of Pentecost after Jesus was crucified, the apostles presented them with a whole new way of life. A gospel for everyone. They were being told that they could now enter into a New Covenant with Christ through baptism. Whereas 3,000 people died at the giving of the Law in Exodus, 3,000 people received the Holy Spirit in Acts 2.

5. Day of Atonement

In Leviticus, the Day of Atonement is the most holy of days for the Jewish people. It falls on the tenth day of the seventh month (September-October). The Day of Atonement is a day of confession and of wiping the slate clean in order to start over with a new year. The sacrifice that went along with this day was a representation of the death and resurrection of Jesus. This shows that the God of the Hebrews is a God of second chances, and He allows us to wipe our slates clean because of the blood of His Son. He is looking out for us, whether we do or do not accept it.

6. Feast of Trumpets

The Feast of Trumpets is to be celebrated on the first day of the seventh month (September-October). It's a day when trumpets are blown throughout the land and no work is to be done. There isn't much more to it than that. It's a feast of rest and worship. As the other feasts represent something that has happened in history that benefits us as believers, this one is in the future still. We don't know when or how, but it is still bound to happen. Many people believe that the Feast of Trumpets will be fulfilled through the rapture—if you believe in the rapture.

7. Feast of Booths

The Feast of Booths was a time of celebration on the fifteenth day of the seventh month (September-October) and lasted seven days, but in reality, it is celebrated for eight days. The Israelites were to look back at the forty years of wandering in the wilderness and they were commanded by God to rejoice over the fact that He provided them with a roof over their heads while they didn't know where to go. This feast points to the fact that one day the Lord will again dwell with His people as He comes to reign over all the world. So I know that was a lot, but the book of Leviticus is dedicated to worship and the holiness of God. There is no book like it in the Bible. As intimidating as Leviticus may seem, the benefits of studying it far outweigh the cost of being bored or uncomfortable. Even though Israel was constantly falling short, God made a way for their sin to be covered. God was always coming up with ways for Israel to be close to Him. This theme remains true for us today. God has a plan for us to know Him. ■

▶ In five words, what were your preconceived thoughts on Leviticus before you read it this week?

▶ Did your views change at all after diving into the book? How?

▶ Does your lifestyle reflect holiness? If not, how could it?

▶ What did Jesus have to say about the Law (Matthew 5:17)? How did He expound on it (Matthew 5:21–48)?

▶ Does your understanding of the Law now change your view of Jesus? If yes, how?

▶ After reading about the offerings, what are some ways you can perform an offering to the Lord today?

▶ As a Christian, do you feel the need to celebrate any of the seven feasts? Why or why not?

▶ After learning about the priesthood in Leviticus, how does that impact your understanding of what Peter says about you in 1 Peter 2:9?

▶ After learning about the sacrificial system, what do you think Paul means in Romans 12:1–2 when he says to present our bodies as a living sacrifice?

NUMBERS

AUTHOR
The author of Numbers is Moses.

DATE
Numbers was written before Moses died and during the end of the Israel-ites' forty years of wandering, making the date around 1405–1406 BC.

AUDIENCE
Moses was writing to the second-generation Israelites whose parents had passed away during the forty years of wandering.

REASON
Moses wrote to document the history of the Israelites' wanderings through the desert in order to show the new generation what not to do once they entered the Promised Land.

THEME
Shows what happens when Israel wanders away from God's plan.

KEY VERSE
"For forty years—one year for each of the forty days you explored the land—you will suffer for your sins and know what it is like to have me against you" (Numbers 14:34 NIV).

SECTIONS
Preparing the Israelites (ch. 1–10), falling away from the plan (ch. 11–14), the Lord's discipline (ch. 15–36).

KEY WORDS
Wander, wilderness, covenant, sin, atonement

STORY OVERVIEW

Numbers is a historical look at the Israelites' journey from Mount Sinai to Kadesh and up through Moab to the edge of the Promised Land. It's a book of rebellion and disappointment. The wanderings were not part of God's plan, but He adjusted to their decisions.

This book is called Numbers because it begins and ends with a census, showing us that Israel was a nation of around 2.5 million people. That's a lot of people wandering through the wilderness together, so it's no wonder that rebellion spread among them. It's important to note that there weren't sound systems or megaphones back then, so whatever Moses said had to be passed amongst the people verbally.

This wandering they were doing in the wilderness for forty years was a punishment for not seizing the Promised Land when they had the opportunity. God decided to wait for the first generation to die off so that the second generation had the same opportunity for obedience.

The Promised Land was God's will for their lives. The Israelites just needed to have faith and desire it. Moses wasn't even allowed into the Promised Land because of his lack of obedience to God while leading the people. If you remember, he struck a rock for water instead of speaking to it as God commanded. And just like that, Moses wasn't allowed in.

In this book, Moses also shares with us how the tribes were called to camp around the tabernacle during the forty years. He was extremely strategic in laying out the tribes around the tabernacle, based on importance and their role, similarly to many military strategies of their day. We also see that the tribe of Judah was placed in the most important spot of all, right in front of the tabernacle.

Later when we look at the life of Jesus, we'll see that He was also sent to the wilderness for a testing period of forty days with Satan. Whereas the grumbling and complaining of the Israelites caused them to miss the Promised Land, Jesus's spoken word of Scripture allowed Him to prevail against the tests of Satan and to begin His ministry.

When the Israelites first made it to the edge of the Promised Land, Moses and Aaron sent out twelve spies to see what they were going to be coming up against. The spies knew the promise of God, but when they saw giants among the land, ten of the spies retreated in fear even though the land itself was perfect. On the other hand, two of the spies, Joshua and Caleb, saw it as an opportunity and had faith that God would pave the way before them. They held onto the truths God gave to Israel and believed in a brighter tomorrow. It didn't matter though. The tribes sided with the ten over the two and, in return, God punished them all for forty years.

When the Israelites finally mustered up enough courage to take over the Promised Land and were standing on the shores of the Jordan River, they were met with resistance from the Moabites and Ammonites, who didn't want them to come into their land.

So they called on the prophet Balaam to come and curse the Israelites. Every time that he tried to curse them, a blessing came out of his mouth instead.

After many failed attempts, God gave Balaam's donkey a word of wisdom and the donkey spoke it to Balaam—knocking some sense into him. The downside of all of this is that Balaam did find a way to defeat the Israelites and it was through the use of Canaanite women.

From there, Moses and Eleazar were called to perform another census and introduce more laws to the nation of Israel before the conquest of the Promised Land. God was going to do whatever He could to make sure they were prepared for their great inheritance. But, as you'll soon see, the temptation was too strong. . . .

We see two distinctly different generations represented in the book of Numbers. The first generation was a group of slaves who were born and raised under the Egyptian culture. So to be free all of a sudden was quite a change of pace for them. Yet, they remained stuck in their ways. They didn't believe that God was looking out for them because all they really knew were pagan rituals.

The second generation was the opposite. Even though they made mistakes and weren't perfect at all (as none of us is), they still trusted in God's plan and were about to experience the blessings they grew up hearing about. One thing that you also must remember is that the second generation were most likely all children during the time of the plagues in Egypt, Moses's splitting of the Red Sea, the manna falling down from the sky, etc. Miracles were a way of life for them, not an oddity. ∎

▶ What does the book of Numbers show you about the importance of obedience?

▶ Have you ever failed to obey God's plan and, consequently, you didn't receive your Promised Land—God's best for you? If yes, what happened?

▶ What role does the tribe of Judah play in the future of Israel?

▶ Write out three promises of God from the Bible that you can hold on to when you begin to complain, so that you don't miss walking into your Promised Land:

    1.

    2.

    3.

▶ Describe a time when your faith outweighed the faith of your peers. What was the end result?

▶ Has God ever used a strange circumstance to share His thoughts with you? What happened?

▶ Looking at the two generations represented in Numbers, which one can you most easily identify with? Being stuck in ritualistic ways? Or having faith for God to move miraculously in your life?

▶ What are some changes you can make in your life to become more like the second generation?

AUTHOR
Deuteronomy is the fifth and final book written by Moses. You'll notice that the final chapter deals with the death of Moses, which was most likely added by Joshua.

DATE
Deuteronomy was written at the end of the forty years of wandering, right before the Israelites entered the Promised Land.

AUDIENCE
Moses was writing to the second-generation Israelites who were about to enter into the Promised Land. He also wrote with the intention of future generations reading this book.

REASON
In Greek, Deuteronomy means second law, which conveys this is the second giving of the Law in the nation of Israel. This time it is given to the second generation of Israelites as a renewal of the covenant with God's people.

THEME
Covenant renewal with blessings and curses attached.

KEY VERSES
"He said to them, 'Take to heart all the words by which I am warning you today, that you may command them to your children, that they may be careful to do all the words of this law. For it is no empty word for you, but your very life, and by this word you shall live long in the land that you are going over the Jordan to possess" (Deuteronomy 32:46–47).

SECTIONS
History of wanderings (ch. 1–4), review of the Law (ch. 5–26), curses and blessings attached (ch. 27–30), farewell of Moses (ch. 31–34).

KEY WORDS
Covenant, observe, blessing, curse

DEUTERONOMY

STORY OVERVIEW

This is the second giving of the Law to the nation of Israel. This time it is given to the second generation of Israelites as a renewal of the covenant with God's people. Deuteronomy, simply put, is a covenant renewal with blessings and curses attached.

Many people become confused when they read Deuteronomy for the first time because they don't understand why there is another book in the Torah that dictates the Law. Didn't we just go through the Law when studying Leviticus?! Yes, we did just go over everything, but the audience is different now. The Law was originally given to the first-generation Israelites who had escaped Egypt. God was so disappointed in their lack of faith He decided that none of them would see the Promised Land.

Enter: their children. This was a new group of faces representing Israel, and God was giving the nation a fresh start. Before entering into the Promised Land, God let them know they were going to be held accountable to the covenant. THIS is the reason for us hearing about the Law a second time.

Instead of the Promised Land being an untouched paradise, as so many people tend to view it, the Israelites were looking across the Jordan into a land that was definitely flourishing BUT was full of people who were very different from them.

The first sermon Moses preached to these people of God was the story of their parents' time in the wilderness. They could have entered into the Promised Land in less than two weeks, but their grumblings turned it into forty years. What a waste of time! And in the end, they weren't allowed to enter at all. And

if you remember correctly, Moses wasn't allowed to enter either, because of his disobedience.

Can you imagine how Moses would have felt after striving toward this promise for so long? The thing we need to remember is that Moses *saw* God on Mount Sinai and His glory shone upon his face.

Moses describes all the laws the Israelites are to follow once they have conquered the Promised Land. It's nearly an impossible list to follow, but God demanded holiness in every area of life, otherwise they couldn't be on good terms with Him. Thank God that we are under the New Covenant today. And thank God for grace. He still demands holiness in every area of our lives, though, not just by going to church on Sunday and being a "good person." Being a Christ follower is about full-life transformation.

The text says God takes these rules very seriously because He is a jealous God. Jealousy was always a hard concept for me to understand because I felt it was a negative trait to have. But I've learned that isn't the case. When I began studying the jealousy of God, my views completely shifted. God wants us to himself because He knows what is best for us. He always wants to bless us with the best. So, no, it isn't a negative trait in that sense.

Even though this new generation of Israelites weren't the ones who rebelled against God after they were delivered from Egypt, the problems that rebellion caused were now their responsibility.

Let's take note of that idea again: not their fault, but their *responsibility*. God didn't care if they were

BLESSINGS

CURSES

a new group. He takes generations very seriously, which is why He continually reminds the Israelites to raise their children to obey the Law.

After going over the Law, Moses appointed Joshua to be their new fearless leader. He was going to take charge of the conquest and pick up where Moses left off. The first thing they were commanded to do was go to Mount Ebal and Mount Gerizim to recite the blessings and curses among themselves, making them responsible for their actions. Now it was almost time for them to enter into their inheritance. They just had to wait for Moses to die and then mourn him. Sad but true.

As we continue to dive into the history of Israel, one thing to remember is that we, as Gentiles, have been grafted into this history, so it now becomes our own.

Also, God doesn't change (see Malachi 3:6). He is the same yesterday, today, and tomorrow. Yes, there are new stipulations in the covenant, but He still takes holiness just as seriously. God wants the best for us, even if that looks different from what society expects. By studying the Torah, we have seen that God's Law has very high standards. With the introduction of the New Covenant, adhering to the standards of the Law is no longer required of us, but obedience to God's Word is. And obedience brings blessing, just as we saw in the book of Deuteronomy. ▪

▶ In the book of Genesis, God told Abraham that something had to happen in the Promised Land before His people could take over. What did He tell him (Genesis 15:16)?

▶ What is more important in your life, achievements, or spending time with God? Why?

▶ What does it mean for God to be jealous for His people?

▶ Parents: How can you better raise your children by God's Word and principles?

▶ Children: How can you improve in respecting your parents' teaching?

▶ How has God blessed you for being obedient to His Word?

▶ What other personal applications can you pull out of your study of Deuteronomy?

AUTHOR
The author of this book is Joshua, Moses's military general and assistant. Just as we saw at the end of Deuteronomy, someone else had to have concluded this book by adding in the passage about Joshua's death.

DATE
Joshua wrote this book right around 1390 BC, just before his death.

AUDIENCE
The audience of Joshua was the third-generation Israelites, whose parents had conquered the Promised Land.

REASON
Joshua wrote this book to have an account of how the Israelites conquered the Promised Land, to record the land allotments, and to show God's faithfulness to His covenant with them.

THEME
Possession of the Promised Land.

KEY VERSE
"So Joshua took the whole land, according to all that the Lord had spoken to Moses. And Joshua gave it for an inheritance to Israel according to their tribal allotments. And the land had rest from war" (Joshua 11:23).

SECTIONS
The conquest (ch. 1–12), land allotments (ch. 13–21), farewell of Joshua (ch. 22–24).

KEY WORDS
Possession, inheritance, land, covenant

JOSHUA

STORY OVERVIEW

Let's remember what has just taken place in the book of Deuteronomy: Moses has led the Israelites to the Promised Land, and they had set up camp outside of it. They are called to obey the commands of God to show His character to the other nations, and Joshua has taken over leading God's people after Moses's death.

We see that Joshua is in charge of the people now, which would have been a major task—to follow in the footsteps of Moses. Like Moses, Joshua commanded spies to go and check out Jericho. However, this time he sent two instead of twelve because when Moses sent twelve, only two came back with the right word. Joshua's two spies ended up at the house of a prostitute named Rahab, who offered them protection because she believed in their God. In return, the spies said that God would protect her from the destruction of her city, Jericho.

As the spies returned to the camped-out Israelites, Joshua made the call to proceed. That's when God steps in to show off. Whereas the Israelites' parents crossed through the parted Red Sea after Pharaoh let them go, now we see that God parted the Jordan River for their children the moment the priest's feet touched the water.

Joshua leads the people across the Jordan River toward the land with the ark of the covenant. Joshua set up a monument of twelve stones on the other side of the Jordan after the group passed through, a remembrance for generations to come.

Afterward, all the men who weren't circumcised underwent circumcision as a physical representation of their covenant with God.

The book of Joshua is the first of six that are known as the *historical books*. With the first five books of the Law complete, it is time to put everything into action throughout the rest of the Old Testament. Israel's obedience ebbs and flows for the rest of their history, but Joshua shows that they begin on a high note after conquering the Promised Land.

There is a whole lot of war and conquering going on in this book. The first city the Israelites defeated was Jericho, with the only resident survivors being Rahab and her family. For six days, God's people marched around the city following the ark of the covenant and blowing trumpets. On the seventh day, they marched around it seven times, blowing their trumpets and giving a shout at the end, and all the walls of the city of Jericho fell down! This approach is all for the glory of God. He gets the credit here, and Israel sees His faithfulness.

Then comes a loss that the Israelites experienced during their conquest of the Promised Land against the city of Ai. God allows for their defeat because on his way out of Jericho, Achan stole treasures for himself, including precious metals, which went against God's command. Achan is proof that the disobedience of one man can negatively influence an entire nation. Not only was Achan killed, but his entire family was too, in order to destroy any generational sin.

As the Israelites were fighting against the Amorites at Gibeon, Joshua prayed for God to extend the day by making the sun stand still so that they could assure their success. God agreed and allowed the sun to stand still for about an entire day. CRAZY!

Once the Israelites defeated all the cities in the Promised Land, we learn that Joshua divided the land among the twelve tribes. The one tribe that didn't receive a physical inheritance in the Promised Land were the Levites because God himself was their portion.

Joshua foreshadows Jesus, and the story as a whole foreshadows our spiritual journey. Many believers spend their lives wandering through the wilderness, remaining in their old ways and never being allowed to experience their Promised Land. On the other hand, there is a small group of believers who get to the Promised Land right away and are able to experience all that God has for them.

The book of Joshua is purposeful in reminding us of God's faithfulness and His plea for us to be faithful to Him. ▧

THE PROMISED
LAND

▶ What was Rahab commanded to do in order to be protected from the falling walls (Joshua 2:18)?

▶ How does the command to Rahab compare to the story of Exodus (Exodus 12:5–7)?

▶ In what contexts do we read about Rahab in the New Testament (Matthew 1:5; Hebrews 11:31)?

▶ Is there any sin in your life that has been passed down from generation to generation that needs to be broken? If so, put together a prayer strategy below to defeat it.

▶ Has God ever helped you win a battle through miraculous intervention? What happened?

▶ How would you feel as a Levite, being in the Promised Land and knowing that you don't have any physical inheritance? Would having God be enough?

▶ How can you experience your "Promised Land" today and live under the inheritance that God wants to bless you with?

AUTHOR
The author of Judges is unknown, but most believe the likely candidate is the prophet Samuel.

DATE
Samuel would have written this between David's anointing in 1025 BC and before he captured Jerusalem in 1004 BC. I choose to favor a date closer to the latter.

AUDIENCE
Samuel wrote to the Israelites whose ancestors continuously rebelled against God.

REASON
The book of Judges was written as a defense for King David and as a record of Israel's sin cycles under their appointed judges.

THEME
Israel's disobedience and the need to be saved.

KEY VERSE
"In those days there was no king in Israel. Everyone did what was right in his own eyes" (Judges 21:25).

SECTIONS
The reason for falling away (1:1–3:6), the twelve judges (3:7–16:31), the outcome (ch. 17–21).

KEY WORDS
Sin, repent, judge, faithfulness

JUDGES

Joshua had asked the Israelites to be faithful to their covenant with God after arriving in the Promised Land through obeying the commands in the Torah. This faithfulness would show all the other nations what God is like. So we have the book of Judges beginning with the death of Joshua and going on to show the complete disaster the Israelite people became.

Before entering the Promised Land, the nation of Israel had one major leader, Moses. Then the conquest itself was led by one man, Joshua. Now that the Israelites were spread out among the Promised Land according to each tribe of Israel, they needed to modify the leadership in some way. This is where our judges enter.

A judge was a deliverer of the people. A hero. A savior. Judges were sent by God as soon as the people cried out for help, and their job was to bring them back to obedience (for at least a short time).

But the people ended up falling back into their sinful ways and "did what was right in their own eyes" instead of what was right in God's eyes. The faithfulness of God is ever present in this book because every time they fell away, He would come to their rescue by sending a deliverer.

As mentioned, the author shows us the cycle of sin the Israelites were stuck in. They would fall away, cry out to God, He would provide a deliverer, things would get better, then they would fall right back into it. Twelve times.

The judges God sent for the people varied in importance and effect. We know a lot about some of them and almost nothing about others. When God sent a deliverer to the nation, it was usually in a way that caused the destruction of their enemies.

Reading these stories, we come to realize that the judges were far from perfect and also far from godly, according to today's standards.

I mean, you see the left-handed Ehud killing the fat king of Moab and getting his sword stuck in his belly. You have Shamgar, who killed 600 Philistines with an ox goad, and Samson, who killed 1,000 men with the jawbone of a donkey. Those are wild stories!

One of the judges we are given a little more information about was a man named Gideon. God reduced Gideon's army from 32,000 to 300 so that Gideon would rely on God for protection and provision.

Then we read the full story of the judge most people know about—Samson. Samson's parents offered him up as a Nazarite before he was born, so he wasn't allowed to drink alcohol, shave his head, etc. There were rules attached to his life so that God could use him in mighty ways. Samson had one weak spot, though: women.

The most famous relationship Samson had was with a woman named Delilah. She was a snake. Delilah did everything possible to find out the secret behind Samson's great strength.

So many people portray Samson as this big, burly man, but every time he does something out of insane strength, the Spirit of the Lord comes upon him first. It's never his own physical strength, but always the supernatural. God does that on purpose to show that He can use anybody and to boost the faith of those around those He chooses.

Every time God sent a judge to the people of Israel, the Holy Spirit played a major role in the delivering process. It was never out of their own strength—the Holy Spirit always stepped in to work through them, and then He left when the job was done.

Samuel wraps up the book of Judges with two stories that should definitely NOT be taught in Sunday School. They were included to show how far the sin cycle had spun downward and how even the Levites were consumed with moral decay. It shows what happens when God is taken out of the picture and Israel's sinful nature takes hold. It isn't pretty.

Although Judges highlights a list of stories of Israel being rescued, the book ends with the people's desperation for a leader, except this time it will be a king.

So the author sets the stage for the lineage of King David and shows the consistent theme of God's people in desperate need of His grace. ▪

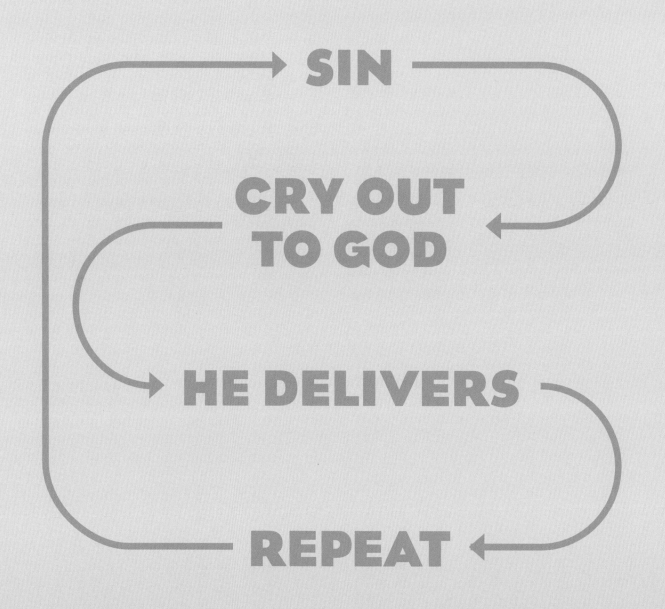

▶ What caused the Israelites to continue falling back into their sinful ways (Judges 2:10, 12)?

▶ What sin cycle do you keep falling back into? What truths or promises from God's Word can you start speaking over your life to remain free?

▶ How can you justify a God of love sending someone to slaughter their enemies?

▶ Has God ever reduced your resources (as He did with Gideon) to draw you closer to Him and so you would depend on Him? What happened?

▶ Has God ever used you in supernatural ways to fulfill certain tasks even though you were clearly not qualified? How?

▶ What can you take away from the two stories at the end of Judges?

AUTHOR

Many scholars as well as Jewish tradition hold that Ruth, attached to the end of the book of Judges in the Hebrew text, was also written by Samuel.

DATE

As we saw when studying Judges, Ruth was most likely written between David's anointing in 1025 BC and before he captured Jerusalem in 1004 BC.

AUDIENCE

Ruth was written to all Israelites after the time of the judges, who would be able to look back and see what their ancestors dealt with.

REASON

Samuel wanted to show the sin of the tribe of Benjamin (King Saul's tribe) at the end of Judges and then go right into the divinely inspired connection with the king of Judah, King David. Ruth is also used to show Gentile acceptance within Israel, and it gives us a road map for how to work together with the Jewish nation today.

THEME

Foreshadowing our Kinsman-Redeemer.

KEY VERSE

"But Ruth said, 'Do not urge me to leave you or to return from following you. For where you go I will go, and where you lodge I will lodge. Your people shall be my people, and your God my God'" (Ruth 1:16).

SECTIONS

The return to Moab (ch. 1), Ruth and Boaz meet (ch. 2), Ruth's request (ch. 3), the kinsman-redeemer (ch. 4).

KEY WORDS

Kinsman-redeemer, glean, redemption

RUTH

STORY OVERVIEW

Ruth is a pretty short narrative, but it is actually a very theological book that shows how God desires to be intimately involved with the details of our lives.

Ruth is a book of high importance to the church. It foreshadows the acceptance of Gentiles within the nation of Israel and is the key that saves them from the time of the judges.

When Naomi's husband and sons died, she was left with her two daughters-in-law. But Naomi was mourning, and in her bitterness, she told the daughters to go find a new life somewhere else. Orpah obeyed. Ruth did not. And Ruth's decision changed the course of humanity.

Not only did Ruth, a Gentile, choose Naomi, but she also chose Naomi's people and Naomi's God. And from then on, she found favor with the Lord and He blessed her abundantly.

There are three laws we must understand in order to place ourselves in this story.

First, the law of gleaning. This law stated that you were allowed to harvest your crop one time every day, but whatever you missed was to be left for the widows and the poor.

Then there is the law of redemption, which states that if you could no longer afford your land, or if the landowner died, your next of kin (aka kinsman-redeemer) had the first right to take it over, but all obligations were included.

And finally, the law of levirate marriage, which dictated that if a husband died, his brother was to as- sume the marriage in order to properly raise up the husband's seed/children.

Ruth stumbled into the field of Boaz looking for some grain because she was familiar with the law of gleaning. This "random" field she went into ended up changing everything for us. Boaz was a nobleman of high standard and strength. People looked up to him because he knew what he was doing. Boaz was also a very generous man. We see that he gave a double portion for Ruth to glean.

And it just so happens that the mother of Boaz was Rahab, the Gentile from the book of Joshua with a heart for the Jews.

Naomi realizes Boaz is a kinsman, so she sees this as a massive opportunity to bless Ruth as well as herself. Being seasoned in Jewish thought, Naomi counsels Ruth on how to draw Boaz to herself. We then see Ruth approach Boaz while he is asleep on the threshing floor. It was harvest season, so land- owners would sleep next to their good crop to pro- tect it from being stolen. Uncovering Boaz's feet was a way of letting him know that she was interested, and Boaz takes the bait but realizes he needs to get around the law of redemption first, since his kinsman was allowed first priority.

The good news for Ruth is that the nearest kinsman passed on the offer, so Boaz could purchase the land that included Ruth as a bride, and he would become her kinsman-redeemer.

The book of Ruth ultimately comes together in verse 4:17, which says, "And the women of the neighborhood gave him a name, saying, 'A son has been born to Naomi.' They named him Obed. He was the father of Jesse, the father of David."

That means Boaz is the great-grandfather of King David.

Samuel ended the last chapter in the book of Judges on a low note regarding King Saul, since he was from the tribe of Benjamin, and ends Ruth on a high note for King David, since this story shows his family's character. And shortly, we will see how David reigns supreme.

The story of Ruth foreshadows the history of God's people in amazing ways:

> Boaz can be seen as the Lord of the Harvest.
> Naomi represents Israel.
> Ruth is the Gentile Bride.

Now go back through the story looking at it with this new understanding. Everything lines up perfectly. Naomi and Ruth both play a crucial part in the story of redemption. They couldn't do it without each other, and in the end, both are blessed for their actions. ■

YOUR PEOPLE
YOUR PEOPLE
YOUR PEOPLE
YOUR PEOPLE
YOUR PEOPLE
YOUR PEOPLE
YOUR PEOPLE
YOUR PEOPLE
YOUR PEOPLE

YOUR GOD
YOUR GOD
YOUR GOD
YOUR GOD
YOUR GOD
YOUR GOD
YOUR GOD
YOUR GOD
YOUR GOD

▶ Have you (like Ruth) ever made one small decision that changed your entire life? What was it?

▶ What do you think was going through Ruth's mind while she was waiting for Boaz to get permission from his kinsman? Did she have faith that God would pull it off?

▶ How does this story impact your views of the Jewish people today?

AUTHOR
The author of the two books of Samuel is anonymous, but experts believe that they were most likely a compilation of stories by Samuel, Nathan, and Gad.

DATE
The events recorded in these two books ended around 960 BC, making the dating sometime between 960 BC and shortly after the death of Solomon in 931 BC.

AUDIENCE
The audience was the nation of Israel living under the reigns of David and Solomon. Both books would also be read by following generations as a historical guide.

REASON
The author wrote to show the role God played in the life of a God-fearing king and to inspire future kings to use David as a role model.

THEME
The building of a godly monarchy.

KEY VERSES
"And Samuel said to Saul, 'You have done foolishly. You have not kept the command of the LORD your God, with which he commanded you. For then the LORD would have established your kingdom over Israel forever. But now your kingdom shall not continue. The LORD has sought out a man after his own heart, and the Lord has commanded him to be prince over his people, because you have not kept what the LORD commanded you'" (1 Samuel 13:13–14).

"Your house and your kingdom will endure forever before me; your throne will be established forever" (2 Samuel 7:16 NIV).

SECTIONS
1 Samuel: The final judge, Samuel (ch. 1–12), the rise of Saul and David (ch. 13–31).

2 Samuel: King David's successes (ch. 1–10), King David's failures and troubles (ch. 11–24).

KEY WORDS
Judge, king, evil, sin, spirit

1 & 2 SAMUEL

We are going to put First and Second Samuel together so you can see them as a whole book. This time period represents a turning point in the history of Israel's leadership as they transition from the time of judges to the time of kings. Samuel is the final judge and prophet, while Saul becomes the first elected king. We then see how everything went downhill from there, until we get to the model king, David.

The books of Samuel cover a period of 150 years of history. That's a lot crammed into a couple of small books, but the Greeks split them up in order to make it more manageable. For organizational purposes, we are going to look at them combined.

Samuel begins the story with a barren woman named Hannah, who promises God that if she is given a son, she will dedicate his life to the Lord's work.

When the Lord visited Hannah and answered her prayer, He didn't do the minimum—He went above and beyond to make sure that she was taken care of because God loves blessing those who love Him. Sometimes all it takes is to ask for it.

A lot of people complain today that God doesn't bless them or their situation, but many times people don't spend time in prayer asking for the blessing, even though Matthew 7:7 and Luke 11:9 promise, "Ask, and it will be given to you; seek, and you will find; knock, and it will be opened to you."

Moving on, in 1 Samuel chapter 4 we learn that the Philistines capture the ark of the covenant from the Israelites. That's a big no-no. The Philistines didn't fully understand the ark, though, because they thought God was now on their side since they possessed it. Their understanding was in the physical realm, not the spiritual. Samuel let the Israelites know they lost against the Philistines because of their sin. Ultimately, this gets them to destroy their pagan gods and clean up their act.

Many times throughout the Old Testament, we will see that whenever Israel disobeyed God, He would send an enemy against them as a form of punishment. This time, once the Israelites repented, God intervened in order for the ark to make its way back into the hands of Israel.

The Israelites began to demand a king that their enemies could actually see. They looked at all the other nations who were successful with a kingship and wanted to be like them. That wasn't God's plan, but He chose to give the people what they wanted. As a result, the Israelites chose a handsome, macho man: Saul, from the tribe of Benjamin.

Saul started off great, but just as with the judges, his time in office ended badly because he wasn't striving after the Father's heart. He loved to do things his own way.

Having a king gave the Israelites rules and parameters on how to live their life. All people wanted was a checklist to follow so they could perform a certain way and live the rest of their life on their own. A similar mindset has continued through the ages, and many Christians today desire the same thing. But

THIS IS THE DAY THE LORD

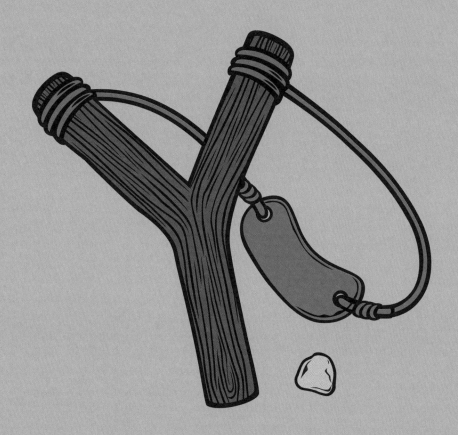

WILL DELIVER YOU INTO MY HAND

that ends up erasing the relationship-with-Jesus part of our faith and the need for a transformed life.

As I said, when Saul became king, he started off great, but eventually fell. The text even says that the Spirit came mightily upon him, meaning that he was walking in the Spirit for the time being and he feared the Lord. However, this didn't last, and eventually God's Spirit left him during his kingship.

Even though Saul was still king, God directed Samuel to seek out Jesse and anoint one of his sons. Jesse was obviously proud, so he showed off his boys to Samuel, leaving out David because he was at the bottom of the totem pole. Samuel didn't sense the Holy Spirit guiding him to anoint any of them, so he asked Jesse if he had any other sons.

When David showed up, Samuel knew right away that he was the one. The anointing process took place, and his time of kingship awaited him sometime in the future.

A few years after his anointing, David ends up being allowed to fight against Goliath as the representative for Israel. Obviously, this story is one of the most popular Sunday school stories, which makes absolutely no sense. It's brutal! David kills Goliath and cuts his head off. That's a pretty gruesome children's story, if you ask me!

After David kills Goliath, the Israelites praise him for his strength and skill. Jealousy rose within Saul when he heard of their praises, and he made it a point to defeat David. Little did he know that his plan was going to be harder than it sounded.

We really see David's character shine in the next few chapters as he had two chances to kill Saul in return for the threat upon his life but chose to let Saul live. Each time, though, David messed with Saul a little bit.

In the first instance, David comes across Saul when he is sleeping and clips off the edge of his garment. It's important to understand that back then, the edge of the garment was where your authority was held. It was similar to stripes on a military uniform today. So first, David is taking away Saul's authority.

In the second instance, David comes across Saul when he is sleeping again. This time he takes Saul's weapon and his water: two things necessary for survival. David hinted that Saul was going to die soon, but he didn't make the move himself.

Closing out the first book of Samuel, Saul dies in battle by falling on his own sword and his sons are slain as well, killing off the family bloodline.

We saw quite a bit of David's character come through during the first book, but it's in the second book that we understand him even better. This is where we learn that David is considered a man after God's own heart.

Fast-forward to 2 Samuel chapter 11, where David sins. The great sin of David was his affair with Bathsheba, which resulted in the murder of her husband, Uriah, the Hittite. It's a terrible story of what lust can make you do when it has a grip on your life.

God sends Nathan as a gift to David to open David's eyes and rebuke his actions after he commits these acts. David knew his sin, acknowledged it, repented, and moved on with his life. That's all that needed to happen for David to get right with God. God has a lot of grace for repentant sinners, which is a huge message for us to grab hold of in these books.

The second book of Samuel closes out with David purchasing a threshing floor upon which to build a temple for the Lord. He has all of the resources imaginable and wants to bless God, but God tells him that He wants David's son, Solomon, to be the builder.

So he gathered the resources, put together a plan, and sat on it, waiting for the day that Solomon would build this great temple for the Lord.

One of my favorite people in history is King David. He was THE man. He was the only man in the Bible who was considered by God to be "a man after his own heart," which happens to be the greatest title you could ever be given.

King David was the whole package, in God's eyes.

He trusted God and had unstoppable faith. He was courageous. He looked out for other people. He knew how to repent of his sins. He learned from his mistakes. He continually worshiped God throughout the day.

The cool thing about studying David's life is that David messed up. He wasn't perfect at all. He messed up so badly that he should have been put to death. But that wasn't God's plan for his life.

No matter how much we fail, we're never in too deep for God to use us for His plan.

Although the Bible isn't a ten-step program for how to live life, it does give us principles and people to model our lives after. David is one of those people.

While First and Second Samuel are all about David, they end with a future hope of another king: a Messiah. This King will one day come and restore humanity back to God's original intent. ■

GOD'S OWN HEART MERC

NOINTED PRAISE & WOR

IP HUMBLE FEARED GOD

OUS MA

N HEART

PRAISE

LE FEAI

DURAGE

GOD'S O

NOINTE

DAVID WAS:

RAISE & WORSHIP HUME

FEARED GOD GRACE CO

RAGEOUS MAN AFTER G

▶ Similar to Hannah, what other barren women did God use in the Old Testament? (Hint: Genesis)

▶ Samuel was a prophet. What do you know about prophecy today? What does Paul say we should do regarding the gift of prophecy (1 Corinthians 14:1)?

▶ What are your thoughts on God blessing His people today (Jewish and Christian alike)?

▶ Having a king caused the people to incorporate rules and parameters on how to live their life. Why do you think people like being told what to do in their faith? How do you think God feels about that?

▶ What does it mean to fear the Lord? How do you fear the Lord?

▶ What was Saul's downfall? Could it have been avoided?

▶ How do you think not knowing the timing of his kingship affected David? Do you think his family treated him differently?

▶ What "Goliaths" are in your life that you need to defeat with a sling and a stone? Write out a prayer asking God to help you take them on just like David did with Goliath.

▶ List the top five strengths of David that you admire:

1.

2.

3.

4.

5.

▶ What are some practical ways you can mold your life to be similar to David's?

▶ What is the Davidic Covenant that is promised in 2 Samuel 7:8–16?

▶ What does this book teach you about the character of God? How does that influence the way you view your life?

▶ David was forgiven of a great sin. If you repent of your sins, are you confident that you, too, will be forgiven?

▶ Who is someone you model your life after? Why?

1 & 2 KINGS

AUTHOR
The author of the two books of Kings is unknown, but many people attribute the writings to the prophet Jeremiah.

DATE
Kings was written during the Babylonian exile, sometime between 560–550 BC.

AUDIENCE
Jeremiah wrote to the Jews in exile so they would remember their roots and be able to pass their history down to their descendants.

REASON
Jeremiah recorded the history of Israel and Judah, giving the Jews a bird's-eye view of why they were exiled in the first place.

THEME
Failing to live for God leads to judgment.

KEY VERSES
"And this occurred because the people of Israel had sinned against the Lord their God, who had brought them up out of the land of Egypt from under the hand of Pharaoh king of Egypt, and had feared other gods and walked in the customs of the nations whom the Lord drove out before the people of Israel, and in the customs that the kings of Israel had practiced" (2 Kings 17:7–8).

SECTIONS
1 Kings: Reign of Solomon (ch. 1–11), division of kingdom and the kings that followed (ch. 12–22).

2 Kings: Fall of Israel and Judah (ch. 1–17), Judah into exile (ch. 18–25).

KEY WORDS / PHRASES
Did what was evil, did what was right, covenant, sin, disobedience

STORY OVERVIEW

Although in our English Bible we have two separate books from Kings, they were originally written as one book telling one big story to follow the book of Samuel.

We finished the book of Samuel with a look at the life of King David and the great man that he was. David was the prime example for kingship among the Israelites and was used as the plumb line for what made a great king.

We saw that David pulled together resources and plans for how his son Solomon should build the temple of God. We begin by looking at the transition in power from David to Solomon and a charge from David before he dies for the Israelites to remain faithful to God. This charge is similar to Moses's and Joshua's farewells.

Solomon then assumes power and starts off on a great foot by asking God for wisdom and then building God's temple. Finally. But once the building is complete, Solomon begins to make some really bad choices, which lead to his downfall. When he dies, Solomon doesn't resemble the kind of king his father was at all.

But Solomon made some great decisions that positively impacted the people as well. One thing he did very well was unite the people toward one focus. As soon as he died, the kingdom split into two groups, the northern and the southern kingdoms.

The north, aka Israel, consisted of ten of the tribes joining forces, while the south, aka Judah, consisted of only two tribes.

Even though the southern kingdom was small, they had three very important things going for them: the city of Jerusalem, the temple, and the bloodline of David. For these reasons, they lasted over 100 years longer than the northern kingdom. They definitely weren't perfect, but they had far more good kings than the north.

The northern kingdom didn't have anything physical that connected them to God, and they gave in to their pagan neighbors by worshiping idols and living out very sinful lifestyles. In return, they never had the opportunity to be led by a good king.

They were all terrible and sinful, bringing the state of the northern kingdom further downhill until their eventual fall in 722 BC to Assyria.

After studying the history of Israel, some people may call God unfair for not giving them a way out, but time and time again, He sent different prophets,

like Elijah, with a word of repentance and a chance for reconciliation. But God's people never listened. These prophets weren't genies. They spoke to the people on God's behalf and challenged Israel to repent.

Elijah and Elisha were two of the most famous prophets from the north. In the back half of 2 Kings, we see Elijah boldly go against the rule of a terrible king by the name of Ahab, and God helps him. Multiple times. Before Elijah is taken to heaven by God himself—that's right, God took him—he passes his leadership to his student Elisha, who asks for a double portion of Elijah's authority.

We see Elisha go on to confront Israel and attempt to get them to turn around with a total of fourteen different stories of God using him, but they remain in their ways.

At the end of 2 Kings, the Israelites are exiled and scattered across the world, and the author blames it on their rebellion and disobedience.

Judah is then overthrown by Babylon and the line of David finally comes to an end. It seems dark, but as we know, God doesn't abandon Israel or the line of David, and as we move forward, we will see how things begin to turn around.

So serving as a recap, the book of Kings lays out Solomon's rule, explains the divided kingdom of Israel and Judah, and concludes with God's judgment of Israel's disobedience through exile. One thing that I find very helpful is to create a timeline to see all of the kings, prophets, and major events of the time. Especially since the Old Testament isn't written chronologically, this can help in understanding what was happening at the time of all the books. ▧

TIMELINE

Instead of answering questions this week, we are going to do a timeline of the kings, prophets, and major events. You will find a list of dates, names, and events on the next few pages. Then, the following pages have a blank timeline on them, so it is your job to fill in the names/events and color code the kings as to whether they are good, bad, or so-so.

Key Kings

Saul: 1050–1010 BC		*Bad*
David: 1010–970 BC		*Good*
Solomon: 970–930 BC		*So-So*

KINGS

Northern Kings

Jeroboam: 930–909 BC		*Bad*
Nadab: 909–908 BC		*Bad*
Baasha: 908–886 BC		*Bad*
Elah: 886–885 BC		*Bad*
Zimri: 885 BC		*Bad*
Tibni: 885–880 BC		*Bad*
Omri: 885–874 BC		*Bad*
Ahab: 874–853 BC		*Bad*
Ahaziah: 853–852 BC		*Bad*
Jehoram: 852–841 BC		*Bad*
Jehu: 841–814 BC		*Bad*
Jehoahaz: 814–798 BC		*Bad*
Jehoash: 798–793 BC		*Bad*
Jeroboam: 793–753 BC		*Bad*
Zechariah: 753 BC		*Bad*
Shallum: 752 BC		*Bad*
Menahem: 752–742 BC		*Bad*
Pekahiah: 752–732 BC		*Bad*
Pekah: 742–740 BC		*Bad*
Hoshea: 732–723 BC		*Bad*

Southern Kings

Rehoboam: 930–913 BC		*Bad*
Abijam: 913–910 BC		*Bad*
Asa: 910–869 BC		*Good*
Jehoshaphat: 872–848 BC		*Good*
Jehoram: 853–841 BC		*Bad*
Ahaziah: 841 BC		*Bad*
Athaliah: 841–835 BC		*Bad*
Joash: 835–796 BC		*So-So*
Amaziah: 796–767 BC		*So-So*
Azariah / Uzziah: 767–750 BC		*So-So*
Jotham: 750–732 BC		*So-So*
Ahaz: 732–725 BC		*Bad*
Hezekiah: 725–686 BC		*Good*
Manasseh: 687–642 BC		*So-So*
Amon: 642–640 BC		*Bad*
Josiah: 640–609 BC		*Good*
Jehoahaz: 609 BC		*Bad*
Jehoiakim: 609–598 BC		*Bad*
Jehoiachin: 598–597 BC		*Bad*
Zedekiah: 597–586 BC		*Bad*

PROPHETS

Obadiah: 850 BC

Joel: 835–796 BC

Jonah: 770–750 BC

Amos: 760 BC

Hosea: 750–715 BC

Isaiah: 700–680 BC

Micah: 700–686 BC

Nahum: 663–612 BC

Zephaniah: 640–621 BC

Jeremiah: 626–585 BC

Habakkuk: 609–605 BC

Ezekiel: 593–571 BC

Daniel: 530 BC

Haggai: 520 BC

Zechariah: 520–518 BC

Malachi: 430 BC

EVENTS

Divided Kingdom: 930 BC

Fall of Samaria: 722 BC

Fall of Nineveh: 612 BC

First Battle of Carchemish: 609 BC

Second Battle of Carchemish: 606 BC

Second Deportation: 597 BC

Fall of Jerusalem: 586 BC

Fall of Babylon: 539 BC

Cyrus's Decree: 538 BC

First Return: 536 BC

Temple Finished: 516 BC

Second Return: 458 BC

Third Return: 444 BC

NORTHERN KINGS

| 930–909 | 909–908 | 908–886 | 886–885 | 885 | 885–880 | 885–874 | 874–853 | 853–852 | 852–841 | 841–814 | 814–798 | 798–793 | 793–753 | 753 | 752 |

PROPHETS

| 850 | 835–796 | 770–750 | 760 |

SOUTHERN KINGS

| 930–913 | 913–910 | 910–869 | 872–848 | 853–841 | 841 | 841–835 | 835–798 | 796–767 | 767–750 |

KINGS

| 1050–1010 | 1010–970 | 970–930 |

GOOD KING

BAD KING

SO-SO KING

EVENTS

930

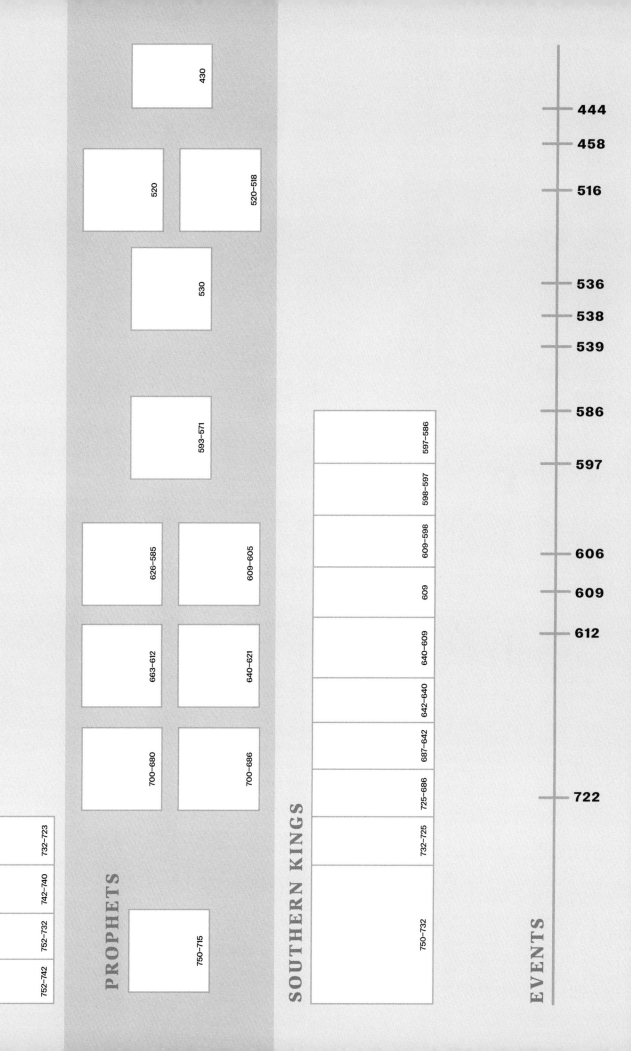

NORTHERN KINGS

| 752–742 | 752–732 | 742–740 | 732–723 |

PROPHETS

| 430 |
| 520 | 520–518 |
| 530 |
| 593–571 |
626–585	609–605
663–612	640–621
700–680	700–686
750–715

SOUTHERN KINGS

| 750–732 | 732–725 | 725–686 | 687–642 | 642–640 | 640–609 | 609 | 609–598 | 598–597 | 597–586 |

EVENTS

444
458
516
536
538
539
586
597
606
609
612
722

1&2 CHRONICLES

AUTHOR
The author of Chronicles is unknown, but Jewish tradition states that Ezra was the author.

DATE
The books of Chronicles were written after the Israelites had returned from exile and were back in Jerusalem. The time is 450–440 BC.

AUDIENCE
Ezra was writing to the returned exiles.

REASON
Ezra wrote to restore the Israelites' identity and bring them back to the law of Moses.

THEME
The kings of Judah and God's covenant with David's household.

KEY VERSE
"If my people who are called by my name humble themselves, and pray and seek my face and turn from their wicked ways, then I will hear from heaven and will forgive their sin and heal their land" (2 Chronicles 7:14).

SECTIONS
1 Chronicles: Reestablishing history (ch. 1–10), building of the temple (ch. 11–29).

2 Chronicles: Reign of Solomon (ch. 1–9), history of Judah and the temple (ch. 10–36).

KEY WORDS
Kingdom, law, temple, covenant

STORY OVERVIEW

Even though the two books are separate in our Bible, they were originally written as one book like Samuel and Kings but divided due to length. So we're going to study them together.

Chronicles is interesting because it repeats content from the books of Samuel and Kings. But look back at the stories and notice how the books are much more positive than Kings. Whereas Kings was dark and focused on the sin of the kings, Chronicles is more positive and centered around the good. Ezra keeps his focus on the royal line of David and their religious history, whereas Kings' is on their political history.

But it probably still seems strange that we have the books of Kings back-to-back with the books of Chronicles, right? Well, in the Hebrew Bible these two books are split up. Chronicles is actually the last book they read, so their Bible ends on a much happier note than our Old Testament does with Malachi.

In Chronicles, Ezra focuses almost solely on the southern kingdom because that was where the temple was located, and his priestly calling connected him to the goodness of the Law and the importance of the temple. He spends his time writing about eight main kings that positively impacted the nation.

One of the most important things this book did was show the returned exiles their genealogy. Now, I know genealogies may not be that big a deal to

you and me, but to the Jewish person, a genealogy is *everything*. It displays where they came from and also gives them something to place their pride in. Through these genealogies we have the anticipated line of the Messiah and the line of the priesthood, the lineage of Moses's brother Aaron.

An interesting take on Chronicles is that the negativity surrounding King David's rule is not mentioned as it was in Samuel. Chronicles also puts an emphasis on David's heart for the building of God's temple. David is even compared to Moses! These details about David are included to make one point very clear: There is a better king, a better David coming, and He will be from the same lineage, but this time, He will be the Messiah.

The dream for the temple was that it would be a place for the Messiah to come, rule, and unite all His people. The temple was the livelihood of the priests because it gave them a purpose and a place to worship God. They could now get right with God after being in exile for seventy years. This was their time to shine.

So we have two messages being conveyed throughout the writings of Chronicles. First, there is the hope for the Messiah, and second, there is the hope for a new temple.

Chronicles also revisits the different kings and shows how some obeyed and were blessed for their faithfulness and how others rebelled and were ruined. So what does all of this mean? It means for the Israelite readers to remain faithful to the Torah!

The key section that links Chronicles to the beginning of Ezra is found in the last two verses of Second Chronicles. They talk about Cyrus allowing the Jews to return to Jerusalem in order to rebuild the temple. Since they didn't have the Holy Spirit inside them, the only way to be connected to God was by having a place for Him to reside, which was the temple.

An ironic part of the last two verses is that they end in an incomplete sentence! And this is no mistake. It symbolizes that the ending is incomplete. The hope again is pointed to the Messiah's arrival and all that comes with it. So, the final book of the Jewish Scripture calls the Israelites to remember everything that has happened in order to anticipate what is to come. So cool!

Ezra does a great job at focusing on the positive defining moments of Israel's past to set the people up on a good note. It's almost as if their failures were wiped away and God was showing them where He was in all of it. He still does that TODAY! When we become new creations, all the sin from our past/present/future is wiped away, and we have a fresh slate with a new identity attached to it.

The books of Chronicles point directly at the New Testament, Jesus, and a completed future that is on the horizon. Chronicles serves us with a clear message: God loves His people. Even when we cannot feel it, He is moving. He's working. And the southern kingdom of Judah ultimately receives more attention here because of that. ■

▶ What did the kings do to bring the people back into the right relationship with God?

▶ Just as Ezra did in this book, list three positive defining moments from your past, and focus on those when the enemy tries to condemn you for your failures.

1.

2.

3.

EZRA

AUTHOR
Ezra and Nehemiah were originally compiled as the same book in the Hebrew Bible. They called it Ezra-Nehemiah. With that said, the author of both books is Ezra the priest, the leader of the second return to Jerusalem.

DATE
Since we know that Ezra came back to Jerusalem in 458 BC and Nehemiah went back to Babylon in 433 BC, it is safe to say that Ezra wrote these two books sometime after 433 BC.

AUDIENCE
Ezra and Nehemiah were written to the returning Jews of the Babylonian captivity. The temple was already built, and they were finally getting to work on the city of Jerusalem.

REASON
Ezra wrote to show the history of their rebuilding after exile and to spark a fire in their lives.

THEME
Rebuilding of the temple and restoring of their faith.

KEY VERSES
"And the elders of the Jews built and prospered through the prophesying of Haggai the prophet and Zechariah the son of Iddo. They finished their building by decree of the God of Israel and by decree of Cyrus and Darius and Artaxerxes king of Persia; and this house was finished on the third day of the month of Adar, in the sixth year of the reign of Darius the king" (Ezra 6:14–15).

SECTIONS
First return (ch. 1–2), the rebuilding (ch. 3–6), Ezra's return (ch. 7–8), restoring faith (ch. 9–10).

KEY WORDS
Temple, law of Moses, decree, restore

STORY OVERVIEW

Just as we will see in other books, as in Jeremiah 25 and Isaiah 44, God promised to bring His people back into the land after the time of their exile was complete through a decree by a man named Cyrus. When Cyrus of Persia led the takeover of Babylon, Daniel approached him with a copy of Isaiah's prophecy and proclaimed freedom for God's people. Cyrus was a peacemaker with the gods and wanted to bless them all in hopes of being blessed in return. Little did he know that the God of Israel is the one true God that would actually be able to bless him.

So Cyrus made a decree in 538 BC that allowed all of the Jews to go back to Jerusalem and he even gave the Jewish remnant—what was left of the Jewish people—all the materials necessary for rebuilding the temple.

The returning remnant then had a plan. They knew God wasn't happy with them, but also recognized that they were being given another chance to make things right. So the consecration and rebuilding began. This time they were going to get it right, so the builder spent a great deal of time getting a firm foundation set for the temple. Having a solid foundation sets the tone for what's to come.

No matter where we go in the world, if we are walking in the Spirit, we will be met with some sort of resistance because the devil doesn't want God's plan to come to fruition. In this case, the Samaritans were trying to get Artaxerxes, who was Cyrus' replacement, to stop the Jews from continuing on. But they were out of luck.

And in 515 BC, the second temple was finally finished being rebuilt, twenty-three years after the Jews' return. But this temple wasn't nearly as magnificent as Solomon's. That bummed some of the people out because Cyrus had provided enough materials for it to be GREAT, but the remnant didn't take advantage of their gifts.

One thing to note is that by the time Ezra is sent to Jerusalem, the temple had already been built for almost sixty years. That's something we may miss when reading through such a short book. Ezra was sent with a mission: to restore their faith.

Ezra showed up to set the stage for Nehemiah. He was there to remind Israel of the commands in the Torah and to help reestablish the community. So he showed up with the Law and a bunch of Levites to assist in the rest of the restoration process.

The king of Persia was backing the mission legally and financially because he wanted the Persians to be blessed.

But when Ezra showed up, he realized that the Israelites were in rough shape. Their entire downfall, from the beginning, upon entering the Promised Land was that they lusted after the Canaanite women and that's exactly what we see here: They married Gentiles. And even though he did not participate in the sin with the people, Ezra, as a great leader, still prayed to God using "our" and "we" because he was included in God's people. It was a "when one man falls, we all fall" mindset.

That's why Ezra stood out. He truly cared for the people. That was a very godly perspective because God himself made a covenant with the entire people group, not just one individual.

We see that Ezra's prayer life brought revival. It's another example of God moving when His people ask. In this case, an entire nation confessed and came back into a right relationship with God. Through the prayers of ONE man.

The book of Ezra is a testimony of God fulfilling His promises. God promised that He would one day bring His people back into their land, and that's exactly what we see here.

Ezra is meant to bring hope to the hopeless. Life to the lifeless. Joy to the depressed.

The Hebrew root word for *testimony* means "to do again." Just as this book shows God fulfilling His promises, we should be praying into the testimony of Jesus and the promise of His return every day. It's through these testimonies that we can ask God to "do it again." ▪

▶ Who was Zerubbabel (Ezra 2:2; 3:2–8; 5:2)?

▶ Why do you think only 50,000 people returned from exile?

▶ In what ways can you build a firm foundation in your faith?

▶ Have you ever been faced with resistance when walking out God's plan for your life? If so, in what way?

▶ Now that your foundation is being set by studying the Bible, what can you do to make sure your temple becomes like Solomon's (the best it can be) and not like the second temple?

▶ How did Ezra react to the sin of the people (Ezra 9:3–15)?

▶ How does Ezra's prayer life encourage yours? What are some practical ways of growing in your prayer life?

▶ What promises are you waiting on God to fulfill? How does the book of Ezra increase your faith in those areas?

IMPORTANT DATES

Dates to Remember

539 BC	Fall of Babylon
538 BC	Decree of Cyrus
537 BC	Return under Zerubbabel
515 BC	Temple Rebuilt
458 BC	Return under Ezra
444 BC	Nehemiah Arrives

NEHEMIAH

AUTHOR
When studying the book of Ezra, we learned that both Ezra and Nehemiah were originally one book entitled Ezra-Nehemiah. While Ezra was a priest, Nehemiah was a working man, a man's man. And he came to get the job done.

DATE
Ezra, the priest, wrote these books sometime after Nehemiah's return to Babylon in 433 BC.

AUDIENCE / REASON
Ezra wrote to record the temple restoration process for the future generations to read and appreciate.

THEME
Restoring the city and the people.

KEY VERSES
"So the wall was finished on the twenty-fifth day of the month of Elul, in fifty-two days. And when all our enemies heard of it, all the nations around us were afraid and fell greatly in their own esteem, for they perceived that this work had been accomplished with the help of our God" (Nehemiah 6:15–16).

SECTIONS
Nehemiah's return (ch. 1–2), rebuilding the city (ch. 3–7), revival under Ezra (ch. 8–13).

KEY WORDS / PHRASES
Law of Moses, city, covenant, prayer

STORY OVERVIEW

Ezra was a priest, and Nehemiah was a working man who came to get the job done.

The beginning of this book shows Nehemiah sitting back comfortably in the king's court. He was a cupbearer, a high-authority position. He was a godly man who knew his Scripture well and knew the God of the Scripture even better. If he was called to do something, obedience was the only available option.

Nehemiah's friend Hanani updated him on what was happening in Jerusalem, and it didn't sound good at all. Nehemiah knew that God had set apart His people in a specific way, so any time that they weren't doing well, it broke Nehemiah's heart. Ezra shares that the king noticed Nehemiah was sad one day, and Nehemiah was able to tell him how he felt.

The king, obviously being influenced by God, was willing to help to the fullest. Anything that Nehemiah needed to help make things right, he was given. He was even given an armed escort!

So Nehemiah arrived with an extra skip in his step. Nobody knew who he was, but his presence was to be admired. He inspected the wall and knew what needed to be done. So the delegation began.

Nehemiah was now the new governor in town. He was the big man on campus. He was sent by the king with working orders, so everybody had to listen to him. Unlike the previous governors, who increased social injustice and were just there for personal gain,

Nehemiah knew what needed to be done and how they were going to complete it. And he chose anyone and everyone to do it.

Just as we saw in Ezra, there was a lot of opposition toward the Jews' rebuilding project. There were two men named Sanballat and Tobiah who weren't the friendliest of the bunch. Sanballat and Tobiah, the Arabs (or Ammonites), and the Ashdodites all teamed up together and were angered at how fast the wall was being built. It was the evil inside of them that made them oppositional. They couldn't stand seeing how good a job the Israelites were doing and how hard it soon would be to destroy them.

But God doesn't always protect His people if they aren't willing to put in the work. So they rallied the troops with sword in hand and continued working on the walls, but puffed up their chests in case they had to attack. They knew that the enemies wouldn't come right away, but if they did, they were ready. So a plan was in motion. If anything were to come against them, they knew what to do.

When the last nail was pounded and the final bolt was tightened, the door was set up and the people were placed in their official positions under the direction of Nehemiah.

Whereas the first seven chapters were based on the wall and opposition, the content following is now redirected to the people. It went from renovating the city to renovating the nation. Both were needed

All Things New

All Things New

All Things New

All Things New

All Things New

All Things New

All Things New

All Things New

for the nation's success. And Ezra enters the scene again.

While Nehemiah was the champion of social and political influence, Ezra brought them home from a spiritual perspective. When Ezra spoke, everyone listened. The people actually begged for more. This was a defining moment for the people of Israel and the future nation as a whole.

After celebrating the Feast of Booths all week, the people drove themselves to mourning. They separated themselves from foreigners and confessed the sins they had committed as well as the iniquities of their fathers.

They wanted to start fresh. To be new. Improved. Doing things differently this time around. So what did the people do to confirm their change of heart? They made a covenant. Just as they saw their ancestors do in the past, the Jews did the same. This wasn't your normal, everyday covenant though. This one was with the God of the universe.

From here on out, they promised to be holy as a group, not as an individual like a typical covenant. It was to be between God and His people alone. They promised themselves that they would be set apart from the land and would follow God's law completely.

New laws were to be instituted because the people could no longer live the way that man had always taught. They had new obligations. The Lord's one desire for His people from the beginning was to have them live as a solid representation of His glory. Nehemiah and Ezra, equipped with the law of the Lord, were there to bring revival. To teach the people what needed to be changed in order to receive the blessing of the Lord upon their new city/nation.

This was the reformation of a nation for the history books. There was none like it. Nehemiah shows that it is possible to be a strong leader and a man of God at the same time. He even makes it look enjoyable!

From the beginning, we see that Nehemiah takes prayer very seriously. He drops to his face when he hears of the current state of Israel. Ezra also knows the importance of prayer in leadership, so he makes sure to include all of the one-line prayers Nehemiah says throughout the day because if the Lord knows your heart, one line is all you need for Him to move. And Nehemiah's prayer life is remarkable. Every single time he prays, Nehemiah begins with praising the Lord, then he gives his opinion and desires, and finally, he ends with more praise. His life was filled with praise, and that is apparent throughout his successes. The Lord listened to Nehemiah and He moved.

▶ What did Nehemiah do when the news came through about what was happening in Jerusalem (Nehemiah 1:4)?

▶ How does that compare with your initial reaction when receiving bad news?

▶ How willing are you to be used in God's plan? What holds you back from going all in?

▶ We see the people working on the walls with one hand and a sword in another. How does this image compare with a body of believers today? Are you plugged into a community that fights alongside each other and for each other?

▶ Has anything happened in your life that caused you to change from your old ways? If so, did you change cold turkey, or was it a gradual process?

▶ How can you incorporate Nehemiah's prayer strategy into your prayer life?

▶ We are all leaders to some extent. What tips and tricks can you pull from Nehemiah's leadership style?

ESTHER

AUTHOR
I have absolutely no idea who wrote the book of Esther and neither does anybody else. There is a chance that it was Mordecai himself, but an unknown Persian Jew may seem a more reasonable candidate.

DATE
The book of Esther was most likely written shortly after the events occurred, around 460 BC.

AUDIENCE
Esther was written to the Israelites who remained under Persian control and were familiar with the recorded events.

REASON
Esther records the origin of Purim and shows that God was still involved with the Jews who remained in exile.

THEME
Saving God's people.

KEY VERSE
"For if you keep silent at this time, relief and deliverance will rise for the Jews from another place, but you and your father's house will perish. And who knows whether you have not come to the kingdom for such a time as this?" (Esther 4:14).

SECTIONS
Esther becomes queen (ch. 1–2), threat against the Jews (ch. 3–4), victory of the Jews (ch. 5–10).

KEY WORDS
Queen, Jew, banquet, decree

STORY OVERVIEW

The book of Esther is an amazing story of how God protected His people from extinction, yet again. We're dealing with those Jews who chose not to return to Jerusalem from exile because of either social or work-related reasons. And God still chose to protect them.

The book of Esther begins in a party at the king's quarters. This isn't just any party that the king decided to throw. It's a rager. Lasting for 180 days. That's a full six-month party! These parties were happening to show how big a deal the king was.

Ahasuerus is the Hebrew name for the Persian King Xerxes, and his reign lasted from 486–465 BC. So King Ahasuerus called for his wife, Queen Vashti, to come and dance for his generals, but she said no. That put the king in a very tough situation because he was technically in charge of her. He was enraged.

Many people claim that she was just an independent woman who was being modest, but they overlook the fact that her son, Artaxerxes, was born in 483 BC. Queen Vashti very easily could have been pregnant with him and not been able to dance. Or she could have had the baby already, and that's what this celebration was about, but she didn't want to show off her post-pregnant body. In any case, her title was taken away because they feared that other women would use Vashti as an example for rebelling themselves.

After four years of not having a queen, Ahasuerus became lonely and called for his people to create a beauty contest for him to select a new queen. Being the king of 127 provinces meant there would be a ton of women to choose from, but they set out on a mission and pulled together all the single women. And out of all the women, one of them was a Jewish girl from the tribe of Benjamin named Esther.

Esther was raised in captivity by her cousin Mordecai, who was a very smart man. He knew that she had to keep her background a secret in order to remain eligible for royalty.

In Chapter 3, we are introduced to Ahaseurus's general, Haman, who had a massive ego, and whose pride would eventually result in his death. Haman was a Canaanite descendent and didn't like Mordecai because he was a Jew who refused to bow to or honor Haman when he walked by.

So he put together a plan to exterminate all Jews.

The king accepted Haman's plea to wipe out the Jews, which meant that if anybody found out Esther's true nationality, she would be killed as well. Persian law was final, and even the king wouldn't be able to save her. Mordecai then realized that Esther's positioning was a part of something bigger than they knew. She was there to save the Jews.

So Esther walked boldly into the king's presence, even though the queen was not allowed there without an invite. And the king reached out his scepter toward Esther, allowing her to speak and then he fulfilled her request.

Esther threw the king two feasts before asking him anything, which meant that she had a major request. And during the second feast, after God had been working behind the scenes, Haman ended up pleading for HIS life.

God stepped up and protected His people once again, and Haman was hung on the same gallows that he prepared for Mordecai. I guess what goes around comes around, huh?

Even though Haman was dead, the edict against the Jews was still out there. It couldn't technically be revoked at this point, according to Persian law, but a stipulation could be added to it to combat the original intent.

So that's what Esther begged for, and the king allowed one to be written up. The stipulation didn't allow the Jews to initiate attacks, but it did say that the Jews could defend themselves. And that is exactly what they did, killing 75,000 during the battle. And the Jewish people became highly respected among the Persians.

As we saw when studying Exodus, the Jews inaugurated holidays and feasts to remember how God used His people and worked on their behalf. These holidays and feasts are always about God, which is pretty remarkable.

Since Haman cast lots to see which day the Jews should be persecuted, it only made sense that they would name this new feast after that. So Purim was added to the main feasts from Exodus to show God's faithfulness to the covenant, making it a beautiful holiday to be celebrated.

One heavily debated part of Esther is that the name of God is never mentioned, and a lot of people have a problem with that. Martin Luther didn't even think Esther should be included in the Bible, based on that reason alone.

When reading Esther, it's easy to see how detail-oriented God was with the actions of people who didn't even follow Him. Here, He used a Persian king who was cool with any type of religion, but definitely didn't consider the Lord to be his one and only God. In this case, the king's God-inspired actions changed the course for the Jewish people. They were saved from a mass genocide because of insomnia and a random evening's chosen reading. God's hand was all over it.

So, what's the point? In the book of Esther, we see that God doesn't abandon His people. Ever. He works with the messiness of humanity. God's commitment to restoration outweighs the faithlessness of people. God is *always* at work.

And that's what we can learn from the book of Esther. ▨

QUEEN ESTHER
PERSIAN EMPIRE
WORLD CHANGER

▶ Give at least one historical example of an attempt to wipe out the Jewish people:

▶ What role does Satan play in anti-Semitism (hatred toward Jewish people)?

▶ How should the church respond to anti-Semitism?

▶ How can we use Esther's boldness as an example in approaching our King, Jesus?

▶ What are your thoughts on the absence of God's name in the book of Esther? Do you think it's a big deal? Why, or why not?

▶ Do you believe everything happens for a reason?

AUTHOR
Nobody knows for sure who the author of Job was.

DATE
The author most likely wrote the book of Job around 2000 BC, during the Patriarchal period.

AUDIENCE
Since we are dating this book around 2000 BC, we do not have a clear idea of who it was written to, but we can conclude that they were both righteous and suffering at the same time.

REASON
The book of Job was written to show that God's people still suffer and that the righteous will be blessed even more greatly if they continue in righteousness.

THEME
Dealing with suffering in the lives of the righteous.

KEY VERSES
"My ears had heard of you but now my eyes have seen you. Therefore I despise myself and repent in dust and ashes" (Job 42:5–6 NIV).

SECTIONS
The testing (ch. 1–2), dialogue with three friends (ch. 3–31), Elihu's thoughts (ch. 32–37), God's thoughts (ch. 38–41), Job's restoration (ch. 42).

KEY WORDS
Suffering, righteous, sin, restore

STORY OVERVIEW

One thing to note while looking into this book is that the theology behind Job's friends' arguments was wrong, which means you should not quote them as truth. Now, let's take a closer look!

From the first interaction in the book of Job we see that there is a lot more going on behind the scenes of heaven than we realize. Many times, what happens here on earth is a direct result of what happens in the spiritual realm. And that can bring a lot of confusion to our situations.

We see Satan believed that people only followed God for the blessings He gives them. That's the concept behind this story, but Job proves him wrong.

So Satan approaches the throne of God. And after their discussion, God allows Satan to tempt Job for a period of time because of His confidence in Job's steady character. The key here is that Satan always needs permission before he touches the righteous. And then Job goes on to lose everything. Literally. Family, livestock, property—everything.

After Job loses everything, three of his friends come to him to do their best at counseling him through it. Normally we would look at that as a good thing, but their theology was skewed by a lack of understanding in the ways of God. They didn't understand the goodness of God and claimed that Job's suffering was a result of him displeasing God in some way.

Most of what those three said about Job's situation was false, and it came from a poor understanding of God. Job knew the Father better than that. He knew God was good, which is why Job is extremely honest

during the entire book. However, the back-and-forth dialogue between the three friends did pose three main questions:

> Is God truly just?
> Does God have an understandable strategy in the ways He measures justice?
> Why is Job suffering?

Job's buddy Elihu eventually steps on the scene and, even though he was younger than the others, he shared some of the best advice Job received all week. Elihu also thought there was a higher purpose behind the suffering, and he sort of set the stage for God to come in and answer Job.

Up until Elihu's conversation with Job, the three friends had operated under the standard cultural understanding of suffering. You suffer because you did something wrong. In other words, you suffer because it's a form of punishment. However, Elihu took a different stance on suffering and alluded to it being connected to a warning from God or even a way God can build character in our lives.

After hearing Elihu out, Job then demands to speak with God himself. When God shows up, He doesn't give Job answers, but He does show Job who He is. James 1:17 NASB says, "Every good thing given and every perfect gift is from above, coming down from the Father of lights, with whom there is no variation or shifting shadow."

God first checks Job by showing him His vastness through the details of creation and all the work that goes into maintaining the universe. This check shows

Job that God's ways cannot be boxed in by human understanding. And this includes our assumptions of how justice and suffering work. God's ways and thoughts are higher.

Justice is more complicated than we can understand, and the way God chooses to carry it out sometimes falls outside of our understanding. The conversation between God and Job wraps up by God showing Job that although the earth is good, it's not perfect. This reality is God's way of saying that suffering is unavoidable. So we need to put our trust in Him.

Job hears the message loud and clear from God and has a complete change of heart. He's apologetic for the accusations he made against God and repents. These actions from Job lead to God honoring the honesty Job displays. Job brought all of his emotions to God. He held nothing back.

So God restores Job. He gives him everything back that he lost before, but this time, it's multiplied. An important thing to note about Job's ending is that it has nothing to do with Job's suffering. More or less, God's decision to restore Job is done out of His wisdom. So what does that mean? It means we must trust God in our trials and difficulties and not always attempt to make sense of the why—as enticing as that may be.

The book of Job teaches us that God cannot be boxed in by our limited understanding. He's the Creator and we're the creation. Time and time again in modern teachings we see that God takes the rap for Satan's tasks. Yes, God may *allow* hard times, but they are always for our good and His glory.

God is love and He always takes care of His people. In this case, yeah, Job had to deal with some junk, but in the end he received a greater blessing than he had before.

We need to remember that God is good. That's the message that was present through it all, even when the outcome was uncertain and death appeared to have the upper hand. Not only that, but it also provides counsel to others who are dealing with similar issues. Never lose sight of God's goodness, because He is good. ∎

testing brings perseverance

testing brings perseverance

testing brings perseverance

testing brings perseverance

testing brings perseverance

testing brings perseverance

testing brings perseverance

testing brings perseverance

testing brings perseverance

Not all advice is good advice

▶ What can we learn about Satan from this interaction between him and God?

▶ Have you ever suffered? What happened? How does this new understanding from Job alter your views of what you went through?

▶ Do you know anybody who has fallen away from their faith because of a trial they went through that they ended up blaming God for? What would you say to them?

▶ Unlike what Eliphaz, Bildad, and Zophar did, what is the best way to comfort a friend who is going through a hard time? Why?

▶ What are some things God says to Job to show how powerful He is (Job 38–39)?

▶ Has God ever given you an even greater blessing after a time of suffering? If so, what happened?

▶ What are your thoughts on suffering? Has the book of Job changed your views on it? If so, in what ways?

PSALMS

AUTHOR
The book of Psalms is a collection of pieces from many different individuals including King David, Moses, Solomon, the sons of Korah, the sons of Asaph, and others.

DATE
All in all, the Psalms were written over a period of nearly 1,000 years. It was an ongoing collection of works that was continually added to over the ages, so there was no distinct time of writing.

AUDIENCE
The audience of the Psalms was varied, based on what period the author was writing in, but nearly all of the psalms were originally directed toward the Israelites.

REASON
These psalms were arranged to be a collection of prayers and praises for the Jewish people toward God.

THEME
God is good all the time.

KEY VERSE
"Let the words of my mouth and the meditation of my heart be acceptable in your sight, O Lord, my rock and my redeemer" (Psalms 19:14).

SECTIONS
Book I: (ch. 1–41), Book II: (ch. 42–72), Book III: (ch. 73–89), Book IV: (ch. 90–106), Book V: (ch. 107–150).

KEY WORDS
Praise, prayer, thankful, hope

STORY OVERVIEW ──────────────────────

The book of Psalms is the longest book in the Bible and the easiest to relate to. Every psalm was written from an emotional state that we deal with today, whether that's joy, love, thankfulness, anger, etc. These psalms were used as a devotional for the Jewish people, yet they are also for you and me today.

Since this is such a unique book of the Bible, we are going to do the study a little differently this week.

I would encourage you to read one psalm every day for the next 150 days. This week, write three of your own psalms/poems on the next few pages, covering topics that can be found throughout the book.

Examples include creation, joy, prayer, love, the Messiah, peace, war, anger, gratitude, worship, praise, judgment, hope, trust, glory, etc. ■

MY PERSONAL PSALM:

_____

_____

_____

_____

_____

_____

_____

_____

_____

_____

_____

MY PERSONAL PSALM:

MY PERSONAL PSALM:

THE PSALMS ARE
THE PSALMS ARE
THE PSALMS ARE
THE PSALMS ARE
THE PSALMS ARE
THE PSALMS ARE
THE PSALMS ARE
THE PSALMS ARE
THE PSALMS ARE

GOOD

FOR

YOU

THE

PSALMS

ARE

PROVERBS

AUTHOR
The book of Proverbs was almost entirely composed by King Solomon. There are six chapters of Solomon's proverbs compiled by Hezekiah's men and two chapters written by guys named Agur and Lemuel. Some scholars believe Agur and Lemuel are nicknames for Solomon, making the entire work Solomonic.

DATE
These proverbs were composed sometime during the middle of Solomon's life (990–931 BC) and fully edited by Hezekiah's men around 700 BC.

AUDIENCE
Solomon wrote to the young, wise men of Israel.

REASON
These proverbs were written as a teacher's manual for how to live wisely day-by-day.

THEME
Sharing wisdom.

KEY VERSE
"Let the wise hear and increase in learning, and the one who understands obtain guidance" (Proverbs 1:5).

SECTIONS
Father-to-Son wisdom (ch. 1–9), proverbs of Solomon (ch. 10–22), common wisdom (ch. 23–24), proverbs of Solomon 2.0 (ch. 25–29), wisdom from Agur and Lemuel (ch. 30–31).

KEY WORDS
Wisdom, knowledge, understanding, righteous, wealth

STORY OVERVIEW

In 2 Chronicles 1, if you remember, God asked Solomon what he wanted in life. Instead of saying wealth or honor, as most people would pick, Solomon chose to be granted wisdom and knowledge. Because of this choice, "God said to Solomon, 'Because you had this in mind, and did not ask for riches, wealth or honor, or the life of those who hate you, nor have you even asked for long life, but you have asked for yourself wisdom and knowledge that you may rule My people over whom I have made you king, wisdom and knowledge have been granted to you. And I will give you riches and wealth and honor, such as none of the kings who were before you have possessed

nor those who will come after you'" (2 Chronicles 1:11–12 NASB).

Solomon was the wisest person to ever live, and we should be forever grateful that he left us with a collection of 900 proverbs on how to live a good life. How cool is that?!

Since Proverbs is another unique book of the Bible, we are going to read it like we are currently doing with the Psalms. Your goal is to read one chapter per day for the next thirty-one days, then write out your favorite proverb from each category listed below: ■

THE TONGUE:

_____

_____

_____

_____

_____

_____

_____

_____

WEALTH:

_____

_____

_____

_____

_____

_____

_____

_____

HEALTH:

_____

_____

_____

_____

_____

_____

_____

_____

_____

FEAR OF THE LORD:

_____

_____

_____

_____

_____

_____

_____

_____

JOY:

_____

_____

_____

_____

_____

_____

_____

_____

WORDS OF WISDOM

PROVERBS

THE PROVERBS TO EMPOWER YOU TO REIGN IN LIFE

ECCLESIASTES

AUTHOR
The book of Ecclesiastes has widely been attributed to King Solomon over the years and there is no reason, in my mind, to believe otherwise.

DATE
Solomon wrote Song of Songs, Proverbs, and Ecclesiastes, all at different stages in his life. This book was most likely written during the final years of his life and before the division of the kingdom in 931 BC, dating it around 940–931 BC.

AUDIENCE
Ecclesiastes was written to the wise Israelites of the time.

REASON
Solomon wrote this book to show that material things fade away and the real meaning of life can only be found in things from above.

THEME
Everything under the sun is vanity.

KEY VERSE
"Then I considered all that my hands had done and the toil I had expended in doing it, and behold, all was vanity and a striving after wind, and there was nothing to be gained under the sun" (Ecclesiastes 2:11).

SECTIONS
Introducing the issue (1:1–11), looking at the meaning of life (1:12–12:8), importance of focusing on God (12:9–14).

KEY WORDS / PHRASES
Vanity, under the sun, wealth, wisdom

STORY OVERVIEW ———————————————————————

As we know, King Solomon was the definition of what society deemed as successful. He was the wisest, richest person to ever live, and people traveled thousands of miles just to witness his grandeur. He was the MAN.

But even though he had the world at his fingertips, it still didn't satisfy his appetite. In fact, he felt he had wasted his life by pursuing meaningless things. So a huge takeaway from the book of Ecclesiastes would be to pursue things in life that are not temporary.

The list could look something like this:

Spend more time with family.
Chase after your dreams instead of money.
Spend more time in prayer.

The list can go on and on.

So what is the meaning of life? First, we need to look at God. The Creator of life. God is perfect. His being is flawless, and His glory is indescribable. The most selfless thing He could have done was to create mankind so we could enjoy His glory along with Him. So that's what He did.

Solomon is speaking directly to this reality by steering his readers' attention and motivations away from things that won't lead to fulfillment. True meaning in life is found in looking at God redeeming and restoring humanity to its original intent. This hope propels us to live lives of character, faithfulness, and integrity, despite most of life remaining a mystery.

In other words, we are taught through Solomon to fix our eyes on Jesus. The author's final conclusion on life's meaning, however, is the most crucial: Fear God and keep His commandment, for that is the whole duty of everyone. ■

WHY AM I HERE?

WHAT IS MY PURPOSE?

▶ How can you fear God daily?

▶ What would you say is the meaning of life?

▶ Are you living out your full potential? If not, what is holding you back?

▶ Who is one person you admire who is walking in their purpose? What do they do differently?

Song of Songs (also known as Song of Solomon) is by far the most debated book in the Bible—from who the author is to how you should view the book to why it's included in the first place. With that said, our study is going to present multiple views that allow you to decide for yourself.

AUTHOR
A large portion of evidence for the authorship of Song of Songs suggests King Solomon, but many scholars disagree. In reality, nobody knows for sure.

DATE
Since I believe that Song of Songs was written by Solomon, I believe he most likely penned it during the beginning or middle of his reign, possibly around 950 BC.

AUDIENCE
Song of Songs was most likely written to the people of Israel who looked up to King Solomon.

REASON
Solomon wrote to show the importance of a holy marriage and how a romantic relationship was to unfold.

THEME
God's view of marriage and sex.

KEY VERSES
"Set me as a seal upon your heart, as a seal upon your arm, for love is strong as death, jealousy is fierce as the grave. Its flashes are flashes of fire, the very flame of the LORD. Many waters cannot quench love, neither can floods drown it. If a man offered for love all the wealth of his house, he would be utterly despised" (Song of Songs 8:6–7).

SECTIONS
Praising the physical attributes (1:1–2:7), becoming more intimate (2:8–3:5), the procession and marriage (3:6–5:1), missing her husband (5:2–6:9), the romance (6:10–8:4), what the future holds (8:5–14).

KEY WORDS
Beloved, love, beautiful

SONG OF SONGS

STORY OVERVIEW

Your view of Solomon's Song of Songs is heavily reliant on your interpretation of the text, and through which lens you choose to view it.

The three ways of interpreting Song of Songs:

The Literal Interpretation looks at this story as God's view of a holy marriage.

The Allegorical Interpretation looks at the Song as an allegory of God's love for Israel.

The Typical Interpretation looks at it as being a "type" of Christ and the Church.

All three of the interpretations are true, and you can learn incredible truths by viewing the Song through each lens.

Many people have a problem with this book because of the sexual content. They tend to disregard it because they don't believe sex is a spiritual experience, considering how sex is viewed in our society. In reality, sex is a gift from God and should be treasured. Satan has continually distorted our view of sex to keep believers from experiencing God's plan and the fullness of it. What society tells us is that what is right doesn't look anything like the true intimacy that is associated with a godly relationship.

Allegories of God's love for His people are also woven throughout the text, creating a beautiful picture of what God intended love to be. It shows us unity and safety in a sacred relationship. It shows us that God's type of love stands alone and is higher than any other form of love there is. Anything less is counterfeit. Sex is meant to exist only in the confines of marriage. Those marriage desires are displayed here beautifully and transparently. This holy union is the way Christ sees the church. He is eager to be united with it, and loves it unconditionally. ■

▶ Through which lens do you interpret Song of Songs?

▶ What are your views on sex? What does your church teach about the topic?

▶ How can sex be a holy experience?

▶ List five key points from this book that can be applied to your love life.

1.

2.

3.

4.

5.

AUTHOR
The book of Isaiah was written by the prophet Isaiah.

DATE
Isaiah was kind enough to note which kings were reigning during his ministry and we can conclude that he wrote his prophecy shortly afterward, around 700–680 BC.

CONTEMPORARY PROPHETS
Hosea around 750–715 BC
Micah around 700–686 BC

AUDIENCE
Isaiah wrote his prophecy mainly to the southern kingdom of Judah, but also to the northern kingdom and to all the Gentile nations willing to listen.

REASON
Isaiah was written mainly to show how serious God takes His covenants and to give His people hope for the future.

THEME
Judgment and salvation.

KEY VERSES
"You will say in that day: 'I will give thanks to you, O Lord, for though you were angry with me, your anger turned away, that you might comfort me. 'Behold, God is my salvation; I will trust, and will not be afraid; for the Lord God is my strength and my song, and he has become my salvation'" (Isaiah 12:1–2).

SECTIONS
Judgment (ch. 1–39), salvation (ch. 40–66).

KEY WORDS
Woe, remnant, salvation, redemption, glory

ISAIAH

STORY OVERVIEW

Isaiah is the first *major prophet* book of the Old Testament. As you will see, the major prophet books are BIG and jam-packed with content that encompasses entire studies inside themselves, so we take it pretty easy with some of these huge prophetic books and encourage you to do a deep dive once you complete the yearlong study. Focus on the big picture and go back for the details later.

Isaiah was trying to get two points across, and his prophecy is laid out in those two major sections: judgment and salvation.

Some people may struggle with the judgment of God that's so prevalent in the Old Testament. I get it, especially when we are seeing things from a New Testament, grace-filled perspective. Just remember that God is the same now as He was back then. And the presence of judgment shows that it's necessary for salvation to occur. Before we can have salvation, we must have a need for it! So the bulk of those early chapters in Isaiah details judgments against the people who have turned their back on the Lord, showing us that those who persist in their rebellion will receive judgment. On the other hand, we also see God's faithfulness to His promise. He will preserve a small number of faithful believers, those who will continue into the perfect renewed world He has prepared for His children in the end times.

Something cool to note is that Isaiah is known as "the messianic prophet" because of his vast array of messianic prophecies sprinkled throughout the text—more than 300 of them in total. It actually provides us with the most comprehensive prophetic picture of Jesus Christ in the entire Old Testament. And the New Testament quotes from Isaiah more than any other prophet because he had so much to say about the coming King, Jesus.

Isaiah speaks to the complete mission of His life: first the announcement of the Messiah coming to earth, then the fact that He will be born from a virgin, then the reality of the Good News message He'll bring, accompanied by the sacrifice that His death was, and finally His return for the church. Because of these and numerous other Christological texts in Isaiah, the book stands as a testament of hope in the Lord, the One who will save His people from themselves.

One thing that makes Jesus hard for the Jewish people to understand is that He didn't present himself as a conquering king like Isaiah prophesied about, but He did come as a suffering servant. You see, Isaiah represented what seemed like two different people: A king and a servant. So that is what the Jews expected. It's the great mystery of Isaiah that we, as believers, are blessed to understand.

Isaiah shows that upon Jesus's arrival, a new kingdom would be created. God's Kingdom would be brought to earth. And that's exactly what Jesus does with His life. Isaiah points to Jesus and the reality that His coming will bring restoration. ■

STRENGTH

STRENGTH AND SONG

MY STRENGTH AND SONG

Using your New Testament understanding of the Messiah, along with Isaiah 53, take the next page to explain to a Jewish person why Jesus is their Messiah after all. It's not an easy task, but it's important to be able to do it. Have fun with it!

WHY IS JESUS THE MESSIAH?

_____

_____

_____

_____

_____

_____

_____

_____

_____

_____

_____

_____

_____

_____

_____

_____

AUTHOR
The book of Jeremiah was written by Jeremiah, son of Hilkiah the priest. That would make Jeremiah another priest/prophet, like Samuel.

DATE
The ministry of Jeremiah took place between 626–580 BC, and he wrote these prophecies over that forty-six-year time span.

CONTEMPORARY PROPHETS
Nahum around 663–612 BC, Zephaniah around 640–621 BC, Habakkuk around 609–605 BC, Ezekiel around 593–571 BC

AUDIENCE
Jeremiah wrote his prophecies to the southern kingdom of Judah, more specifically Jerusalem.

REASON
The main reason Jeremiah wrote these prophecies was to warn Judah of the coming judgment ahead, in hopes of sparking nationwide repentance.

THEME
The fall of Jerusalem and the reason for their exile.

KEY VERSES
"For thus says the Lord: When seventy years are completed for Babylon, I will visit you, and I will fulfill to you my promise and bring you back to this place. For I know the plans I have for you, declares the Lord, plans for welfare and not for evil, to give you a future and a hope" (Jeremiah 29:10–11).

SECTIONS
Jeremiah's call (ch. 1), warning to Judah (ch. 2–29), future restoration (ch. 30–33), before and after the fall of Jerusalem (ch. 34–45), warning to other nations (ch. 46– 51), final outcome (ch. 52).

KEY WORDS
Sin, wickedness, judgment

JEREMIAH

STORY OVERVIEW

Jeremiah was known as "the weeping prophet" because he really put his heart into his prophecies. His words hit you on the inside, and you get to know his personality much better than the other prophets'.

Jeremiah is the second-longest prophecy in the Bible, coming in at fifty-two chapters in length. The only one longer is Isaiah. The majority of this book is about destruction and judgment that was to come to Judah and the surrounding nations for remaining unrepentant. Same story as most, just a different prophet.

The prophecies of Jeremiah offer us a unique look into the mind and heart of one of God's faithful servants. This presents Jeremiah not merely as a prophet brought on the scene to deliver God's message but also as a real human being who was burdened for his people and desired justice for evil, and as a man concerned about his own safety as well. Another thing to note is that the book of Jeremiah also provides us the clearest glimpse of the new covenant God intended to make with His people once Christ came to earth. This new covenant would be the catalyst of restoration for God's people, as He would put His law within them, writing it on hearts of flesh rather than on tablets of stone. Rather than fostering our relationship with God through a fixed location like a temple, He promised through Jeremiah that His people would know Him directly, a knowledge that comes through the person of His Son, Jesus Christ.

Because Jeremiah prophesied in the final years of Judah before God's people were exiled to Babylon, it makes sense that the book's overarching theme is judgment. The first forty-five chapters focus primarily on the judgment coming to Judah because of its disbelief and disobedience. However, an element of grace is also present in these events.

The fall of Jerusalem comes nearly nine hundred years after the original covenant between God and the Israelites in the Sinai desert. This extended period of time witnesses to God's great patience and mercy. He allowed His people the opportunity to turn from their sinful ways—a lifestyle they began not long after they struck the original covenant with God.

Another cool feature in Jeremiah is that he writes in poetry for the whole book. It shows that the Father is communicating His heart toward the audience instead of His mind, as we see when a writer uses prose. Poetry is deeper and shares the feelings of the Father. Prose is more effective to get the point across.

Not only did Jeremiah write from the heart and share the Father's heart, but he also spoke a lot about the importance of getting your heart right with God instead of being religious with your actions. So often, we tend to get caught up in the actions of our faith and think that's good enough. We go to church every Sunday, attend a small group on Tuesdays,

PLANS TO PROSPER YOU PLANS TO GIVE YOU A HOPE AND A FUTURE

JEREMIAH 29:11

have fifteen to thirty minutes of "quiet time" every day, and think we are set when in reality the Father desires intimacy with His children and doesn't look at what you are doing to be a "good" Christian. So if you're missing out on that intimacy while attending your church, small group, and having a quiet time, then you may be missing the relational aspect of the Christian life.

I get it, though. There was a time in my life when I was in the same position. All I wanted was to know the Bible well and learn as much as I could about what I believed. So I filled my head with as much knowledge as possible, but my heart remained untouched. I've been in a process lately to change that. To go from my head to my heart. . . . And I'm finally able to see God move more and hear what He has to say. ∎

ACTIVITY

Pray this prayer:

"Father, it's clear that Jeremiah knew Your heart, and You knew his. He expressed Your feelings with confidence and knew his identity in You. I want that. So, Father, I'm asking You to align my heart with Yours. Take what I know in my head and teach it to my heart. Show me how to apply Your heart to my current situation and show me what You think about me. Amen."

Now, be still and spend this page writing down what you sense God might be saying to you:

_____

_____

_____

_____

_____

_____

_____

_____

_____

_____

_____

_____

LAMENTATIONS

AUTHOR
The author of Lamentations is considered to be anonymous, but the majority of scholars attribute it to Jeremiah.

DATE
Lamentations was written at the beginning of exile, around 586–580 BC.

AUDIENCE
Lamentations was written to his fellow Jewish people in exile.

REASON
Jeremiah wrote to express his deep sorrow over the destruction of Jerusalem.

THEME
Sorrow over Jerusalem and the compassion of God.

KEY VERSES
"The steadfast love of the LORD never ceases; his mercies never come to an end; they are new every morning; great is your faithfulness" (Lamentations 3:22–23).

SECTIONS
Destruction of Jerusalem (ch. 1), the anger of the Lord (ch. 2), the Lord's comfort (ch. 3), past vs. present (ch. 4), prayer for forgiveness (ch. 5).

KEY WORDS
Sin, anger, transgressions, Zion

STORY OVERVIEW

Lamentation: Noun

"The passionate expression of grief or sorrow." (Oxforddictionaries.com)

We saw while looking at the book of Jeremiah, that he was known as "the weeping prophet" because of how emotional he was in his writing. Lamentations is the proof of that; in this follow-up book, he expresses his deep sorrow over the destruction of Jerusalem.

After multiple prophecies of Jerusalem's future destruction, their time was finally coming to pass because they had failed to repent as Jeremiah had pleaded. Jerusalem was destroyed before their eyes, and the people were taken away to exile. It was a horrific time to be alive. And Jeremiah wept. Oh, how he wept. Lamentations is the record of that weeping.

It's one of the saddest books you could ever read. But there's hope! Jeremiah realized that in God's mercy, He chose to keep a group alive. The prophet was seeing the good inside the bad and found something to be thankful for even when the situation looked terrible. Jeremiah took that revelation and prayed into it that God would one day be so merciful that the nation of Israel would be restored. And history shows us that the Lord answered. Hallelujah!

When they were surrounded by war, pain, and suffering, the people of Israel repented and cried out to God for restoration in the lament poems. These poems serve as outlets to process emotion and confusion at the chaos and to tell God how they truly felt. Reading Lamentations teaches us to bring our emotions and frustrations to God. He can handle it!

In the middle of Lamentations, we see hope for restoration. This glimmer of hope is clearly spelled out in the middle of Israel's pain. It's a message that God is not done with them, despite their disobedience. Another clear representation of the Gospel inside the Old Testament. ∎

ACTIVITY

Spend a few minutes listening to the song "Mercy" by Amanda Cook.

▶ Then use the rest of this page to journal what you sense God saying to you through that song and what His views of judgment and mercy are.

_____

_____

_____

_____

_____

_____

_____

_____

_____

_____

_____

_____

_____

_____

_____

EZEKIEL

AUTHOR
The book of Ezekiel was written by the priest/prophet Ezekiel, who was one of the captives during Nebuchadnezzar's second siege of Jerusalem.

DATE
Ezekiel was written around 593–571 BC.

CONTEMPORARY PROPHETS
Jeremiah around 626–585 BC.

AUDIENCE
Ezekiel directed his prophecies toward the exiles in Babylon who were steadily losing hope.

REASON
Ezekiel wrote to show that God was still among them while in exile, and that He would be faithful to His promise of future restoration.

THEME
God's sovereignty over all people and His glory.

KEY VERSES
"Then they shall know that I am the Lord their God, because I sent them into exile among the nations and then assembled them into their own land. I will leave none for them remaining among the nations anymore. And I will not hide my face anymore from them, when I pour out my Spirit upon the house of Israel, declares the Lord God" (Ezekiel 39:28–29).

SECTIONS
Judgment against Judah (ch. 1–24), judgment against other nations (ch. 25–32), future restoration (ch. 33–39), the future temple (ch. 40–48).

KEY WORDS / PHRASES
Know that I am the Lord, covenant, glory, temple, holy

STORY OVERVIEW

The book of Ezekiel has a lot of prophetic destruction that may not really apply to us, but there are some gems that can speak into our lives and our current situation. Those are the ones we are going to focus on.

Being that Ezekiel was both a prophet AND a priest makes him stand out from most of the prophets in the Old Testament.

His original calling in life came through this crazy vision that we see in chapters 1–3. Ezekiel knew that he was now in the presence of God. He was experiencing holiness firsthand, so he dropped to his face in worship. That's all you can really do when you're in that position.

And then from chapters 4 through 37 there are ten things God makes Ezekiel do to get His point across to the people. After everything God calls Ezekiel to do, He promises a future restoration for the people of Israel. The restoration was not a reward for their good behavior or anything they could physically do, because when it came down to it, they always ended up failing. The restoration was completely for God's sake so that He would be represented accurately. God takes His name very seriously and expects us to represent Him well. Calling yourself a Christian means that you associate yourself with Christ, AND He also associates with you. It's two-sided and should benefit both.

Ezekiel goes on to share a very popular prophecy about a bunch of bones coming to life. It's an image of God pouring His Spirit out on the lifeless and bringing them to life or resurrecting them. It's important to note that Ezekiel clarifies this is a spiritual and physical restoration of Israel, which we began to see in 1948 when Israel became a nation.

Right after the dry bones prophecy, Ezekiel goes into a highly debated prophecy: The War of Gog and Magog. The prophecy suggests that Israel will be attacked from all sides and God will step in at the last minute to protect His people. History shows that He has done it before, and prophecy shows that He will do it again. If you keep an eye on Israel, you can see God's hand in all of it.

In chapters 40–48, Ezekiel ends by speaking of a *grand* temple that was going to be built with the reinstatement of the sacrificial system. This section is another highly debated prophecy among scholars today. Some people go with a symbolic interpretation of the passage, while others go with a literal interpretation. One thing we know for sure is that this temple Ezekiel is speaking of has never actually been built. The symbolic interpretation states that the temple is a spiritual temple that was fulfilled through the church today. The literal interpretation states that there will one day be a third temple in Jerusalem, and that the sacrificial system will be reinstated during what is known as the millennial reign.

All in all, the book of Ezekiel is a book of hope. Hope for the future—all because of one man named Ezekiel.

God gave this prophet many visions in order to promise future restoration. You see, when God promises something, it has to come into fruition because He can't lie. God's actions don't always line up with our desired outcome, though. Then we get mad and wonder where God was the entire time. Sound familiar?

Every time that happens to me, I always reflect and can see God's hand all over the situation. Most of the time the outcome was even better than I could have conjured up in my own mind. Sometimes He does stuff that doesn't make sense to me, though. Sometimes life is tough for no apparent reason at all. But that's where trust comes in. Trusting that

God's ways are the best ways. Trusting that He is for you and not against you. Trusting that it *will* all be better in the end.

Ezekiel was one of the only guys in exile God shared His plan of redemption with. Ezekiel could either share it or keep his insight to himself. He chose to share it because it provided hope to all of the Israelites since they just had their entire lives stripped from them. He provided hope in order to show them that life was actually worth living.

No matter what you go through in life, if you have accepted Jesus as your Savior and Lord and have a personal relationship with Him, then you can have hope and confidence in the fact that you will one day be in the new earth for eternity. And that's what we see with Ezekiel. ■

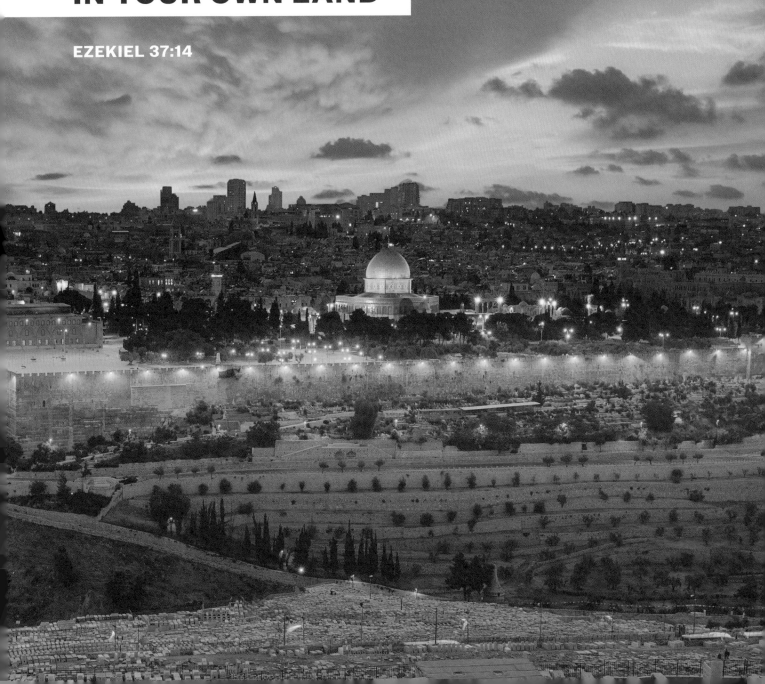

I WILL PUT MY SPIRIT IN YOU

AND YOU WILL LIVE

AND I WILL SETTLE YOU

IN YOUR OWN LAND

EZEKIEL 37:14

▶ What do you think each piece from Ezekiel's vision in chapters 1–3 represents?

Lion:

Ox:

Man:

Eagle:

Wheels:

▶ Have you ever been overcome by the Lord's presence like Ezekiel was? If so, what did it feel like? How did you respond?

▶ From chapters 4 through 37 there are ten things God makes Ezekiel do to get His point across to the people. List them below:

(4:1–3)

(4:4–8)

(4:9–17)

(5)

(12:1–16)

(12:17–20)

(21:8–17)

(21:18–24)

(24:15–24)

(37:15–28)

▶ Would you say you are a good representation of Christ? In what ways could you improve?

▶ What are your thoughts on the temple that we see in this book? Do you think we should take it literally or symbolically?

DANIEL

AUTHOR
The book of Daniel was written by the prophet Daniel, an exile during the Babylonian reign.

DATE
Daniel was taken into exile as a child during the first deportation of the Jews in 605 BC and recorded events up until 540 BC. Therefore, the book of Daniel must have been written shortly after that time, around 540–530 BC while he was in Persia.

CONTEMPORARY PROPHETS
Jeremiah around 626–585 BC
Habakkuk around 609–605 BC
Ezekiel around 593–571 BC

AUDIENCE
Daniel wrote to the other Hebrew exiles in Babylon and later in Persia.

REASON
He wrote to show them God's hand in all that was happening.

THEME
No matter what happens on earth, the kingdom of God will reign supreme for eternity.

KEY VERSES
"His dominion is an everlasting dominion, and his kingdom endures from generation to generation; all the inhabitants of the earth are accounted as nothing, and he does according to his will among the host of heaven and among the inhabitants of the earth; and none can stay his hand or say to him, 'What have you done?'" (Daniel 4:34–35).

SECTIONS
Stories of Daniel's influence (ch. 1–6), prophecies of future victory (ch. 7–12).

KEY WORDS
Dream, kingdom, authority, time

STORY OVERVIEW

The book of Daniel is full of stories and prophecies, both natural and supernatural. Daniel is known as the "Revelation of the Old Testament" because of its focus on the end times. Some revelations are easy to understand, and others are a little harder and unclear. There's some mystery involved, but the life lessons are numerous.

Daniel presents us with the inside scoop. He is given the backstage pass to Babylonian royalty and ends up being one of the leading actors. Not only is this Daniel's story, but it also shows how God was protecting His people, even during their punishment in exile.

When Nebuchadnezzar took over a new city, he would start by bringing the wisest men back to Babylon first to bring advancement among his dominion. So by the time Daniel and the first round of exiles were taken captive, Babylon was highly advanced in wisdom, wealth, and spirituality.

When Daniel and his buddies were being immersed in the ways of the Babylonians, they remained faithful because they knew who the one true God was. In return, their obedience called for a large amount of favor from the Lord. He also gave them skills and wisdom to be the best of the best. That favor resulted in Daniel being an official in Babylonian royalty for nearly seventy years, which is insane!

Daniel's first prophecy over Nebuchadnezzar involved the interpretation of one of his dreams, about a statue of Nebuchadnezzar. Just as we will see with the other prophecies in this book, the statue represented the rise and fall of the earthly kingdoms and the ultimate reign of the kingdom of God.

If you want a breakdown of the statue's meaning:

> The gold on the statue represented Babylon from 606–539 BC.
> The silver represented Persia from 539–332 BC.
> The brass represented Greece from 332–68 BC.
> The iron represented Rome from 68 BC onward.
> The iron and clay is not a completely new world power, but a variation of Rome.

There are many speculations on what the final world power will be, but nobody knows for sure.

Continuing on, the stone cut without hands signifies the Second Coming of the Messiah. And his vision of the mountain is God's kingdom taking over the whole earth before the new heaven and new earth are introduced.

Then Nebuchadnezzar reacts. He made a statue of himself made entirely of gold to show that his kingdom couldn't be taken over by any other world power and he forced all of the people to bow down and worship the statue of him. Daniel and the boys didn't agree with this new law, so Nebuchadnezzar turned up the furnace heat and called for Daniel's friends to be thrown into the furnace. God remained true to His character and saved the guys through the fire, and we see another person with them in the fire, which we know is Jesus protecting them.

BOLD AS A LION

BOLD AS A LION

In chapter 4, Nebuchadnezzar had another dream that prophesied his demise. Daniel had grown keen on Nebuchadnezzar, so this time it was hard for him to share what the dream meant. The king still had so much pride and an unrepentant heart that God allowed Satan to torment him for seven years, with the desired outcome being repentance. It was a second chance to humble him.

Many years after Nebby's conversion, his grandson Belshazzar began his command and Daniel was around eighty years old at this time. Belshazzar decides to throw a party that resulted in the fall of Babylon. After desecrating the temple jars with wine, the words *Mene, Mene, Tekel, Peres* were written upon the wall next to them. Mene means numbered, Tekel means weighed, and Peres or Parsin means broken, or divided. The words were all Aramaic so it wasn't that the people couldn't read them, they just didn't understand their meaning.

Daniel was called in and interpreted that the words meant their time was up. It just so happens that Persia took over Babylon that very same night.

Another classic Old Testament story that we find in this book is when Daniel is thrown into the lion's den and God closes the lions' mouths for the night to keep Daniel alive. In chapter 7, the book shifts from narratives to prophecies.

Toward the end of Daniel's time in Babylon, he was reading the Scriptures and realized Jeremiah had prophesied that they would only be in exile for 70 years. After doing the math, Daniel realized that the 70 years were almost up! He went straight into prayer and fasting. And God sent Gabriel with an answer. God often provides answers to our questions if we are just willing to ask Him.

As the kingdoms of this world rise and fall and persecution increases, Daniel shows us that the kingdom of God will be eternally victorious. So no matter what stands in our way, God's plan is always for our good and His glory. ■

I WANT THAT

Daniel Favor

▶ Can you think of anywhere in the world that is similar to Babylon today?

▶ How has God shown you favor among unbelievers like we saw with Daniel?

▶ By looking at the life of Daniel, how could you receive more favor?

▶ In what areas of your life have you dealt with fiery trials and seen that God was faithful in helping you through? Give an example.

▶ What does Nebuchadnezzar's time in the wilderness teach us about God?

▶ Metaphorically, have you ever been thrown into a lion's den and had to rely on a godly intervention? If so, what happened?

▶ How often do you ask God the burning questions of your heart? Give an example of how He has answered a question of yours.

▶ How does chapter 10 influence your view of prayer and fasting? Do you understand the power that is within you when you pray?

▶ Look back at Daniel's character and his relationship with God in this book. What are five traits or truths you can pull out and incorporate into your own life?

1.

2.

3.

4.

5.

HOSEA

AUTHOR
The book of Hosea was written by a man named Hosea, a citizen of the northern kingdom, Israel.

DATE
Hosea states that his ministry took place during the reigns of Jeroboam 2, Uzziah, Jotham, Ahaz, and Hezekiah, making it around 755–715 BC. He most likely wrote this prophecy toward the end of his ministry.

CONTEMPORARY PROPHETS
Jonah around 770–750 BC, Amos around 755 BC.

AUDIENCE
The book of Hosea was heavily directed toward the ten tribes in the north who were under the impression that they could "do life on their own," without the help of God.

REASON
Hosea wrote this illustration as a cry of repentance toward the nation of Israel.

THEME
God's faithfulness to the covenant even when His people fall away.

KEY VERSE
"I will plant her for myself in the land; I will show my love to the one I called 'Not my loved one.' I will say to those called 'Not my people,' 'You are my people'; and they will say, 'You are my God'" (Hosea 2:23 NIV).

SECTIONS
Marriage of Hosea and Gomer (ch. 1–3), marriage of the Lord and Israel (ch. 4–14).

KEY WORDS
Adultery, *return*, *sin*, *covenant*

STORY OVERVIEW

Hosea's prophecy is the final cry of repentance for the northern kingdom. He was the last prophet we see before they fall into the hands of Assyria. But this message of romantic imagery was not enough to turn Israel's hearts around.

The first three chapters of this book are a story of Hosea's love life. God then takes that story and spins it into His passionate love for the people of Israel.

Hosea's wife was a prostitute who was stuck in her ways. Even though she was loved by her husband, she still chose to fall back into the evil ways of the world, but God told Hosea to chase after her with unwavering love.

God loved the people of Israel unconditionally. They were His pride and joy, even though they didn't live it out. Instead of God using Hosea as a vessel to share His anger, God shared His love through a personal experience, which made the prophecy hit home even harder for Hosea.

After going through this crazy situation with his wife, Hosea was commanded to share that experience with the people of Israel. Not as a warning of future judgment, but as a love story with a happy ending. Yes, they would suffer for their disobedience, but they would eventually be brought back into a relationship with God.

The biggest character flaw that made them continually fall was their pride. Time and time again, we will see the prophets talk about the pride of the Israelites, which brought them into exile. Pride isn't just a form of confidence over other people. In this case, their pride displayed a false understanding that they could live life on their own. Without God. Solo.

Not only did God warn them about the future exile, He also showed them how to behave once they were in Assyria. But they didn't listen because in their eyes, they were good. Even though the Lord provided them with a way out and was the One behind Israel's success in the first place, they were still ungrateful because they couldn't see that God was behind all of it.

I wonder how many things we miss from the Lord every day due to our self-centered focus. One thing I find very helpful in turning my focus from self to God is the practice of gratitude. I try to thank God as much as possible for what He is doing in my life, and I often challenge the people around me to share what they are thankful for every day. Being thankful was one thing that Israel had a hard time doing.

Since it was their Golden Age, they assumed all of their blessings came from their hard work. Not true. God had their back even when they rejected Him and His ways. Hosea is a crazy illustration of God's

AS I AM

pursuit of His people shown through the marriage of Hosea and Gomer.

She was a prostitute. She didn't know how to be loved. She was used and abused. But she was perfect. Hosea chose her just as God chose His people. They didn't deserve a thing, but they were given it all. This represented true love. Relentless love.

Unexplainable love. The kind of love that only God can be in on.

God doesn't care what you have done in the past or what you are doing right now. He cares about your heart and your willingness to change. He can take any person and use them for His glory in amazing ways. Never underestimate the love of your Maker. ■

► What do you think was going through Hosea's mind when God told him to chase after Gomer? Did he truly still love her or was he just doing it out of obedience?

► Has God ever challenged you to love someone who has betrayed you? If so, what happened?

► How does pride play a role in our society today? Have you ever struggled with pride issues?

► Have you ever thought you were doing things right, only to find out that you were going against God's plan? If so, when?

► Why do you think God remained faithful even when Israel fell away?

▶ What does the Lord promise to do to Israel if they repent and return to Him (Hosea 14:1–7)? How does that compare with us today?

▶ How does the book of Hosea shape your view of God's love? How will you apply this book to your life?

▶ Do you keep a Gratitude Journal? If not, I want to challenge you to create one. It's simple: Buy a journal. Begin numbering off things you are grateful for every day. When you are feeling down, shuffle through your pages of gratitude. You can make a start on the next page.

I AM THANKFUL FOR . . .

JOEL

AUTHOR
The book of Joel was written by a prophet from Judah named Joel, the son of Pethuel. Aside from his prophecy, he was really just an anonymous fellow.

DATE
Joel wrote his prophecy sometime during the reign of Joash, around 835–796 BC.

CONTEMPORARY PROPHETS
Elijah and Elisha in Israel around 875–797 BC, Jonah in Nineveh around 785–775 BC.

AUDIENCE
The book of Joel was directed toward the people in Jerusalem because that was where the temple and priests were located.

REASON
Joel wrote as a warning of future judgment toward the Judahites in hopes of changing their hearts.

THEME
The Day of the Lord will bring judgment if the people do not repent.

KEY VERSE
"I will restore to you the years that the swarming locust has eaten, the hopper, the destroyer, and the cutter, my great army, which I sent among you" (Joel 2:25).

SECTIONS
Judgment and repentance (1:1–2:17), future blessings (2:18–3:21).

KEY WORDS / PHRASES
Day of the Lord, *locusts*, *return*, *land*

STORY OVERVIEW

The prophecy of Joel displays great imagery in comparison to the other minor prophets. He also makes the interpretation a little difficult because of his use of metaphors. Therefore, the reader gets to decide when Joel is talking about actual locusts and when he is talking about an actual army. Israel most likely endured a massive locust attack that wiped them out for a good amount of time, and this is what caused Joel to begin his prophecy.

The first locust plague that had hit Israel messed with their food supply. It forced them to stop worshiping God through grain offerings because there wasn't any more grain to be found. Sadly, the Israelites didn't seem to care. Their views on God were changing, and they began taking things into their own hands. It's easy to follow God when things are going well in your life, but it takes real faith to follow Him even when all hell is breaking loose.

Not only was life tough for the Israelites because of the locust plague wiping them out, but a worse day was on the horizon, according to Joel. The locusts were the warm-up. The Day of the Lord was on the way. Joel was begging the people to fast as a nation and called them to repent of their sin.

The Lord is always faithful to His word. He loves giving second chances, even when people don't deserve it. So Judah's fate lay in their own hands. The Lord wanted to protect the people from the coming attacks, but He gave them a choice. Unfortunately, they chose their own strength over His. Bad move.

Joel was showing that deliverance was *now,* and the Spirit will continue to be poured out until the coming Day of the Lord. That means we are in the last era before Jesus returns. We are the final part of history, whether that's one year or thousands of years. There is no greater time to live than now. We must rise up in our faith and press on harder than ever to fight against the works of the devil and to share Jesus and God's truths with all of those around us.

During the last chapter of Joel, he speaks a lot about the judgment of other nations. Nations that don't believe in God and choose to go against His people. Joel speaks of a time when all the nations will gather, and God will judge them according to their ways. For eternity. It won't be a pleasant time. Hell won't be a party. That view is a trick from the devil to keep many on the broad road that leads to destruction instead of on the narrow road that leads to life.

But there is a way out, and the Lord promises restoration for those who turn back to Him. THANK GOD FOR THAT! ■

▶ Google "locust plague" and write out three things that locusts can do when they swarm:

1.

2.

3.

▶ What are three descriptions that Joel gives of the locusts in 1:1–12?

1.

2.

3.

▶ How do you remain faithful when everything else in your life seems to be falling apart?

▶ Has God ever given you a second chance? If so, how does that influence the way you treat others?

▶ What is the "Day of the Lord" that Joel speaks of? When will it occur?

▶ Read Joel 2:28–32 and Acts 2:17–21. What was happening in Acts at the time? What do Joel and Peter say we should expect to happen? Have you witnessed any of those things firsthand?

▶ Have you ever considered that you may be around during Jesus's return? If so, does that lead you toward evangelism?

AMOS

AUTHOR
The book of Amos was written by a man named Amos from a small town called Tekoa. Amos was unlike the rest of the minor prophets, as he was just a poor shepherd who was called by God to prophesy.

DATE
Amos wrote this prophecy around 760 BC.

CONTEMPORARY PROPHETS
Jonah in Nineveh around 770–750 BC, Hosea around 750–715 BC.

AUDIENCE
Although Amos was living in the southern kingdom, he wrote to the wealthy, oppressive folks in the northern kingdom. That was a massive deal because the two kingdoms didn't get along.

REASON
The book of Amos was written to call the northern tribes of Israel to repent of their materialistic nature and turn from their ways.

THEME
Judgment will come on the northern kingdom because of their materialism and social injustice.

KEY VERSE
"This is what the Lord says: 'The people of Judah have sinned again and again, and I will not let them go unpunished! They have rejected the instruction of the Lord, refusing to obey his decrees. They have been led astray by the same lies that deceived their ancestors'" (Amos 2:4 NLT).

SECTIONS
Judgment of nations (ch. 1–2), judgment against the northern kingdom (ch. 3–6), destruction and restoration (ch. 7–9).

KEY WORDS
Judgment, covenant, righteousness, nations

STORY OVERVIEW

Amos was just a poor shepherd from a small town in the south. He loved God and could be trusted. God knew that He could use Amos because of his obedience, not because of his skills. That's such a common choice by God throughout the entire Bible. He uses the least qualified, and that way He is able to show His power and receive the glory.

The beginning of Amos's prophecy was directed toward all the Gentile enemies in order to get Israel on his side, and then he drops the bomb by giving them their own judgment.

Amos 3:7 is an amazing promise, which says, "For the Lord God does nothing without revealing his secret to his servants the prophets." Some people believe this verse means everything God does will be found in the Scriptures alone, while others believe He still reveals His plan to modern-day prophets as well.

Amos was also a strong man of prayer. He was confident in his relationship with the Father and knew that He cared about what Amos had to say. So when Amos receives terrible visions of judgment coming upon God's people, he pleads on behalf of them, and God ends up showing them mercy by not following through.

The God from back then is the same God we serve today. The Father is more than willing to change His plans if we provide Him with a good reason to do so.

More than almost any other book of the Bible, Amos holds God's people accountable for their mistreatment of other people. It consistently points out the failure of the people to fully capture God's idea of justice. They were selling weaker people for goods, taking advantage of those who couldn't stand up for themselves, oppressing the poor, and the men were using women immorally. Consumed with financial gain, the people had lost the concept of caring for one another; and Amos rebuked them because he noticed from their lifestyle that Israel had forgotten God.

Amos concludes his prophecy with the eventual restoration of the nation of Israel. He says that they will be brought back into their land and remain there forever. One of the most amazing things to witness in history is how God's promises are still coming true today. In 1948 Israel became a nation, which is one of the biggest, most important Old and New Testament prophecies to be fulfilled. Since 1948 we have been one step closer to Jesus's return. Hallelujah!

Looking at the situation as a whole, Amos was just a poor shepherd from a small town near Bethlehem. He wasn't famous. He wasn't even known as a prophet. He was what many people would call a nobody. But God chose to use him. God chose to use him to prophesy about times that we are currently in the midst of.

FAITHFUL SHEPHERD

AMOS

He spoke of the destruction of Israel in 722 BC by the Assyrian exile, but then he also spoke about the rebuilding of the Davidic Kingdom and what was to come after that.

The cool thing about all of this is that God chose to use Amos, just a random shepherd from Tekoa, whose words are coming to life almost 3000 years later. You may never know why God calls you to do certain things. That's the mystery of life. We can be confident, though, that there is a purpose behind it all because God is faithful and intentional in every situation.

My word of advice is to obey without hesitation. Who knows, your words just may influence people 3,000 years from now. ■

▶ Name a few ordinary people in modern culture God has used to do great things:

▶ Why do you think God chose to use a man from the south to prophesy to the north?

▶ Why do you think Israel was going to be judged more severely than the other nations?

▶ Beginning in chapter 4, list the five times that God said, "yet you did not return to me" and the reason behind the statement:

1.

2.

3.

4.

5.

▶ Sharing testimonies of answered prayer builds up faith within us. So what are a few examples of answered prayer in your life?

▶ How has God used you in ways that you didn't originally see?

OBADIAH

AUTHOR
The book of Obadiah was written by a prophet named Obadiah.

DATE
There is much debate around the dating of Obadiah. The answer lies in which invasion of Edom you believe Obadiah is talking about. Either around 850 BC during the reign of King Jehoram, or in 586 BC at the fall of Jerusalem. I tend to agree with the early date, but feel free to decide for yourself.

CONTEMPORARY PROPHETS
Elijah and Elisha in Israel around 875–797 BC.

AUDIENCE
Obadiah wrote to the Judahites who were recently attacked by the Edomites.

REASON
The book of Obadiah was written to bring hope to Judah through the promise of Edom's judgment.

THEME
Edom will be judged.

KEY VERSE
"For the day of the Lord is near upon all the nations. As you have done, it shall be done to you; your deeds shall return on your own head" (Obadiah 15).

SECTIONS
Judgment of Edom (vv. 1–16), hope for Judah (vv. 17–21).

KEY WORDS / PHRASES
Edom, Jacob, Day of the Lord, the nations

STORY OVERVIEW

Obadiah may be the shortest book in the Old Testament, but it sure has a lot to say about Judah's enemy, Edom.

The nation of Edom is located within the boundaries of the Promised Land, but Israel had yet to occupy it. The Edomites had attacked the Judahites, which led to a lot of anger in the eyes of Judah. So Obadiah was prophesying about how the Edomites will eventually get a taste of their own medicine. God had promised to protect His people, so He wasn't going to let a small nation like Edom walk all over them.

Basically, there is just a lot of judgment taking place in this book, but that is what the time called for.

As we have looked at briefly before, Old Testament prophecy was much different than the New Testament prophecy we live under today. You see, before Jesus, the only way to be righteous was to hate wickedness and provide offerings to cover your sins. There was no new creation, being covered by the blood of Jesus, or grace. So, whereas the Old Covenant was based on a lot of hate toward things that were not from God, the New Covenant is based on love and grace.

Back then they would hate their enemies. Now we are called to love our enemies. Back then they would call out character flaws. Now we are to call out the gold in people's lives and speak God's truth over them. Yes, some prophecies today may still warn of future judgment, but that should never be the main focus.

God loves every one of us, Jewish or Gentile, righteous or wicked, and desires all of us to be saved.

So as we are studying the Old Testament prophets, we need to remember how we approach prophecy today and how it differs from the past.

One of the biggest reasons Edom was being judged by God in this book was because of their pride. Edom thought they were the greatest and did everything they could to prove it. That seems to be the case time and time again in the prophetic books. Not only that, but there has been tension between Edom and Israel for centuries because, if you look back, the Edomites came from Esau, and the Israelites came from Jacob.

Obadiah has yet to be fulfilled since he speaks of *all* the nations being judged for how they treated Israel. This complete fulfillment won't be until the final tribulation period, but God continues to protect His people today. Just pay attention to the news.

Today, Israel is one of the smallest nations around and they pose very little threat, yet everybody wants them destroyed for some reason. It's a modern-day Israel—Edom situation.

From what we have studied, we know that one day there will be judgment on the land. That's a promise because God doesn't lie. We are currently in a time that people nearly 3,000 years ago prophesied about. It's time to open our eyes on this truth and not skip over Old Testament prophecies.

Obadiah reminds us to surrender to God's authority. He reminds us to trust His plans and will for our lives and eagerly await the promise of restoration. ■

TREASURE HUNTER

▶ Can you think of any times that God has protected you from harm? When?

▶ What are your thoughts about modern-day prophecy?

▶ Speaking of the Israelites and Edomites, what happened between Esau and Jacob that caused this tension (Genesis 27)?

▶ Do you believe the State of Israel is important in God's plan? Or do you believe these prophecies are only for the spiritual nation of Israel?

▶ How do your views impact your relationship with Israel and Jewish people today?

JONAH

AUTHOR
The book of Jonah was written by a prophet in the northern kingdom named Jonah.

DATE
Jonah most likely wrote this story shortly after the events took place around 770–750 BC.

CONTEMPORARY PROPHETS
Amos around 755 BC, Hosea around 755–715 BC.

AUDIENCE
Even though Jonah was writing about the city of Nineveh, his main audience was his fellow patriots in the northern kingdom.

REASON
Jonah wrote to show that salvation was for the Gentiles too.

THEME
Running from God and eventual revival.

KEY VERSE
"When God saw what they did, how they turned from their evil way, God relented of the disaster that he had said he would do to them, and he did not do it" (Jonah 3:10).

SECTIONS
Running away (ch. 1), turning his heart back (ch. 2), preaching in Nineveh (ch. 3), complaining to God (ch. 4).

KEY WORDS
Nineveh, destruction, compassion, turn

STORY OVERVIEW

This prophetic book is far different from the others, considering it talks about Jonah's experience instead of a prophecy. You see, Jonah was a very patriotic prophet of the northern kingdom. He often preached repentance, yet hoped for doom toward his enemies, especially the great city of Nineveh; they all hated Nineveh, which was the capital of Assyria and basically the pagan capital of the world, housing over one million people.

Nineveh was 350 square miles with 100-foot walls surrounding the city. It was not a city to mess with. And Assyria was the greatest enemy of Israel.

Since Jonah was so patriotic, having God tell him to go to his enemies would have been the last thing he wanted to do. So he ran. He literally tried to run as far as he could from God's presence because he wanted Nineveh to be judged by God. Jonah didn't make it too far before God whipped up a storm to get his attention. You've probably heard the story before.

And it definitely got Jonah's attention, but he was so disgusted that he didn't even want to think about it. Jonah would rather die at sea than have to go to Nineveh. That is some serious pride.

Then the Lord sent a giant fish to swallow up Jonah right when he was thrown overboard. God gives Jonah a second chance, just as He does with countless people in the Bible and continues to do with us today. God loves giving second chances.

If you look at the approach Jonah took in prophesying over Nineveh, it contradicts most of the Old Testament prophets. Jonah preached judgment, not repentance. An important detail to note from the book of Jonah is that it was the *Gentile* king who thought that if they repented, God may change His mind.

It's interesting to see that the people of Nineveh knew exactly what they were doing wrong. They also knew who this God was and how seriously He should be taken. Obviously, Jonah's heart wasn't right this whole time.

That's why he didn't tell them destruction would come if they didn't repent. He just said they would be destroyed in forty days. He was only choosing obedience hoping that things would go the way he wanted them to and Nineveh would be destroyed.

So Jonah watched from the hillside and pouted as the people began to repent. The book of Jonah is one that hits home with me because I tend to really relate to his story. If you don't know, there was a time in my life when I tried running away from God, and it wasn't until I hit rock bottom that I went running right back.

We can't hide from God. He is always present, and He always desires the best for us, whether we realize it or not. God used Jonah to accomplish one of the greatest miracles in the Old Testament, once Jonah chose to walk in obedience to the Lord. So this is a story of hope, no matter how far you have tried to run in the past. ■

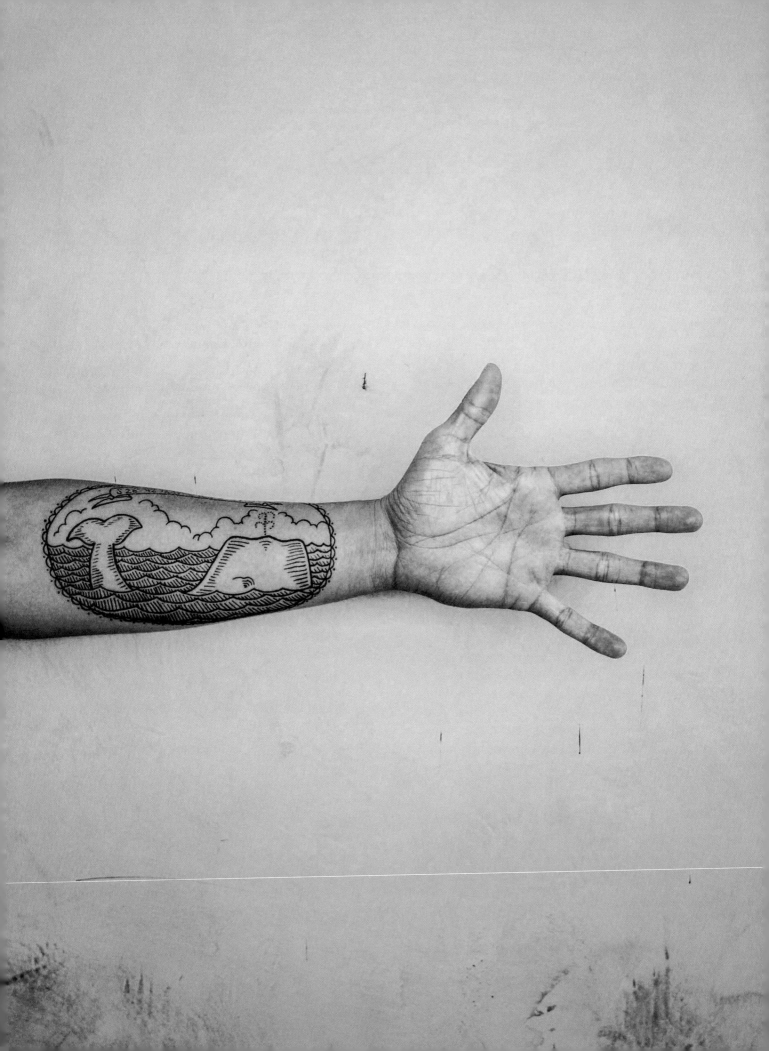

▶ Has your pride ever gotten in the way of your being obedient to God's plan?

▶ What do you think convinced every person in Nineveh, even the king, to change their ways on the spot?

▶ Do you think nonbelievers today know when they are doing something wrong? What do they use to gauge their goodness or wrongdoing?

▶ There are ten miracles in the book of Jonah. List them below:

1.

2.

3.

4.

5.

6.

7.

8.

9.

10.

▶ Have you ever tried to run from God? If so, what happened?

AUTHOR
The book of Micah was written by a prophet from Moresheth Gath in Judah named Micah. Most of his ministry remains a mystery.

DATE
Micah prophesied during the reigns of Jotham, Ahaz, and Hezekiah, which meant he wrote this book around 700–686 BC.

CONTEMPORARY PROPHETS
Isaiah around 700–680 BC.

AUDIENCE
Micah's audience was, for the most part, the political and religious leaders of Judah who were oppressing the poor.

REASON
Micah wrote to share God's heart toward social injustice and to tell of the destruction awaiting the people, but also to offer a way out.

THEME
Judgment against social injustice.

KEY VERSE
"He has told you, O man, what is good; and what does the Lord require of you but to do justice, and to love kindness, and to walk humbly with your God?" (Micah 6:8).

SECTIONS
The judgment (ch. 1–3), hope for the future (ch. 4–5), case against God's people (ch. 6–7).

KEY WORDS / PHRASES
Children of Zion, sin, Jerusalem, Samaria, remnant

MICAH

STORY OVERVIEW

The prophets Isaiah and Micah were contemporaries. Many people believe that Micah was a disciple of Isaiah, calling his book the "Little Isaiah." Both prophets were speaking into the same situation. Both ended up being ignored by the masses.

Unlike Isaiah, Micah came from a small town where he knew the social injustice of the wealthy all too well. These were his people. His life. So you can feel the emotion in his words as he speaks. Micah was going to do everything in his power to stop the injustice from spreading.

It's amazing to see how similar the situation these prophets were dealing with is to ours today. As social injustice runs crazy, we have a job to do. But first, we need to understand the Father's heart behind it. And that's something Micah did very well. Instead of attacking the people with anger, he wept and showed them what true love is. That's a very New Covenant way of approaching injustice. Micah was after their hearts.

Micah then presents a courtroom setting where God describes His legal right to judge His people and their enemies, while Micah was representing the people. No matter how "good" the people have been in presenting themselves, the Lord sees and hears everything. He knows their hearts, and that is what is most important. It's never just about your actions, it's always about the condition of your heart behind those actions.

Back in the day, it was required of people to sacrifice animals in different ways to show their love for God and to restore their relationship with Him. I'm thankful that things have changed because, quite frankly, I don't do well with blood. Micah shows that the sacrificial system was never about the act of the sacrifices. It was about the heart behind them and the pursuit of righteousness.

Not only does Micah tell of future judgment, but he also talks about the restoration that follows. Some things have already taken place; some are still to come. Toward the end, Micah is trying to figure out how he can restore his relationship with God, since Israel had drifted so far away from Him. He brings up the best of the best offerings. They were above and beyond what anybody could afford, but he just wanted to know what it would take because no matter God's response, the action would be worth it.

He told them to do justice, love kindness, and to walk humbly with their God. That's it. Literally. God doesn't care what you bring to the table. He doesn't care what you offer Him. He already has everything He needs. All He wants is your *heart*. It's the cheapest, yet one of the hardest, things that you can give while living in this society. ■

QUESTIONS

▶ Are you involved in any groups against social injustice? Which topic are you most passionate about?

▶ How does Jesus deal with social injustice? With Jesus as an example, what can we do on behalf of those who are hurting?

▶ In Micah 5:2, Micah prophesies something very accurate about the coming Messiah. What was it? How did Jesus fulfill this prophecy?

▶ What is righteousness? How do you become more righteous?

▶ Revisit the key verse. What does the Lord require of you and me?

▶ How do you show God that you love Him?

NAHUM

AUTHOR
The book of Nahum was written by the otherwise unknown prophet Nahum of Elkosh.

DATE
Nahum wrote this prophecy before the fall of Nineveh in 612 BC and sometime after the destruction of Thebes in 663 BC.

CONTEMPORARY PROPHETS
Zephaniah around 640–621 BC, Jeremiah around 626–585 BC.

AUDIENCE
This prophecy was written to Nineveh and Judah. Very different cities. Very different reasoning behind them.

REASON
Nahum was written to share about the coming judgment of Nineveh and to bring comfort to Judah.

THEME
The fall of Nineveh.

KEY VERSE
"The Lord has given a command concerning you, Nineveh: 'You will have no descendants to bear your name'" (Nahum 1:14 NIV).

SECTIONS
The Lord vs. Nineveh (ch. 1), judgment of Nineveh (ch. 2), reason for judgment (ch. 3).

KEY WORDS / PHRASES
I Am against You, Nineveh, evil

STORY OVERVIEW

Nahum seems like a real patriotic fellow, similar to Jonah 150 years before him. They both preached judgment toward Nineveh, and they both had different outcomes.

Nahum is a book of destruction. There is no turning back with his prophecy. Judgment was going to come whether they repented or not. I must admit, that shows God in an entirely different way than we have seen Him in the past. From what we have seen, there is always a way out.

At that time, the best place to be was in Judah, because God promised that He would wipe out their enemies and protect them in the end. God wanted to comfort them even when there was a threat of exile looming on the horizon.

Nahum jumps back to his focus on Nineveh and tells them what God has in store for their future. The city of Nineveh was far past redemption. God knew that they wouldn't change again, no matter what He did for them. Yes, God forgives sin, but if you remain in your sin, you will bear the consequences.

For us, under the New Covenant, being a new creation means that you are moving from glory to glory. You are no longer a sinner. You are now a saint. Remaining in sin contradicts your entire nature. After being saved, you literally have to choose to separate yourself from God and continue to sin. He doesn't want that. And you shouldn't either.

I'm the type of guy who enjoys knowing what is happening in the world. I'd say I'm pretty on top of the news because I find that to be very important. Honestly, I'm amazed that people my age can live their lives ignorant of it all. I just don't get it. Yeah, it's a messed-up world. Yeah, some things can be scary. Yeah, the news doesn't show much good. But if you look closely, you can see God move.

While the book in a nutshell clearly depicts God's concern over sin, His willingness to punish wickedness, and His power to carry out judgment, it also gives us hope. The people of Judah would have found hope in the idea that Nineveh, their main oppressor for generations, would soon be judged by God. ■

JUDGMENT IS UPON YOU

NINEVEH

NINEVEH

JUDGMENT IS UPON YOU

QUESTIONS

▶ What do we know about the "great city" of Nineveh from when we studied Jonah?

▶ There was no way out of the judgment Nahum talks about. What are your thoughts on this?

▶ What does Nahum say will happen to Nineveh?

▶ In what ways can you see God moving behind the scenes of the chaos in the world?

Nahum

211

HABAKKUK

AUTHOR
The book of Habakkuk was written by the Judean prophet Habakkuk.

DATE
Habakkuk ministered to the people of Judah during the end of the seventh century BC and most likely wrote this book around 609–605 BC.

CONTEMPORARY PROPHETS
Jeremiah around 626–585 BC.

AUDIENCE
Habakkuk was directed toward the religious and political people of Judah who were oppressing the working class.

REASON
Habakkuk wrote this prophecy to show God's holiness and to answer some of his own personal questions.

THEME
The righteous will live by faith.

KEY VERSE
"Behold, his soul is puffed up; it is not upright within him, but the righteous shall live by his faith" (Habakkuk 2:4).

SECTIONS
The first question and answer (1:1–11), the second question and answer (1:12–2:20), the prayer (ch. 3).

KEY WORDS
Why, faith, woe, proud

STORY OVERVIEW

Habakkuk was a man who questioned everything. Can you relate? This man wrestled with God until he received an answer that was fitting for his narrow perspective. But Habakkuk wasn't God, so some things would never fully make sense. It is the same today. We can wrestle as much as we want, but in the end, some things will remain a mystery.

In this book, Habakkuk is asking very basic questions that contradict his view of the Father's heart. I think it's a good idea to question things you don't understand in order to align your heart to His and really do a deep dive into doctrine and systematic theology.

So many times, we place God in a box that fits our theology properly but contradicts some of Scripture. That's never a good spot to be in. Habakkuk expected God to act a certain way, and when He didn't, that's when the questions began to fly.

There are so many times when I pray for something, then pray some more, then pray some more, and never get a response. Either that or I get a response that is far different from what I was anticipating. I know many of you can relate. We even jump to conclusions and make excuses for why God does what He does. I think that's a dangerous thing.

Habakkuk hadn't heard from God in a while, and he was getting upset. When God did show up, it was far different than Habakkuk could have imagined. It sucked for his people, actually. He found out that their enemies would eventually destroy them. It had to be devastating.

Question after question arises, and the Lord becomes silent again. The next part is crucial: Habakkuk sits and waits. Listening for God. Praying that He will respond. He doesn't, but it's in that place of silence and prayer that Habakkuk realizes he is part of something far bigger. Something God-sized, where even the things that don't make sense still happen on purpose in regard to the big picture.

It's in the waiting, listening, and praying that Habakkuk comes to acceptance of his position, and it's where humility kicks in. It's the waiting that refines your patience. It's the listening that refines your ear to hear what needs to be heard. It's the praying that refines your character and builds your relationship with God. It's in the times of frustration with God that learning this is most important. ■

▶ What are some of the big questions you tend to wrestle with?

▶ What was the first question Habakkuk asked God (Habakkuk 1:2)?

▶ How did God respond (Habakkuk 1:5–11)?

▶ Does that fit with your view of God today? How?

▶ What was the second question Habakkuk asked God (Habakkuk 1:12)?

▶ How does God respond (Habakkuk 2:2–5)?

▶ In 2:4, Habakkuk says, "the righteous shall live by his faith." What does it mean to live by faith? What happens if you stop believing? Do you think you can lose your salvation?

▶ What prayers are you waiting for God to respond about? What has Habakkuk taught you about the waiting process?

ZEPHANIAH

AUTHOR
The book of Zephaniah was written by the great-great-grandson of King Hezekiah, the prophet Zephaniah. Considering his royal connection, Zephaniah was heavily influenced by politics.

DATE
Zephaniah had his ministry during the reign of King Josiah, before the major religious reform. That means Zephaniah wrote this prophecy sometime around 640–621 BC.

CONTEMPORARY PROPHETS
Nahum around 663–612 BC, Jeremiah around 626–585 BC.

AUDIENCE
Zephaniah was addressed to the southern kingdom of Judah.

REASON
Zephaniah wrote to warn people of the coming Day of the Lord and the judgment that goes along with it.

THEME
Seek righteousness before the Day of the Lord.

KEY VERSE
"Seek the Lord, all you humble of the land, who do his just commands; seek righteousness; seek humility; perhaps you may be hidden on the day of the anger of the Lord" (Zephaniah 2:3).

SECTIONS
Judgment against Judah (ch. 1), judgment against the nations (2:1–3:8), promise of restoration (3:9–20).

KEY WORDS / PHRASES
Day of the Lord, remnant, daughters of Zion, nations

STORY OVERVIEW

The book of Zephaniah is a short prophecy that warned the southern kingdom of Judah about the coming Day of the Lord, and that set the tone for the rest of the book. Israel was already in exile, so Judah is the last remaining group that has a chance of being free from judgment if they turn from their sins. Although, that may be easier said than done.

Zephaniah urges them to join together as one, in order that they all repent and possibly be saved as a nation. God keeps His word, and according to 2 Kings 24:14, there was a group that God protected from exile. It says that all were taken captive except the poorest of the land.

Zephaniah shares about how God will judge the other nations who are the enemies of Israel. He brings up the Moabites, Ammonites, Cushites, etc. The Lord promises to diminish them for their pride and taunting because He always fights on behalf of His people.

No matter what judgment the Lord may have put His people through, He always had the upper hand and protected them in the end. That's why the Jewish people have never been wiped out, no matter how much persecution they have gone through.

Every time the prophets prophesied over the Lord's people, there was always hope attached to the ending. We have seen it time and time again. There is a way out. Either before or after the judgment, they will be taken care of because the Lord always keeps His promises and always holds true to His covenants, even if the Israelites continue to break their side of the deal.

We have studied quite a few of the prophetic books up until this point. We have learned about a lot of destruction and a lot of restoration. Stuff that has already happened and stuff that is still to take place. However, the one trait that all of the books cite as the reason for destruction is PRIDE. It's only the humble who God saves from His wrath.

You can think you're a big deal, but you must understand that you can't do it all on your own. God is in charge right now. You can accept that fact or you can wait and learn later. I'd suggest the former. The proud never win. If you struggle with pride, spend some time meditating, and ask God to show you places in your life where you are not being truly humble. Then ask God to forgive you of any pride and to reveal to you a plan of attack to defeat it.

Like the writings of many of the prophets, the book of Zephaniah follows a pattern of judgment on all people for their sin followed by the restoration of God's chosen people. We have to allow Zephaniah to remind us how seriously God takes our life and our relationship with Him. ■

SEEK
THE
LORD

THE LORD. SEEK RIGHTEO
S. SEEK HUMILITY. SEEK TH
. SEEK HUMILITY. SEEK TH
ILITY. SEEK RIGHTEOUSNESS. SE
SEEK RIGHTEOUSNESS. SE
TEOUSNESS. SEEK THE LORD. SEE
THE LOR EEK RIGHTEO
S. SEEK H NESS. SE
SEEK RI ORD. SEE
ILITY. SI HUMILI
TEOUSNI IGHTEO
THE LORD. SEEK TH
S. SEEK HUMIL RIGHTEOUSNESS
RD. SEEK RIGHTEOUSNESS. SEEK THE LOR
HUMILITY. SEEK THE LORD. SEEK H
ITY. SEEK THE LORD. SEE

SEEK HUMILITY.

▶ From what we have seen in the Old Testament so far, what do you remember about the Day of the Lord?

▶ Why do you think the poorest of the land were more inclined to repent in this story?

▶ What is the main reason for all the judgment in Zephaniah (Zephaniah 1:4–6; 3:11)?

▶ What can they do to prevent it (Zephaniah 2:3)?

▶ What does the Lord promise for the future of Israel (Zephaniah 3:14–20)?

AUTHOR
The book of Haggai was written by the prophet Haggai.

DATE
Haggai dated his prophecies more precisely than any other Old Testament author. We know that all four of his messages were written over a five-month period in 520 BC.

CONTEMPORARY PROPHETS
Zechariah around 518 and 480 BC.

AUDIENCE
Haggai wrote to the returning remnant who began building the temple in 536 BC but soon became discouraged and allowed it to lay untouched for sixteen years until Haggai and Zechariah came along.

REASON
To encourage the remnant to finish the temple instead of spending all of their time focusing on making their homes great first.

THEME
Finish rebuilding the temple.

KEY VERSE
"Is it a time for you yourselves to dwell in your paneled houses, while this house lies in ruins?" (Haggai 1:4).

SECTIONS
Call to action to rebuild the temple (ch. 1), God's presence will return (2:1–9), blessing the defiled people (2:10–19), Zerubbabel will lead the way (2:20–23).

KEY WORDS
Temple, house, consider, Lord of Hosts

HAGGAI

STORY OVERVIEW

Whereas most Old Testament prophets prophesied over a long span of time, Haggai had four short messages that he shared in under five months. And his tone was also different from most prophets'. Haggai wasn't preaching judgment like the others; he was encouraging them to keep going with the temple. He knew they weren't living up to their capacity, so he chose to speak words of encouragement regarding their talents. Haggai shares with them how pleased the Father will be once the building is completed.

The Lord doesn't necessarily even care what the building looks like or how it is decorated; He just wants it to *exist* so that He can live among them. It's the ability to live together and the obedience of the people that He cares most about.

Since the foundation of the temple was laid, the Israelites thought the prophecy had come to pass, so now they decided to kick back and work on their own houses instead. They didn't think that they had to put in a large amount of work toward the temple. That's very similar to many believers today. Since they have grace, many don't think they need to put in any work on their own temple, which is incredibly far from God's heart toward grace.

Haggai must have been a great communicator because after he encouraged the people they turned and were motivated to keep building. An interesting thing to note is that the Lord stirred up their spirits *after* they decided to start working again. He reassured their decisions and motivated them further. We all have destinies that we're waiting to step into. God always equips those who are willing to go after His plan, but He will never force you into obeying His plan. He gives us a choice so that our response is genuine, and He often asks us to step out in faith—not knowing in advance all of the details.

The third message Haggai delivered was to the priests because they were the ones who knew the Law best. He made it clear that just because they were touching/working on the temple, that didn't make them holy. The Lord cares about the heart and that's it.

After Haggai shows how the Lord will take care of the surrounding nations, he says that God will raise up His Servant, which was a reference to Jesus coming from the line of David's descendant Zerubbabel, and He would be used to stamp ownership on the earth. The royal line would be reestablished through this man, and something interesting to note is that the two genealogies of Jesus from Matthew 1 and Luke 3 both contain the name of Zerubbabel. So he was an ancestor on both his father and mother's line, just as David was. Amazing.

When considering the temple they were supposed to build, I think, *Man, I've been to big churches and I've been to small churches. Churches worth millions of dollars and churches worth nothing.* I've seen God move in places that you wouldn't expect it, and I've seen Him silent in places that you wouldn't expect Him to be. By the end of Haggai, we see that it's not about the temple and what it looks like. It's about the heart behind the people building it and finally having a place where God can reside among His people.

As we have seen in so many of the previous books, God cares about your HEART. That's all He wants. It's everything to Him. Because from the place of a pure heart is where change can happen, and God can use you for His greater purposes. Don't go to church for entertainment. Go for the relationship. ■

▶ Describe a time when you went above and beyond your usual ability because of an encouraging word from another person:

▶ Why did the Israelites stop working on the temple in the first place (Haggai 1:9)?

▶ What are a few ways that you can continue building your temple while dealing with the busyness of life?

▶ Have you ever stepped out in faith? How did God provide for your needs?

▶ Many believers are either full of head knowledge or heart knowledge, with a small percentage blending the two together. With that said, with which area do you more closely relate? How can you get better at the other?

▶ List three ways you can align your heart to be closer to the Father's:

1.

2.

3.

AUTHOR
The book of Zechariah was written by the priest/prophet Zechariah.

DATE
Zechariah wrote his prophecy over a long time period. Chapters 1 through 8 were most likely written in 518 BC, while chapters 9 through 14 were around 480 BC.

CONTEMPORARY PROPHETS
Haggai in 520 BC.

AUDIENCE
Zechariah was writing to the same people that Haggai was, the returned remnant who were slacking on the rebuilding of the temple but advancing in their home remodeling.

REASON
Zechariah wrote to encourage them to finish rebuilding the temple and to give them hope for the coming Messiah.

THEME
The current temple and the future temple.

KEY VERSE
"And the LORD will be king over all the earth. On that day the LORD will be one and his name one" (Zechariah 14:9).

SECTIONS
Call to repentance (1:1–6), eight visions (1:7–6:15), future restoration (ch. 7–8), deliverance by the Messiah (ch. 9–14).

KEY WORDS / PHRASES
Temple, I Saw, Covenant, King, Nations

ZECHARIAH

STORY OVERVIEW

Zechariah is also one of the most messianic books in the entire Old Testament. I'm sure you noticed that it is jam-packed with prophetic visions of the immediate and distant future. The Lord loves speaking through visions and says that the "young will see visions and the old will dream dreams" during the end times. Visions in the Bible are not necessarily the easiest things to understand. And in some cases, the interpretations are in the eye of the beholder, while at other times they are obvious.

Since we are looking at Zechariah's visions from the future, we can pick out what has already happened and what still needs to take place. In the first vision, God shows Zechariah that he is going to give the nation of Israel a break from all the fighting. He understood that they needed time to regroup and get their bearings. Otherwise, He was just setting them up for failure.

The second vision shows four horns and blacksmiths. Zechariah shares a vision of a golden lampstand and olive trees in chapter 4. In chapter 6, Zechariah shows that Joshua, the high priest, was being crowned and the office of the priest was now the highest authority in Jerusalem. You see, the nation of Israel was not allowed a king at the time because they were still under Persian rule, but they could crown their priests and allow them to lead the people. This was a major deal because even when Jesus was born the two leaders at the time were Caiaphas and Ananias, the high priests. So we know that it stuck.

I'm blown away by how well the Jews knew the Hebrew Bible, yet so many of them missed the Messiah when He was right at their fingertips. Zechariah shows prophecy after prophecy that was *directly* fulfilled by Jesus, all the way down to the fact that He would ride in on a donkey. But when the time came for Jesus to enter Jerusalem, they missed it. They didn't want a Prince of Peace. They wanted a conquering King.

Zechariah gives us a lot of insight into what will happen during the end times as well. He speaks of all the nations gathering against Israel, at which time God will fight on their behalf and show the world that He is alive and well. He even shares that the Jews will mourn for not realizing that the Messiah was who He said He was the first time around.

In Zechariah, there are actually thirty Messianic prophecies. Some are big pictures; some are very detailed. The detailed prophecies really intrigue me. It's always so cool to see how God makes statements hundreds of years in advance and they come true in the exact fashion that they were foretold.

Jesus would be betrayed for thirty pieces of silver. His body would be pierced. He would be the Cornerstone and the Branch. Israel would be scattered as a result of His death. And the list goes on. It all blows my mind, how spot-on it is. ■

▶ Has the Lord ever spoken to you through visions and/or dreams? If so, when?

▶ Have you seen them fulfilled?

▶ In chapter 3, who was Joshua and what did he represent in this vision? What would be so important about his being cleaned up? What do you think that means for the future of the Jewish people?

▶ Jesus is referred to as "the Branch" here. Who are the branches in John 15:5?

▶ What office(s) does Jesus hold? King? Priest? Prophet? All of these?

► List ten Messianic prophecies from Zechariah that were directly fulfilled in the Gospels:

   1. Zechariah 6:12–13 and Hebrews 8:1

   2. Zechariah 9:9 and Matthew 21:6–9

   3. Zechariah 10:4 and Ephesians 2:20

   4. Zechariah 11:7 and Matthew 9:35–36

   5. Zechariah 11:8 and Matthew 26:3–4

   6. Zechariah 11:10–11 and John 14:7

   7. Zechariah 11:12–13 and Matthew 26:14–15

   8. Zechariah 12:10 and John 19:34–37

   9. Zechariah 13:7 and Matthew 26:31

   10. Zechariah 13:7 and Matthew 26:31–56

► Which one of those strikes you as the most obvious?

MALACHI

AUTHOR

The book of Malachi was written by the otherwise unknown prophet Malachi, whose name means "My Messenger."

DATE

Malachi wrote this prophecy around 430–420 BC, 100 years after the last prophecies of Haggai and Zechariah.

AUDIENCE

Malachi wrote to the remnant of Israel, who had lost their passion for the Lord.

REASON

Malachi was written to rebuke the priests and people for falling so far away from the Lord and to warn them of the future Day of the Lord.

THEME

Judgment will come unless they return to the Lord.

KEY VERSES

"For I the Lord do not change; therefore you, O children of Jacob, are not consumed. From the days of your fathers you have turned aside from my statutes and have not kept them. Return to me, and I will return to you, says the Lord of hosts" (Malachi 3:6–7).

SECTIONS

Israel's blessings (1:1–5), rebuking of priests and the people (1:6–2:16), the coming Day of the Lord (2:17–4:6)

KEY WORDS

Covenant, priests, sacrifices, curse

STORY OVERVIEW

At the time that Malachi was writing this prophecy, Jerusalem was in rough shape. The Israelites were doing alright by their own standards, but the main city was far from their main focus. They became selfish. Content. Satisfied. A good relationship with God was the last thing they were focused on because they felt God had left. And the priests didn't take it seriously, so why should the citizens?

The Lord directs His attention to the wickedness of the priests right off the bat and calls them out for their polluted offerings. All that they offered was in vain, so the Lord wouldn't accept it as sincere. He demands worship. Awe. Only when people treat Him as He deserves to be treated will the offerings be accepted the way that they want them to be accepted: as purification and blessing.

The main problem the Israelites were dealing with is that they were messing with God's name—who He is. That's a big no-no. He has a reputation to uphold, and anything or anyone that tries to defame Him is not taken lightly.

The Lord's covenant with Levi was still in effect. Since it was a covenant, it could not be broken by God, no matter how badly He may have wanted to break it. He is faithful to His word, He means what He says, and it is impossible for Him to lie. The problem

was that Judah profaned the covenant for no reason at all. They profaned the temple and married foreign women; two unacceptable things in the Lord's eyes. The Judahites still didn't understand why the Lord wasn't accepting their offerings, though. They were blind to their own actions, and it caused them to stumble even harder.

Malachi teaches us that the Lord does not change at all. Thank goodness for that. No matter what the New Covenant brought, His promises were still the same. He would NEVER wipe out His people completely. Yes, they will go through struggles, and many will die, but He will always keep His promises to Abraham until the end. Even if His people didn't play their part, He would still be good to them in that sense.

The timeframe that is spoken of by Malachi is at the end of the world, during the tribulation period and just before Jesus's Second Coming. Sometimes the Day of the Lord means a time when the Lord is stepping in, but this great day is on a whole different level. This is "the BIG ONE." The last hurrah. And it's coming in hot. A time when all wickedness will be judged and only the righteous will be left standing.

The last three verses of the Old Testament are centered around two of the greatest men in the Old Testament: Moses and Elijah. It's God's last appeal

och luttra dem, likasom silf-
skola de då offra spisoffer uti
anom.

Jerusalem ...er skall w...
likasom f... ...dags och i...

fastän i annar...
nalkas eder till ..., och skall
vittne† mot de trollkarlar, hor-
...e, och emot dem, som wåld och
...gakarlen††, enkan och den fader=
...främlingen, och icke frukta mig,
...oth.

...ge bland eder sjelfwe, och icke blott bland hed-
...de dröjande, såsom I knoten uti egenrättfärdig-
...är domen o... öfwer eder sjelfwe, skall den w...
...snar. † ...ap. 2, 14; ty st...
...n. †† eg... ...a dagakarlens

...Herren, som ... förändras*;
...skolen icke ... ...an förgås...
oföränderlige, t... ...c. 11, 29. Isra...
ej genom den ... ...sdomen, utan
...ntetgöras genom ..., utan förädlas

allt ifrån ... ...tid afw...
...och icke hålli... ... omwänd...
...så will jag ock wända mig till eder...
baoth. Så sägen I då: Hwarutin...
...wända oß?
...tt, att en menniska beswiker Gud,
...u mig? Så sägen I då: Hwarmed
...Med tionde och häfoffer*.
...till försång för mitt tempel och deß tjenare, ber-
...mig och ber...en, att tukta... till bättring göres

...aren I ... e*; ty ...
...famman**.
...ingen wälsignelse ... ...an idel brist och ...
...), den förderswade ..., i motsats mot...
...p. v. 16.

...er mig tion... ...mmans uti n...
...i mitt hus ... s wara: och
...härutinnan* ... ...en Zebar...
... upplåter ed... ...fenster, o...
...else neder tillfyllest**.
...b. ** ordagrant: till icke nog, det är: till mer än

14. I sägen: Det är förgäf...
tjenar, och hwad båta...
och fö... ...tt st... ...lef...
...för
...sorgd... ...hans wakt.
...swåra si...
15. ... ...stolte
wåra t... ...o, och
* de ... ...syndare
garne... ...as, det är:
16. ... ...sig de som
den ene med den andre: och Herre...
...det, och der wardt en tänkeskrift i...
...wen, för dem** som frukta Herra...
hans namn.

* den lilla hopen af werkligt fromma, som
knorrande skrymtare. ** dem till godo. Det
lyses af seden hos Perserna, att de som gjort sig
antecknades i en minnesbok, för att i sinom

17. Och de skola, ...ren
min eg... ...som ...den ...en
och jag ... ...asom en
egen so... ...en h...
18. ... ...ter
åtskillna... ...ttfärdig...
aktige, ...de ...n Gudi
som ho... ...

Kap. 4.

Herrans tillkommelses dag, förberedd af den...

1. *Ty si, den dag** kommer, so...
likasom en ugn: så skola då alle stolte
wara halm, och den tillkommande da...
tända dem, säger Herren ...ebaoth, o...
dem hr... ...en ro...der q...

* I ... ...ert... ... Kap. 3 me...
Christi ... ...af gamla för...
då bomen ... ...och goda aff...
som det f... ... ...både och
gar wid ... ...
kommelse...

2. Me... ...frukte...
rättfärdig... ...het** u...
wingar;... ... ...het, och spr...
gödde kalfw...

* den rättfärdiggörande nådens sol i Christi per...
Luc. 1, 78. ** eg.: läkedom. † strålar, wärmande...
och uppblifwande såsom den rusande fogelns wingar

...ner*, och luttra dem, likasom silf=
...skola de då offra spisoffer uti
...offer, såsom ... aj, ... min...
... G. 6, 7 ... uppfyllelsen
...alems ... skall väl
... fordo... ... i de
... ...an form.

...all nalkas eder till dom*, och skall
* wittne† mot de trollkarlar, hor=
...dare, och emot dem, som wåld och
...dagakarlen††, enkan och den fader=
...fa främlingen, och icke frukta mig,
...ebaoth.

...färdige bland eder sjelfwe, och icke blott bland hed=
... ... Såsom I knoten uti ...
...är öfwer eder sjelfwe ... wäl
... och hämnare ... ...ffet
...entligen: ... karlens lön.
...Her ... som ... ...as*; och
...icke alle ... ...örgås**.
...lige, trosasta ... 9. Israels
...es ej ... den luttran... ...n, utan be=
... ...enom min tu... ...as till

...n allt i...an edra fäder ... upwikit
...d, och icke hållit dem. Så omwänder
...mig, så will jag ock wända mig till eder,
...Zebaoth. Så sägen I då: Hwarutin=
...omwända oß?

...rätt, att en menniska beswiker Gud,
...iken mig? Så sägen I då: Hwarmed
...ig? Med tionde och häfoffer*.
...ällen till förbana för mitt tempel och deß tjenare, der=
... ...bewisen, att tuktan till ...ina göres
... ock förban... ... ...be=
... **.
... ...gen ... ...gnelse i lan... ...rist och nöd.
... der ...erswade stora ... ...tsats mot de

... tionden ... ...an uti min
...tt ... hus må ... ...bе...oth.
... ..., säger ... ...oth.
...upplåter eder himmelen ...per, och
...ignelse neder tillfyllest**.
...armed. ** ordagrant: till icke nog, det är: till mer än
...werslöd.

...jag will för eder näpf frätaren*, att

14. I sägen: Det är förg...
...tjenar, och hwad ...
...före ett strängt ...
...grant: tage wara ...
...for ... (såsom de ...
15. ...rföre pri...
... ..., de försöka ...
..., öfwermo... ...
... * ordagr... ...et
16. Då besprå...ade ... de
den ene med den andre: och He...
...det, och der wardt en tänkeskrif...
...wen, för dem** som frukta He...
hans namn.

* den lilla hopen af werkligt fromma,...
knorrande skrymtare. ** dem till godo.
lyses af seden hos Perserna, att de som gjo...
...tecknades i en minne... ...att fin

...7. Och de skolo, ...er
...ndom på den ...
...jag ... ...ll skona den ...
... ...en honom ...
18. ...I skolen ...ber ...
...r emellan ...
... ..., emellan ...
...om h...om icke tje...ar.

Kap. 4.

Herrans tillkommelses dag, förberedd af

1. *Ty si, den dag** kommer,
likasom en ugn: så skola då alle st...
wara halm, och den tillkommande
...anda dem, säger He... ...ebaoth,
...hwarken rot eller

* ...reiska texten fortsätt...
...ommelses dag wid ...
...om ... i Israel affli...
... ...e i ännu st...
...christliga w...
...per, som mitt ...
...ens sol ...
... och I skole ...
...göda ...alfwartt††

...rättfärdiggörande nådens sol i Christ...
Luc. 78. ** eg.: läkedom. † strålar, wärm...
och upplifwande såsom den rusande fogelns wi...
†† I skolen gå ut, och hoppa c., det är:
... ...na frihet, såsom

to Israel before 400 years of silence. He told them to get back to the way of Moses and God would give them another chance. He would send one more prophet to them, Elijah, who would prepare the way for the Messiah.

We saw this happen through the life of John the Baptist in the New Testament, but many people believe the real Elijah will come back to earth before the Second Coming. Nobody knows for sure . . . we'll just have to wait and see!

One of my favorite verses in this book, Malachi 3:10 NLT, says, "'Bring all the tithes into the storehouse so there will be enough food in my Temple. If you do,' says the Lord of Heaven's Armies, 'I will open the windows of heaven for you. I will pour out a blessing so great you won't have enough room to take it in! Try it! Put me to the test!'" It's interesting because in Proverbs it talks about the same concept. If you bless God or His people, He will bless you in return.

Some Christian groups are big advocates of God taking care of your needs—and if He isn't yet, give more. It's a very strange concept if you've never seen it in full effect, but if you have, you know how true it is.

One week, when I was out in Australia, we had a "giving morning" to kick the week off. It was a time when, if you had a need, you would write it on the board, and anybody could go up and anonymously pledge to help you out with it. We gave over $40,000. In thirty minutes. Between 100 people. Three-quarters of whom were under the age of thirty. That's insane!

People who had money were giving. People who didn't have money were giving. It was like a big game of Monopoly with all the money being passed around. One of the coolest parts about all of it was that nobody was stressing out. They had so much faith in God that they knew He would provide for their needs. This was just a group of 100 people walking out what they believe. It was truly a transformational thing to witness. If you have never seen God provide in your life and are stingy with your money, give some of it away. Something big enough to make a dent. He's the One who told His people to test Him and promised blessings in return. Why not give it a shot?

And that, in short, is the book of Malachi. Now we have 400 years of silence before the New Testament begins. ■

▶ In what ways can we give offerings to the Lord today?

▶ As a Christian, how can you better represent God in your day-to-day life? List five ways below:

   1.

   2.

   3.

   4.

   5.

▶ What promises has God given you that have yet to be fulfilled? Is there anything you can do to speed up the process? Do you need to step out in obedience?

▶ Are you generous with your finances? If not, how can you be better?

▶ What is the greatest lesson you have learned from the book of Malachi?

THE
BIBLE
IS
GOOD
FOR
YOU

NEW TESTAMENT

Matthew—Revelation

Gospels	Pauline Epistles	Hebrew Christian Epistles	Revelation
Matthew	Romans	Hebrews	Revelation
Mark	1 Corinthians	James	
Luke	2 Corinthians	1 Peter	
John	Galatians	2 Peter	
	Ephesians	1 John	
Acts	Philippians	2 John	
Acts	Colossians	3 John	
	1 Thessalonians	Jude	
	2 Thessalonians		
	1 Timothy		
	2 Timothy		
	Titus		
	Philemon		

Key Figures in the New Testament

JESUS CHRIST

Jesus Christ is the Messiah, God in the flesh. His ministry spanned over three years, but the impact of it is timeless. Jesus came to earth to redeem humanity back into a right relationship with God. You will learn more about Him in the first four books we will study together, the Gospel accounts of Matthew, Mark, Luke, and John.

DISCIPLES

The word *disciple* means "a follower or student of a teacher, leader, or philosopher," according to a quick Google search (English dictionary provided by Oxford Languages). When we talk about the disciples of Jesus, we refer to His twelve closest friends while on earth. They were Andrew, Bartholomew, James the son of Zebedee, James the son of Alphaeus, John, Judas Iscariot, Jude the brother of James, Matthew, Peter, Philip, Simon the Zealot, and Thomas. One thing to note is that the disciples were quite young, likely between the ages of thirteen and thirty.

JOHN THE BAPTIST

John the Baptist was a prophet who arose after the 400 years of silence that followed the words of Malachi. He was the forerunner of Christ who was to pave the way and prepare the people for Jesus's arrival. John the Baptist was also Jesus's cousin.

JOHN

John was known as the *beloved disciple* because of how much Jesus loved him. He was faithful until the end and was entrusted with taking care of Mary, the mother of Jesus. He wrote one of the Gospels, three letters to churches in Asia Minor, and the book of Revelation.

PAUL

Paul was known as the Hebrew of Hebrews, having studied under Gamaliel, a revered rabbi and member of the Sanhedrin, and was an extreme Pharisee, which meant he took his religion very seriously. Paul experienced a radical conversion to Christ (which we will read about in the book of Acts), and he became the greatest missionary of the early church. Paul founded many churches around the Greco-Roman world, and today we have letters to some of those churches that give us the groundwork for our theology.

LUKE

Luke was a physician as well as a friend and travel associate of Paul's during a portion of his missionary work. Luke was a Gentile (non-Jewish person), according to many scholars, which would make him the only Gentile author in the New Testament, writing a Gospel account and the book of Acts. Some scholars believe he wrote both letters as testimonies for Paul's Roman trial.

PETER

Peter was one of the first disciples Jesus called to follow Him. Jesus knew that Simon would be a great voice for the kingdom. So He changed Simon's name (meaning *reed*) to Peter (which means *rock*), and although Peter had his ups and downs, he gave us some amazing words recorded in his sermon on the day of Pentecost (which we will read in Acts) and in his two follow-up letters, 1 Peter and 2 Peter.

TIMOTHY

Timothy was Paul's spiritual son and was greatly loved by Paul. Timothy also helped write several of Paul's letters and had two letters written to him by Paul as encouragement to stand strong in the faith and continue with the gospel message.

JAMES

James was a brother of Jesus who didn't believe Jesus was the Messiah until after His resurrection. James then became one of the top leaders for the church in Jerusalem and was highly respected among other believers. He ended up writing the book of James as wisdom literature to be added to the New Testament. It has been said that after he was martyred, his friends saw his knees for the first time, and they were like the knees of a camel from spending so much time in prayer.

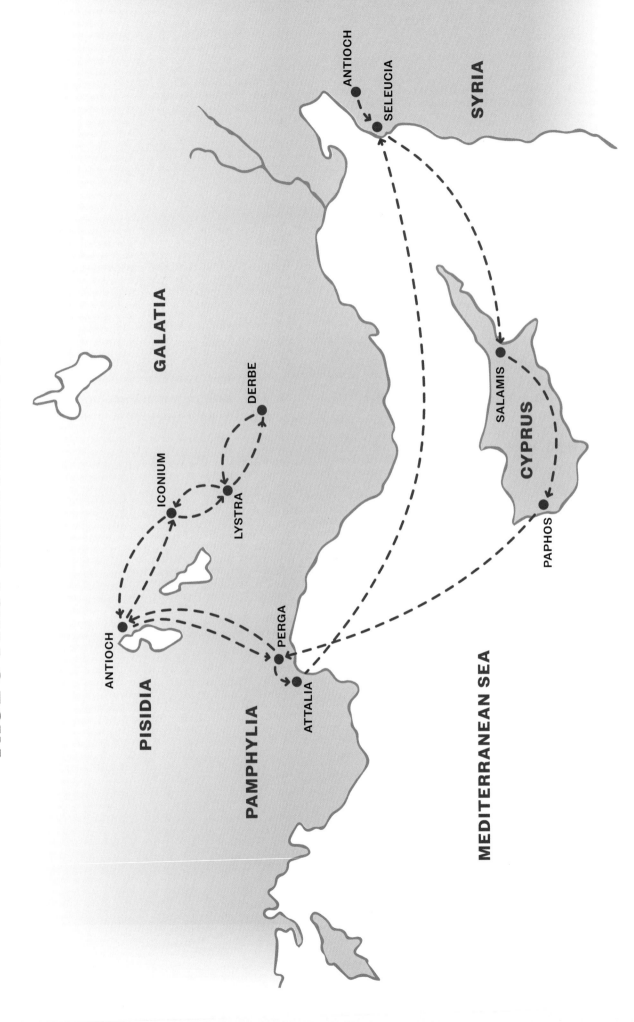

PAUL'S FIRST MISSIONARY JOURNEY

GALATIA

SYRIA

ANTIOCH

SELEUCIA

DERBE

ICONIUM

LYSTRA

CYPRUS

SALAMIS

PAPHOS

ANTIOCH

PISIDIA

PERGA

PAMPHYLIA

ATTALIA

MEDITERRANEAN SEA

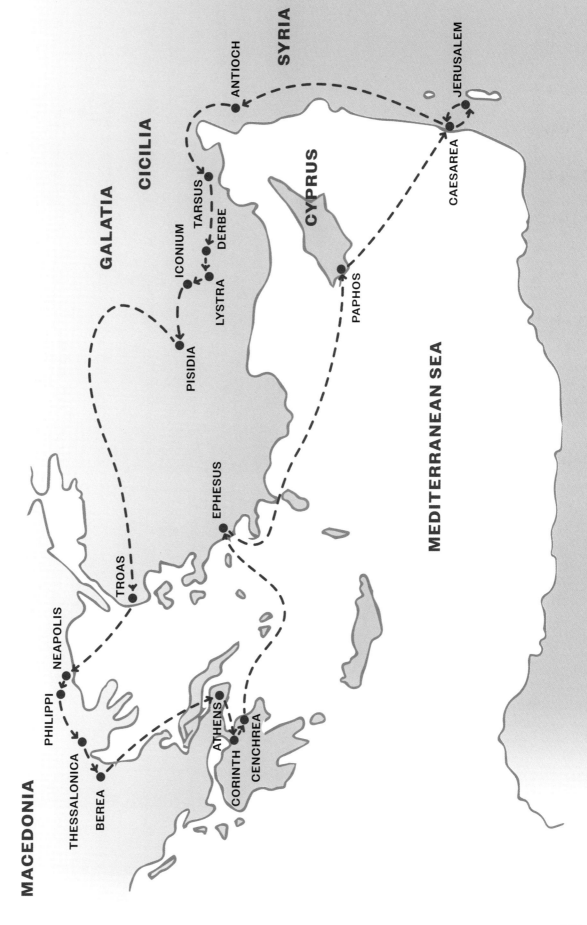

PAUL'S SECOND MISSIONARY JOURNEY

MACEDONIA

NEAPOLIS

PHILIPPI

THESSALONICA

BEREA

TROAS

ATHENS

CORINTH

CENCHREA

EPHESUS

GALATIA

CICILIA

PISIDIA

ICONIUM

LYSTRA

DERBE

TARSUS

ANTIOCH

SYRIA

JERUSALEM

CAESAREA

CYPRUS

PAPHOS

MEDITERRANEAN SEA

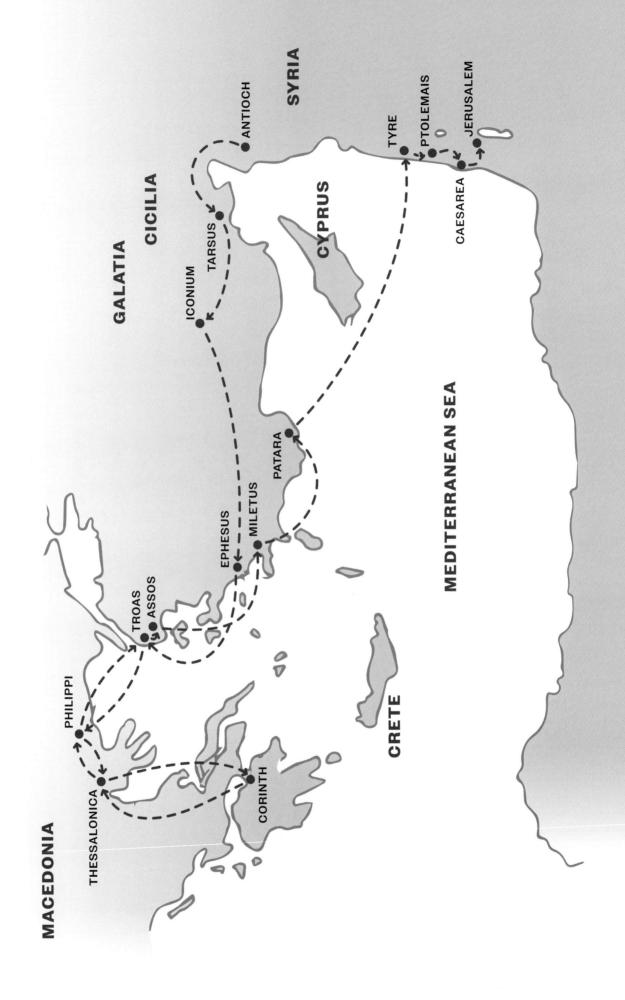

PAUL'S THIRD MISSIONARY JOURNEY

MACEDONIA

THESSALONICA

PHILIPPI

TROAS
ASSOS

EPHESUS

MILETUS

PATARA

CORINTH

CRETE

GALATIA

CICILIA

ICONIUM

TARSUS

ANTIOCH

SYRIA

CYPRUS

TYRE

PTOLEMAIS

JERUSALEM

CAESAREA

MEDITERRANEAN SEA

MATTHEW

AUTHOR
The author of the first Gospel in the New Testament was Matthew, a disciple and former tax collector.

DATE
Matthew wrote his Gospel around AD 50 to 55, most likely from Antioch.

AUDIENCE
The content of Matthew is heavily focused on Jesus being the Messiah, the King of the Jews, which means his audience was almost completely Jewish.

REASON
Matthew was written to show the Jewish people that Jesus was the Messiah they had been waiting for.

THEME
Jesus is the Jewish Messiah, the fulfillment of Old Testament prophecy.

KEY VERSE
"Do not think that I have come to abolish the Law or the Prophets; I have not come to abolish them but to fulfill them" (Matthew 5:17).

SECTIONS
Ministry in Galilee (ch. 1–7), miracles and kingdom parables (ch. 8–13), end of Galilean ministry (ch. 14–18), ministry in Perea and Judea (ch. 19–25), passion, death, and resurrection (ch. 26–28).

KEY WORDS
Kingdom, covenant, fulfilled, Father, Spirit

STORY OVERVIEW

The Gospel of Matthew is the first book in the New Testament, which is important because Matthew is a Jewish man writing to a Jewish audience and he shows them that their Messiah has arrived. It's a phenomenal book of fulfillment. One thing to remember when looking at the four Gospels is to put yourself in the shoes of the original reader so you can better understand what is being taught. In this case, Matthew uses far more Old Testament quotes than the other Gospel writers and doesn't feel obligated to explain the Jewish lifestyle. The audience would have understood all that.

Right off the bat, Matthew records Jesus's genealogy through Mary, the bloodline/legal line of Jesus. He shows how Jesus was a descendant of David and Abraham, two of the people most fundamental in the Jewish faith, both of whom the Messiah was promised to come from.

Genealogies may not be very important to us as Gentiles, but this genealogy alone has caused many Jews to come to faith in Christ. Because genealogies mean everything. It's your DNA. It's what makes you, you.

Notice how Matthew started off the story of Jesus at His baptism. An interesting thing to point out is that the Father, Son, and Holy Spirit were all present during it. Many believe that the Father, Son, and Holy Spirit were also present at Creation.

Right after Jesus's baptism, He was brought into the wilderness to be tempted by Satan for forty days. The number forty is often associated with testing

and trials, which we saw in the Old Testament as the Israelites wandered in the wilderness for forty years.

Once John the Baptist completed his task of finalizing the Old Testament and ushering in the New, Jesus put a spin on the message of salvation and taught about kingdom principles. The word *kingdom* broken down means the "king's domain," and since it's the kingdom of heaven, Jesus was implying that God controls everything where the kingdom is present.

Jesus said that He came to fulfill the Law, not abolish it. Matthew records the term *fulfilled* fifteen times in reference to Christ in his Gospel. Jesus also said that not one jot or tittle, as he put it, would pass from the Law before it was fulfilled. As we just saw while studying the Old Testament, there was a lot that had yet to be fulfilled.

It's amazing to see that Matthew was able to record all five of Jesus's main sermons word-for-word in this book. He had to have been ferociously jotting down notes every time Jesus began a discourse, or the Holy Spirit reminded him of Jesus's words.

Jesus affirms the promise of provision among those who dedicate their life to Him. He promises to provide, so we can hold Him accountable to that promise. The key to provision is seeking first the kingdom and His righteousness. Then our needs will be met. So often I hear people say that they wish they could do "Christian" work for a living. Let me be clear: ALL WORK is Christian work. Every believer is in full-time ministry. We are all missionaries who have

BLESSED are the poor in spirit,
for theirs is the KINGDOM OF HEAVEN.

BLESSED are those who mourn,
for they will be COMFORTED.

BLESSED are the meek,
for they will INHERIT THE EARTH.

BLESSED are those who hunger and thirst
for righteousness, for they will BE FILLED.

BLESSED are the merciful,
for they will be SHOWN MERCY.

BLESSED are the pure in heart,
for they will SEE GOD.

BLESSED are the peacemakers,
for they will be called CHILDREN OF GOD.

BLESSED are those who are persecuted
because of righteousness,
for theirs is the KINGDOM OF HEAVEN.

Matthew 5:3–10 NIV

The Beatitudes

been charged with the task of making disciples in our surroundings. If you work at McDonald's, you are called to preach the gospel message to your peers. If you are the CEO of a Fortune 500 company, you are called to preach the gospel message to your peers. If you are living in a yurt in Africa and preaching the gospel message to your peers, you are called to continue preaching the gospel message to your peers. Once we have that realization and begin acting upon righteousness, God will provide for every one of our needs.

The last words of Jesus that Matthew records are "All authority in heaven and on earth has been given to me. Go therefore and make disciples of all nations, baptizing them in the name of the Father and of the Son and of the Holy Spirit, teaching them to observe all that I have commanded you. And behold, I am with you always, to the end of the age" (28:18–20).

That statement is known as the Great Commission. And it's what we've been charged with as well. To make disciples, to baptize them, and to teach them about the Bible. It's our calling. To keep it all about Jesus.

The Gospel of Matthew is all about Jesus. As a Jew. For the Jews. The climax of faith. Matthew is a genius in his penmanship because he displays one prophecy after the next from the Old Testament, confirming that Jesus Christ is the one true Messiah they had all been waiting for. From the location of his birth to his means of transportation into Jerusalem as the King, it IS all there and it HAS BEEN all there.

From the beginning, God promised a Messiah would come one day and save His people. Jesus is the One. The sad fact is that many people missed it. They couldn't comprehend that the Messiah had actually come because it all seemed too good to be true and He didn't present himself as a conquering king, as everyone expected.

As we see time and time again, Yahweh is a God of second chances. He knows it's hard for us to accept things, especially something as brilliant as the advent of the Messiah, the first time around. The good news is that He is coming back. He will come one day to reign supreme and judge every person accordingly.

But until then, keep studying this book! ■

▶ What were the covenants God had with Abraham and David (Genesis 15 and 2 Samuel 7)?

▶ The five women in Jesus's genealogy are listed below. Who were they?

   1. Tamar (Genesis 38)

   2. Rahab (Joshua 2)

   3. Ruth (Ruth)

   4. Bathsheba (2 Samuel 11–12)

   5. Mary (Matthew 1:18–25)

▶ Right after Jesus's baptism He was brought into the wilderness to be tempted by Satan for forty days. Can you think of another time in the Bible when God's people were brought into the wilderness? How long were they there?

▶ When you meditate on the phrase *kingdom of heaven*, what comes to mind?

▶ Jesus said He came to fulfill the Law, not abolish it. What does that mean for us? What does that mean for Jewish people?

▶ What is the main focus of Jesus's five sermons in this Gospel?

   1. Matthew 5–7

   2. Matthew 10

   3. Matthew 13

   4. Matthew 18

   5. Matthew 23–25

▶ How do they all relate to each other?

▶ Why do you think Jesus speaks in parables (Matthew 13:13–17)?

▶ Matthew describes the Mount of Transfiguration experience, including the appearance of Elijah and Moses talking with Jesus. What do you think our glorified bodies will be like? Will our appearance be different? How old do you think we will be?

▶ In what ways are you fulfilling the Great Commission? How can you improve?

▶ After studying the Old Testament, what are some ways you could show a Jewish person that Jesus is their Messiah?

AUTHOR
The Gospel of Mark was written by Mark, also known as John Mark.

DATE
There is a lot of debate about which Gospel was written first. Some believe that Matthew and Luke were first, with Mark pulling his stories from them, while others believe that Mark wrote first, and Matthew and Luke drew from him. We do not know for sure the Gospel writing order.

AUDIENCE
Mark was written to Christians in Rome. If Mark was written at a later date, we know that there were thousands of Christians being martyred in Rome at the time. We also know that the early church met down in the Catacombs, the graveyard of martyrs—a stark reminder of the risk they were taking. Mark might have read this Gospel to the other believers. Think about how much more impactful that would make the story.

REASON
Mark shows Jesus as a suffering Servant to encourage the readers to press on through any form of persecution that they were dealing with. He shows the power and actions of Jesus more than the other Gospels to prove this servant was truly the King.

THEME
Jesus as the suffering Servant.

KEY VERSE
"For even the Son of Man did not come to be served, but to serve, and to give His life as a ransom for many" (Mark 10:45 NASB).

SECTIONS
Jesus's ministry (ch. 1–10), Passion Week (ch. 11–16).

KEY WORDS / PHRASES
Immediately, authority, Spirit, kingdom of God

MARK

STORY OVERVIEW

Mark is a unique book in that it highlights miracles far more than teachings. He includes eighteen miracles in these sixteen chapters, with only four to ten parables (tallies vary depending on who is counting and how) and one major discourse. Mark does not give any of Christ's ancestry, since the theme is that Christ is a servant, and people don't care about a servant's ancestry.

None of the Gospels identify the author because they don't want the attention to be on themselves.

So, who was Mark?

Mark was too young to be a disciple, but he was fascinated with Jesus, so he hung around Him as much as possible. There is a chance that his house was used to host the disciples in the Upper Room. Some scholars believe he was the naked guy who ran away in the Garden of Gethsemane when Jesus was arrested.

Mark never had the spotlight on himself, but he did end up helping Barnabas and Paul on multiple journeys.

You could say that Mark himself was hyperactive. The word *immediately* is repeated forty-one times—Mark was always on the go from one place to the next. He couldn't sit still and wanted to be front and center in all of the action, and maybe that's why the book of Mark focuses so heavily on the actions of Jesus instead of His sermons.

After years of mentoring the disciples, Jesus is sitting with them at the base of Mount Hermon in Caesarea Philippi. He asks them questions about himself to see if they truly believed that He was who He said He was. And the disciples passed the test. It was at this point, when Peter said he believed Jesus

was the Son of God, that Jesus was able to break the difficult news to them. This was the first time Jesus mentioned the cross, the events of which were to happen shortly. God's plan of redemption was almost complete.

Toward the end of the Gospel, Mark decided to narrow his focus and display the reason for Christ's arrival in Jerusalem.

Mark gives us the most in-depth look at Jesus's final week in all the Gospels. Jesus knew what was going to happen, and it wasn't pretty. His life was to be laid down as an exchange for all the sins of humanity. He actually became sin so we could be seen as sinless. Every disease, every anger issue, every addiction, every evil desire from the past, present, and future were nailed to the cross so we could be set free. What we struggle with today was already taken care of 2,000 years ago. If Jesus is your personal Savior, you are FREE. Like, RIGHT NOW!

Just as we saw when studying Zechariah, everything Jesus said and did was a fulfillment of Old Testament prophecy. And it was fulfilled literally to a T. That's why I believe it is so important for us to study and understand the Old Testament today. Jesus was a Jew who came to save the Jews first. How are we supposed to understand the importance of what He did and said if we don't understand the Jewish mindset? It's nearly impossible, and we would miss out on SO much.

Since Mark was writing this Gospel to Roman Christians, many of whom were Gentiles, it is a great starting point for nonbelievers or new believers because it is written so Gentiles will understand it. It's the basics. It shows what Jesus did and what we are called to do. ■

FISHERS OF MEN

▶ The first eight chapters of Mark are all about healings, miracles, and casting out demons. Which one of these stories is your favorite? Why?

▶ How did Jesus set the demoniac free (Mark 5:1–13)?

▶ What does that teach us about demons?

▶ In chapters 6 and 8 we have the feeding of the 5,000 and 4,000. Why do you think both stories were included?

▶ How much food was left over at each (Mark 6:43; 8:8)? Do you see any significance to those numbers?

▶ What did Peter do after Jesus foretold His death and resurrection (Mark 8:32)? Why did Jesus say to Peter, "Get away from me, Satan" (Mark 8:33 NLT)?

▶ Jesus became sin so we could be completely set free. Anything you deal with today was taken care of 2,000 years ago. Have you had a revelation of that concept yet? How does that change the way you live?

▶ Using concepts from this book, how would you evangelize to a non-Christian?

▶ Remember, your audience won't have any understanding of the Old Testament, so give an overview of the gospel message in the most easy-to-understand way possible.

LUKE

AUTHOR
The Gospel of Luke was written by a friend of Paul's, named Luke. Two important things to note while studying this book as well as the book of Acts are that Luke was a doctor and also a Gentile.

DATE
This gospel was most likely written while Paul was imprisoned in Caesarea around AD 58 to 60 or during his Roman imprisonment in AD 60 to 62.

AUDIENCE
Luke addressed his Gospel to one man only: "most excellent Theophilus." So who in the world is Theophilus?

Scholars have made many different claims over the years as to who Theophilus was. Some say that he was Paul's financial supporter, some believe he was Luke's master, and others believe that he was the Roman official or judge over Paul's trial.

I choose to agree with the last of the three main options. Luke does an amazing job at compiling all of his information from eyewitness interviews and then presents the case that neither Jesus nor Paul had any big issues with the Roman government. Also, Luke ends the book of Acts just before Paul's hearing—the same time that these writings would be presented to the judge.

REASON
As we just saw, this entire Gospel could have been written to win Paul's release so he could continue his journey of bringing the gospel around the world. It is an amazing look at the gospel story from the perspective of a Gentile doctor who focused on the humanity of the Son of Man.

THEME
Christ is the Savior for the Gentiles too.

KEY VERSE
"For the Son of Man came to seek and to save the lost" (Luke 19:10).

SECTIONS
Incarnation (ch. 1–3), Galilean ministry (ch. 4–9), journey toward Jerusalem (ch. 10-19), final week (ch. 19-24).

KEY WORDS / PHRASES
Son of Man, salvation, kingdom, pray

STORY OVERVIEW

When studying the four Gospels, the most important thing you can do is look at the stories through the eyes of the writer. In this case, Luke is likely writing to a Roman judge on behalf of his buddy Paul. Therefore, the content is much more focused on how Jesus interacted with Gentiles, Romans, and women.

Luke is a unique book in the sense that it has many stories the other authors did not have because they weren't able to interview the right people. Luke was not present during the ministry of Jesus so he had to get information from all the eyewitnesses he could, to piece together the proper narrative to secure Paul's release. That might be why the feel of this book seems a little different, compared with the other Gospels.

And Luke, being a doctor, approached Jesus from the perspective of the Son of Man. Hence the reason for Jesus's genealogy dating to the first man, Adam, through the line of Mary.

Luke found it important to spend time looking at the healing miracles of Jesus's ministry, not specifically to show the Romans that Jesus was God, but because, as a doctor, he probably was fascinated with them himself. The recordings are truly unbelievable to those that have not experienced or witnessed the power of God. Luke also looks more closely at the Holy Spirit and the power He produces through the natural man than the other Gospel writers. Luke and the book of Acts are also more focused on being baptized in the Spirit and the actions of Jesus's disciples.

At the beginning of Luke, we get this great story of Mary, who was pregnant with Jesus, visiting Elizabeth, who was pregnant with John the Baptist. When Mary greets Elizabeth, John leaps in her womb. John the Baptist seemed to acknowledge a change in the spiritual realm even though he was not even born yet. How cool!

Luke is also the only Gospel that records anything about Jesus's life before His ministry began. We see this wild story about Him being left in Jerusalem at the age of twelve. How could His parents have left Him behind?! He was God in the flesh! Remember that He had not yet received the Holy Spirit, and this was around eighteen years before His ministry began.

Luke also focuses on women, showing how they were loved and cherished by Jesus. Yet sometimes in the church today we discount women in ministry and exalt male religious leaders instead. Doesn't that seem to be the opposite of what Jesus taught?

Luke really is a Gospel for everybody, Jew and Gentile alike. Since Luke was a Gentile writing to a Gentile, this Gospel should be used as an evangelism tool with Gentiles. In my mind, it's probably the best one because Gentiles would understand it best.

Luke includes many important testimonies that we don't read about in the other Gospels. And all of these are used to teach us new things. Testimonies are among the greatest things we can share with the world. They produce hunger. They produce connections. They can also boost faith in hopes that God will work for us in the same way He has for others. And I believe this book will boost your faith and help you see how good a Father we serve. ■

SEEK

SAVE

▶ Of all of the stories that are unique to Luke, which one speaks to you most? Why?

▶ While John the Baptist was still in Elizabeth's stomach, he seemed to acknowledge a change in the spiritual realm, even though Jesus also was not born yet. How does this story affect your views on abortion?

▶ What does this show about children's discernment of the spiritual realm? How should this influence the way we raise our children?

▶ Why do you think the Holy Spirit made sure the story of Jesus being left behind in Jerusalem was included in the text?

▶ What do you think Jesus meant when He said, "Didn't you know I had to be in my Father's house?" (Luke 2:49 NIV)? Remember, He had not yet received the Holy Spirit, and this was around eighteen years before His ministry began.

▶ How can we better serve the women of our communities today?

▶ Which Gospel would you say is best for evangelism?

▶ After reading about the death of Jesus and also remembering the Passover in Exodus, list things that show Jesus was the fulfillment of Passover:

▶ Your testimony is one of the greatest things you can share with the world. Write out the key points of your testimony below:

JOHN

AUTHOR
The Gospel of John was written by the apostle John. He was the only disciple still alive, and times were changing before his eyes.

DATE
John wrote his Gospel sometime in the AD 80s before the persecution of Domitian began. This was his first book, with more to come before his death in AD 98.

AUDIENCE
The Gospel of John was written to various churches around Asia Minor where he had an influence. John was one of the elders in the church of Ephesus and was looked up to because of his experiences and wisdom.

REASON
John was written to show the reader that Jesus was both fully God and fully man. It was most likely used to provide information that the other Gospels left out and to show more of a theological perspective on the life of Christ.

THEME
Jesus came to give eternal life because He is God.

KEY VERSE
"I came that they may have life and have it abundantly" (John 10:10).

SECTIONS
Ministry and rejection (ch. 1–11), Passion Week and resurrection (ch. 12–21).

KEY WORDS
Believe, heaven, Father, eternal

STORY OVERVIEW

The Gospel of John is ninety percent unique from Matthew, Mark, and Luke, which are called the *Synoptic Gospels*. John explores Jesus as the Son of God, including His preexistent genealogy at the beginning of his Gospel.

Whereas the other Gospels looked at what Jesus did and said, John approaches his story from the inside by looking at how Jesus felt and who He was as a person. He made it a point to show that Jesus is fully human and fully divine at the same time. There was nothing Jesus could do while on earth without help from the Father.

John had decades to map out his version of the gospel message, since he lived longer than the other disciples and wrote his Gospel nearly thirty years later than the others did. He didn't want people wasting their time figuring out who Jesus was, so he put it all out on the table.

In chapter 1, we are introduced to a man named John the Baptist—not to be confused with the author—who was the forerunner to the Messiah. The Old Testament closes with a preview of John in Malachi 4:5.

Back in the day, Jews would study the Torah through their entire childhood, in hopes of one day being selected by a rabbi for training, and eventually becoming a rabbi themselves. At the boy's bar mitzvah, a rabbi would come up to him and say, "Follow me." From that moment forward, the trainee would mimic every move and word of the rabbi so he would be a direct representation of him. Since all the disciples were working in their family occupation when Jesus found them, it meant they had not been chosen by the local rabbis. Jesus gave them a chance. Those two words, "Follow me," were worth dropping everything to learn.

Water to wine seems like a strange miracle to start with, doesn't it? Jesus performed this one privately to the disciples so they could see the power at hand, showing that He truly was the Lord. To run out of wine at a wedding was a major faux pas, so Jesus freed them of their embarrassment and even cranked the party up a level. He was more concerned with bringing joy to the lives of others than what was to come in His future.

The beginning of Jesus's ministry marked the countdown to His death.

What do you think the most popular verse in the Bible is? John 3:16? Notice how it is spoken to one man at night. There is no stage or microphone. It's one-on-one. Just the way God likes it.

Then comes the story of the woman at the well, and people are shocked by Jesus's actions. They couldn't believe that He was talking to a Samaritan woman. The Samaritans were considered half-breed sellouts because their distant relatives intermingled with Gentiles from Samaria after returning from exile, even though they were commanded not to do so. Not only was this woman a Samaritan, but just her being a woman made it astounding that a Jewish man would talk to her in broad daylight. But Jesus didn't care about societal norms. He showed her love from the bottom of His heart.

One thing to notice in all John's books is that he writes in sevens. Seven is the number of perfect divinity and is a very important number in the Jewish faith. The top two things John focuses on in this Gospel are seven major miracles as well as seven "I am" statements of Jesus. Those statements meant everything to John.

When John gets to the Passion week, he shows that as Jesus was entering Jerusalem on a donkey, the people placed palm branches on the road before Him as an act of honoring a King. Despite all of Jesus's teaching, they still expected Jesus to be the political Messiah that was talked about so often by the prophets. They just didn't realize then that there would be two comings. They wanted Jesus to establish His worldly kingdom then and now. Think of how confused they must have been when He headed straight for the temple instead of the throne. . . .

The good news for us is that God's kingdom does reign in the hearts of His children right now and can impact the world around us if we allow it to. Jesus told His disciples to pray for heaven to come to earth, and we should be focusing on the same every day.

The day Jesus rose from the dead was the most joyous day in the history of the world.

It changed EVERYTHING! It's interesting to note that Mary doesn't recognize Jesus right away, but knows it is Him when He says her name.

Remember the verse in John 10:27, which says, "My sheep hear my voice . . . and they follow me." She knew His voice.

At the end of this Gospel, Jesus asks Simon Peter three times if he loves Him. Earlier, Peter had denied three times that he knew Jesus. This was the canceling out of those denials. Looking at Peter's letters in the New Testament, we see that he ended well and continued loving Christ for the rest of his life.

Those are just a few highlights from the Gospel of John. I know you'll find many more incredible treasures as you dive deeper. ■

I AM.

▶ Isn't it amazing that the Creator of the universe came down to His creation to save it? Describe a time when you worked extra hard on a project and it didn't turn out as you planned. How did that make you feel? How do you think God felt?

▶ Who was the "Lamb of God" John baptized? What do you think was the reason for His baptism?

▶ What happened during Jesus's baptism that caused John to realize who He was?

▶ Jesus said, "Follow me," to the disciples, and they dropped everything to follow Him. Would you have dropped everything if you hadn't known who Jesus was?

▶ How do you think their family members felt? What would you do if your son just ran off to follow the new rabbi in town?

▶ John focuses his Gospel on seven major miracles. List them below:

1. John 2:1–11

2. John 4:46–54

3. John 5:1–9

4. John 6:1–14

5. John 6:16–21

6. John 9:1–33

7. John 11:1–44

▶ What do all of these miracles show you about Jesus?

▶ What role does joy play in your day-to-day faith? Where does joy come from (Galatians 5:22–23)? How can you increase it?

▶ The most popular verse in the Bible probably is John 3:16. Why do you think Jesus chose to speak it to one man at night instead of preaching it from a mountaintop?

▶ Who does society tell you that you "shouldn't talk to"? What can you do to show them their worth?

▶ John shares seven "I am" statements about Jesus. List them below:

1. John 6:35

2. John 8:12

3. John 10:9

4. John 10:11

5. John 11:25

6. John 14:6

7. John 15:5

▶ Write a prayer about being more aware of your need for Jesus as a Shepherd:

▶ What do you think it looks like to bring heaven to earth every day?

▶ When others deny Jesus's deity or humanity, what verses could you share with them from John's Gospel? (See John 1:1 for starters.)

AUTHOR

As was the Gospel of Luke, the book of Acts was written by Dr. Luke, a friend of Paul. Luke shows that they were together during many of the travels and experienced the same miracles throughout.

DATE

This book was likely written around the same time as the Gospel of Luke, while Paul was imprisoned either in Caesarea around AD 58–60 or during his Roman imprisonment in AD 60–62.

AUDIENCE

Luke addresses Acts to Theophilus, as he did his Gospel.

Considering that Luke ends this book with Paul still awaiting trial, it seems as if the evidence for this being used as a document in the trial is increasing. As mentioned before, Theophilus might have been a Roman judge at the time.

REASON

The book of Acts possibly was used as a legal document to serve as a testimony on Paul's behalf. Thank goodness that we still have it today because this book is a great historical account of the early Christian church.

THEME

The gospel message is for everyone, everywhere.

KEY VERSE

"But you will receive power when the Holy Spirit has come upon you, and you will be my witnesses in Jerusalem and in all Judea and Samaria, and to the end of the earth" (Acts 1:8).

SECTIONS

To the Jews and Samaritans (ch. 1–8), to the rest of the world (ch. 9–28).

KEY WORDS

Believe, Holy Spirit, baptized, witness, church

ACTS

STORY OVERVIEW

The book of Acts is a historical look at the first 30 years of the early church and, in many cases, could be used as a model for missionary work around the world today.

It starts off with Jesus promising the disciples that they would receive the power of the Holy Spirit shortly and would end up preaching in Jerusalem, Judea, Samaria, and to the remotest parts of the earth.

Each one of those places is another ring outside of their current sphere of influence. They were in Jerusalem, then right outside are Judea and Samaria, and outside of that is everywhere else in the world. This can be used as a great plan for evangelism today no matter where you are located. You have your neighbor, your city, and then the rest of the world.

After instructing the disciples regarding the Holy Spirit, telling them that He was coming to be their Comforter and was going to help them in so many ways, we see that Jesus ascended into heaven and left them with a hope to hold on to.

The disciples picked Judas's replacement, and then in chapter 2, an amazing thing took place among them. They were all filled with the Holy Spirit, and everyone began to speak in different tongues, different languages. So much so that people called them out as being drunk, but others were blown away that they could understand them speaking their language.

In the book of Exodus, we saw that on the day of Pentecost 3,000 people were killed. But fast-forward almost 1,500 years, and in Acts 2:41 Luke shows us that on this day of Pentecost, 3,000 souls were saved. Whereas the Law brought death to 3,000 people, the Holy Spirit brought life. It's an amazing illustration of God's sovereignty.

After this life-changing experience, the church was finally able to begin building itself up based on what they had been taught through Jesus's ministry. It was go time. It's safe to say that they were hit with quite a bit of resistance right off the bat. That seems to be the case any time the Holy Spirit moves in mighty ways, even today.

So we learn about Stephen and how he was spreading the gospel message. At one point he was even able to share with the Sanhedrin, which was like the top-top Jewish group of the time. He preached the gospel to them and was explaining why Jews were following The Way, which is what Christianity was called at that time.

The Sanhedrin wouldn't have any of what Stephen was saying, though, and they stoned him. Stephen's stoning sparked persecution of Christians throughout Jerusalem led by a man named Saul. Saul was a bad dude, a Jewish Roman citizen who studied under Gamaliel, the top of the top among rabbis. Saul was so hardcore in his faith that he made it a point to throw anyone in prison who went against his beliefs, especially these new Christians.

One day when Saul was on the road to Damascus with hopes of throwing more Christians in prison, he was stopped by Jesus himself and ended up being blinded until a man named Ananias later came to heal him of it. Saul was converted on the spot and was baptized.

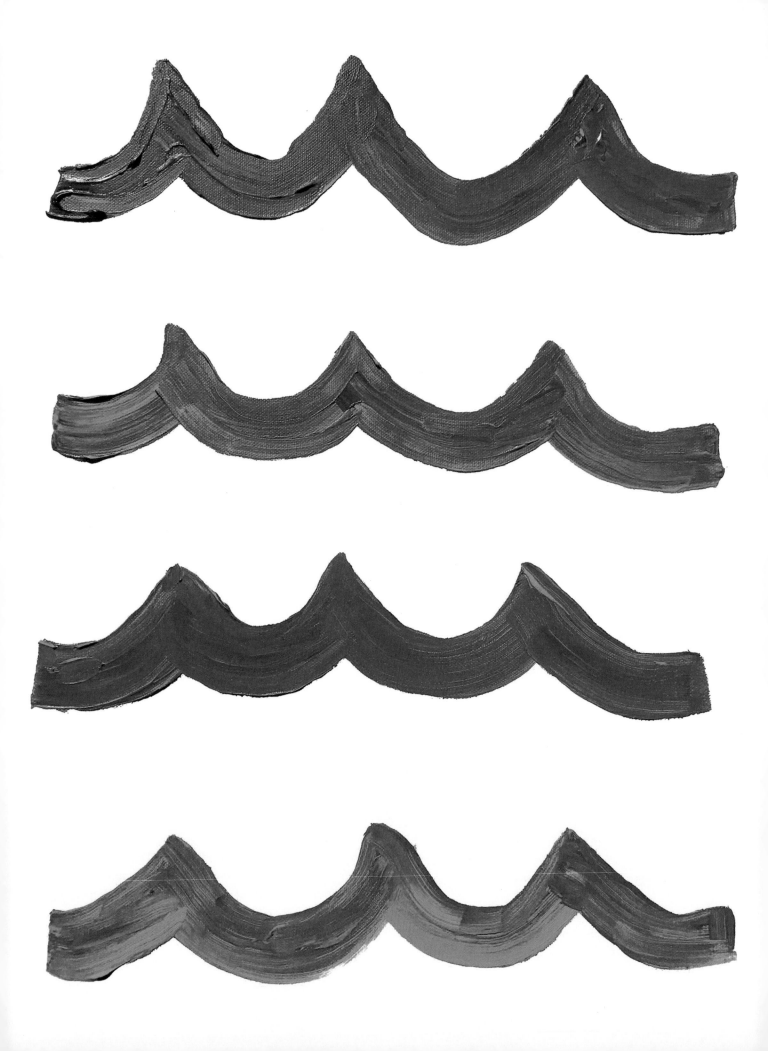

We know that Saul went to his hometown of Tarsus for ten years to preach there and build himself up before going out on any missionary journeys. Many people in the church talk about having a Saul-Paul conversion once they became saved, but that just isn't biblical. Once Saul is converted, his name remains Saul. It isn't until he begins his first missionary journey to the Gentiles that he switches over to his Roman name of Paul. It's only fitting, since he claimed to become all things to all people, and if he was preaching to Roman citizens, it would make sense for him to use his Roman name.

If you flip back to the New Testament Overview in this book, there are maps that show the routes of Paul's travels, and you can follow along as you go back through Acts; you'll also see how many of the cities he visited ended up receiving letters from him later that we now have in our Bibles. Letters to the Corinthians, Ephesians, Philippians, and Thessalonians—it's pretty cool.

Paul went on his first few journeys with Barnabas and John Mark, but he got into a disagreement with John Mark, who wrote the Gospel of Mark. Paul decided to go in a different direction, preaching with Silas and Timothy instead, while Barnabas and John Mark kept going on their own way. Luke also joined in on his second journey, so you'll notice that he began to include "we" in his writing.

An important thing to note is that all the disciples were creating more disciples in each city. They didn't ask people to raise their hands and make a "decision," like today. They mentored them, teaching the new believers from the ground up, nurturing their faith alongside them. It's that real transformation that causes the greatest impact and trickles down to the next round of believers and the next and the next.

In chapters 23 through 26 we see the beginning of Paul's trial. It is likely the reason this book was written. It's Rome vs. Christianity. Paul never harmed anybody on his journeys, he only healed them. So the guards were fairly lenient as they watched over him. Even on the ship, heading to Rome, the crew seemed to listen to Paul's prophecies and wisdom as a higher authority than their own common sense.

They eventually made it to Rome, and Paul was placed under house arrest. He was still able to welcome visitors, though, and continued to preach the gospel message. He also wrote letters to the churches he had built on his journeys while awaiting the trial that was soon to take place.

Considering that Paul was released in AD 62 and was able to depart from Rome on his fourth missionary journey (which we don't have much information on), we can surmise that this letter was a successful witness regarding his life and ministry. If you look at Acts from a personal perspective, it can be a very heavy book because much of the modern-day church conducts itself far differently from what we read of here.

In the eyes of many, signs and wonders being used for evangelism purposes tend to be for the "crazies," but in the Bible they always accompanied the preaching of the gospel. The disciples would FIRST show the power of God and THEN give them the Good News. They shared an experience of the Holy Spirit's presence FIRST because they knew that affecting hearts was far more life-changing than affecting heads. You can tell someone all day about why they should believe the Bible, but it may save you a lot of time and be more impactful if you just show them instead. ■

Acts

275

ADVENTURE
IS CALLING

▶ What is your church's mission statement for missions?

▶ Have you been water baptized? When? If not, have you thought about it?

▶ Do you remember what happened at the first Pentecost in the Old Testament (Exodus 32:25–29)? How do the two compare?

▶ Have you ever experienced the Holy Spirit moving around you? If so, what happened?

▶ What do you think was going through Ananias's mind when the Lord told him to heal Saul, the man who was persecuting all his friends?

▶ Saul went back to his hometown for nearly a decade to preach and build himself up before going on any missionary journeys. What about us? Do our hometowns see the fire in each of us? They need to see our changed life before the world will. How can you use Saul as an example regarding hometown missionary work instead of just doing short-term mission trips every once in a while?

▶ Do you think Paul dealt with any fear of what others thought of him during his first missionary journey? If he did, how do you think he overcame that fear?

▶ What was the council debating in chapter 15? What was the final consensus? What does that mean for us?

▶ Paul was blocked from going to Bithynia in chapter 16. Have you ever been blocked by the Holy Spirit from going somewhere? If so, what happened?

▶ Have you ever been mentored or discipled? Are you currently discipling anyone? How can you use this story as an example for evangelism?

▶ What are your thoughts on using signs and wonders for evangelism purposes?

AUTHOR
The book of Romans was written by the apostle Paul.

DATE
Romans was written on Paul's third missionary journey around AD 55 to 56. He had not actually been to Rome yet, and due to the similarities of 1 and 2 Corinthians, we can conclude it was written in that timeframe.

AUDIENCE
Paul was writing to a church he had never visited before and he did not personally know the leaders in Rome; we can conclude that from the entire chapter he used as a closing statement, to show that he knew the same people they did, which would help build credibility with them. There was a ton of tension in the Roman church between Jews and Gentiles at the time, with both making claims that they were in charge and things would be done their way. Talk about a mess.

REASON
Romans was written to help resolve the tension between the Jews and Gentiles in Rome and to show that both groups were equal in God's sight. It was also written to explain the gospel as a whole, to be used for ministry advancement.

THEME
Basics of Christianity and Jew-Gentile relations.

KEY VERSES
"For I am not ashamed of the gospel, for it is the power of God for salvation to everyone who believes, to the Jew first and also to the Greek. For in it the righteousness of God is revealed from faith for faith, as it is written, 'The righteous shall live by faith'" (Romans 1:16–17).

SECTIONS
Paul's Gospel (ch. 1–8), the gospel and Israel (ch. 9–11), living out the gospel (ch. 12–16).

KEY WORDS
Law, righteous, grace, justified, faith, gospel

ROMANS

Romans is a massive book—not necessarily words-wise, but content-wise. It's so deep that it would take months to really dive into. That's why we are doing an overview of each book for now with the hope that you will take time in the future to go deeper, once you have a better understanding of the Bible as a whole.

So Romans is the gospel. It's a book about grace and it's a book about redemption. This is God's plan for humanity. Therefore, it is extremely important that you take time to really understand this book.

Paul was one of the most influential Jews at the time, and he maintained a Jewish mindset even when reaching out to the Gentiles. Therefore, he understood his faith through the lens of a covenant relationship because that is what the Old Testament is heavily based on. So we also must understand covenants, to get what Paul is talking about.

So first off, how was a covenant cut, or made?

Well to create a covenant was a serious thing. It started out with the kill. The two people entering into the covenant relationship began by finding a pure animal to sacrifice for the covenant ceremony. Once the animal had been selected, the two of them cut it in half along the spine, separating it into two sides. Remember, they didn't have electric saws back then, so at this point they were covered in blood, sweat, and maybe some tears. Completely and utterly exhausted.

The next step was the oath. They would lay out both sides of the animal, cut side open, facing each other, representing the two parties involved. They would each have a group of witnesses on their side. Then they would walk in a figure-eight pattern throughout the halves, repeating the terms of the covenant as they did so. After the terms were stated multiple times, they would take a rock and cut a large slice on their right hand, followed by putting their hands together. As we saw in Leviticus, blood means life. So the covenant parties' blood joining together symbolized their lives joining as well. The two became ONE.

Then they would rub dirt in their wound to create a scar as a visible reminder of the covenant. After all the rituals were complete, the witnesses from each side of the covenant had a large party together. And those in attendance would become responsible for holding the covenant makers accountable for their actions.

To enter into a covenant was a major deal. It meant that you died to yourself and there was no way out of it. Everything you did revolved around the terms of the covenant.

When God entered into a covenant with Abraham in Genesis 15, He put him to sleep during the process and passed between the animal pieces himself, employing fire and smoke. The reason that Abram couldn't do the task was because he was still sinful, and God needed someone sinless to join Him. So God basically made a down payment to show that the covenant was unconditional and eternal. Two thousand years later we see that Jesus was the One without sin. Through Him we enter into that covenant when we are washed clean by His blood. When we come to Jesus, we are saying that we want to join

HERE&NOW
HERE&NOW
HERE&NOW
HERE&NOW

in on His side of the covenant. We want to be a part of that covenant party now that it is complete. His representation allows us to be included in this whole thing. It's amazing!

The Bible as a whole is one big covenant being fulfilled. Since we are under this covenant, God sees Jesus when He looks at each of us. That is our new identity. The old has been forgotten, and we have been made completely new from the inside out. Being one with Him means that we now have the same authority on earth as He did. We are His representatives here and now, spread out across the earth.

Jesus taught us to pray like this, "Your kingdom come, your will be done, on earth as it is in heaven," because He wants to see heaven on earth NOW. We need to stop worrying about getting there and focus more on bringing it here. The covenant we have accepted as our own allows us to do just that. Saying we agree with the covenant means we are charged with a task. Our new identity has expectations associated with it.

Before you were a believer you were a sinner. But once you have been redeemed, you're now a saint! That doesn't mean you no longer sin, but it does mean that's no longer your nature. When you call yourself a sinner, it's easy to justify your sin. But when you're a saint, every time you sin, it hits a little differently, which results in actual change instead of providing an excuse for your actions.

When you go from the mindset of being a sinner to being a saint and understand that you are dead to sin, the negative influence that used to control your life will be turned to a positive one. And you will be set free to be far more joyful.

Our sin was nailed to the cross and has no power over us. When we understand that, we can believe what God says about our salvation. You are truly a new creation all together. Satan legally has no dominion over you anymore. But you have the choice to believe what you want. You choose who you obey throughout the day. God never forces us to do or say anything. One of the biggest lies of the enemy is that we haven't been changed—and unfortunately, many times we believe it and act accordingly!

Being dead to sin means that we are free. It is not a battle going on inside of us, as so many people teach. Yes, there is a battle going on outside that we are fighting, but it no longer has control of us. It's no longer a part of our identity.

Now that we are new on the inside, we must learn how to live by the Spirit. For some of you this is probably an entirely new concept, but it's exactly what God says about us. So if you truly believe in Him, you need to believe what He says. And He says that you are a new creation (see 2 Corinthians 5:17–21; Romans 6:4–6; Galatians 2:20; Colossians 3:9–10; Ephesians 2:10; Ephesians 4:22–24).

Moving on, we get to chapters 9 through 11, which are fairly controversial because of what Paul says regarding physical Israel and the Jewish people. Paul gives a great illustration of what happens between Jews and Gentiles. Israel is shown as an olive tree in which branches that do not bear fruit are broken off and Gentile branches that do bear fruit are grafted in. So we, as believers in Jesus, have been brought into God's plan of redemption that began with the Hebrews and will end with the Hebrews.

In Chapter 12, Paul shows that we have everything we need right now to bring the kingdom to earth—we just need to act on it. We can sincerely love others and encourage them. We can hate what is evil and love what is good. We can bring peace to those who are suffering by introducing them to Jesus.

The New Testament teaches us that we are supposed to be everything that Jesus was as a man. We are in covenant with God, so all those things are now part of our nature. If we don't walk them out, then we are acting against our nature. Jesus was fully God AND fully man, which means He had to make the same moment-by-moment decisions we do. That should give us confidence. We can do this!

Looking at the church today as a whole, I think you'll agree that we are divided, not walking in the unity Jesus desired for us. Oftentimes we don't even try to understand those we disagree with. One of the biggest divisions is between those who believe in the outworking of the Holy Spirit through signs and those who are just focused on head knowledge or learning the Bible. Two different takes on Scripture. Tons of disagreements.

It all reminds me of the Jew-Gentile tension Paul was dealing with when writing to the Romans. His main objective, besides preaching the gospel, was to unify the church. Each group had different views, but each group was necessary for the church to function properly. Just like today. We get so caught up in which view is correct, when in reality, Jesus is coming back for His bride—singular. Not His nondenominational bride. Not His Pentecostal bride. Not His Lutheran bride. He is coming back for His ONE, spotless bride. We are all in this together.

Jesus is coming back for us, the church, and He loves His bride more than anything. So as one group of people is being used by God to perform miracles and is speaking in tongues, and another group is spending their time combing Scripture for answers on the end-times theology, we need to love them both. Spirit and Scripture. Both are necessary.

As I said earlier, and as you now know, Romans is a *massive* book. There is so much important information here that we need to spend time wrestling through. It is my prayer that you take time to continue studying this book at a later date and that God gives you a revelation of your new identity. ■

▶ Do you know what the word *gospel* means? If so, what?

▶ What are the four main covenants of the Old Testament?

   1. Genesis 8

   2. Genesis 15

   3. Genesis 17

   4. 2 Samuel 7

▶ Why did God give the Law to Moses (Romans 5:20–21)?

▶ Since we are no longer under the Law, what exposes our sinfulness now (John 16:8)?

▶ What is justification?

▶ What is sanctification?

▶ What is glorification?

▶ Romans 6:12 NIV says, "Do not let sin reign." As good as that may sound, do you know how we can obey that command?

▶ What have you accepted as truth about your identity as a child of God, when you know it's really from Satan?

▶ What are some ways we can bring the kingdom of God to earth today?

▶ In what ways would you like to be more like Jesus?

1CORINTHIANS

AUTHOR
The author of both letters to the Corinthians was the apostle Paul.

DATE
First Corinthians was written between AD 55 and 56, while Paul was in Ephesus. Second Corinthians was written less than a year later from Philippi.

AUDIENCE
These two letters were written to the church in Corinth and were later shared among other churches in the area. Corinth was a major party city in its time. We would compare it to Vegas today. It was a place of pleasure and indulgence. The Corinthians' focus was self-satisfaction. They weren't an easy bunch to deal with, but Paul was just the right guy for the job.

REASON
Paul was writing to help with church affairs based on reports from his friend Chloe's people and a letter sent by a group of Corinthians.

THEME
Love is the reason for everything.

KEY VERSE
"Let all that you do be done in love" (1 Corinthians 16:14).

SECTION
Reports from Chloe's people (ch. 1–6), questions from the Corinthians letter (ch. 7–16).

KEY WORDS
Spirit, body, love, church

STORY OVERVIEW

From what we can gather in these two letters (1 and 2 Corinthians), we learn that Paul had actually written four letters to the church of Corinth, two of which we have and two that were lost.

The first problem Paul addressed was the division in the church. People disagreed on who they liked best, what leader they preferred, who they were baptized by, etc. Those divisions are very similar to the divisions we see in the church today. In America, there seems to be a different denomination on every street corner. And new ones keep arising, mostly because of theological differences and new forms of interpretation.

Another point to note is that the Corinthians were highly influenced by a Greek mindset when it came to the role of their bodies. They thought spirituality was one thing and the body was another, one being good and the other evil. The two never crossed. Many believers today have the same Greek mindset when it comes to spiritual gifts that involve an outward act. We want to worship inwardly, but when it comes to a manifestation of the Spirit some get freaked out.

So to break it down, there are four main views on spiritual gifts today:

Cessationist: Spiritual gifts were only for the early church and are not relevant today.

Continuationist: Spiritual gifts are for today, but the "sign" gifts need to be looked at and tested with caution.

Charismatic: Spiritual gifts are for every generation, and they should be practiced today. This view is limited by Scripture with no additions to the Word.

Hyper Charismatic: Spiritual gifts are for every generation, and contemporary revelations are equal to Scripture.

The main places in the Bible that we learn about spiritual gifts are from 1 Corinthians 12–14, Romans 12, and Ephesians 4. Some people look at those lists and limit the gifts to them. But since we do not have a complete list, it can be fairly unclear as to what all the gifts are, which creates much disagreement in the church. One big mistake is to deny spiritual gifts altogether. Another mistake is to pick one and think it's better than the others.

The spiritual gifts listed in those three main Scriptures are:

Romans 12: prophecy, service, teaching, encouragement, giving, leadership, and mercy.

Ephesians 4: apostleship, prophecy, evangelism, pastoring, and teaching.

First Corinthians 12: word of wisdom, word of knowledge, faith, healing, miracles, prophecy, discernment, tongues, and interpreting tongues.

If we're looking at a quick overview of spiritual gifts, it's important to note:

- Spiritual gifts are not to be confused with natural talent.
- Every Christian has at least one spiritual gift.
- No Christian has every spiritual gift.
- Spiritual gifts can be abused.
- The Holy Spirit chooses which gifts each of us receive.
- God's will is not accomplished if love is not the main motivation behind the gifts.

When reading 1 Corinthians 12–14, you most likely recognized the famous love chapter that was placed right in the middle. Paul does that deliberately, teaching that loving others is the main focus behind every spiritual gift. If you are exercising your gifts for any other reason, you might as well not use them. Love should be the reason behind everything. ◼

The Breakdown

PROPHECY

Prophecy is the ability to speak truth into an individual's destiny and to reveal future events to the church in order to call for repentance or build them up. People with this gift can easily read others and "just know" things before they happen.

TEACHING

Teaching is the ability to apply Scripture in an easy-to-understand way. People with this gift love to study and are focused on doctrinal application.

GIVING

Giving is the ability to earn money in order to meet the needs of others in a cheerful manner. People with this gift are good at making money and like to give behind the scenes.

MERCY

Mercy is the desire to take care of those who are going through difficult times without expecting anything in return. People with this gift enjoy one-on-one serving and are able to sympathize naturally.

SERVICE

Service is the ability to meet physical needs within the body of Christ and apply a spiritual significance to it. People with this gift like to work behind the scenes and get joy out of helping others.

ENCOURAGEMENT

Encouragement is the ability to motivate others on their faith journey. People with this gift are good counselors and can personally apply Scripture.

LEADERSHIP

Leadership is the ability to direct others in completing a God-given task of specific ministry work. People with this gift can clearly share a vision, and others gladly follow their lead.

APOSTLESHIP

Apostles are those who have a desire to be sent out to start churches and ministries in the local community and around the world. People with this gift are comfortable in other cultures and able to execute a specific vision.

EVANGELISM

Evangelists are those who can easily share the gospel with unbelievers and lead them to a personal relationship with Jesus Christ. People with this gift are very personable and convincing of the truth.

WISDOM

Wisdom is the ability to look at a situation and advise the best strategy for action based on the insight given. People with this gift can see various outcomes and can discern which action is the best to take.

FAITH

Faith is the ability to have a confident belief that God will accomplish the impossible despite reality. People with this gift trust God completely and act in confidence.

MIRACLES

Those with the gift of miracles have the ability to be used as a vessel of God to reveal His power through supernatural acts that alter the natural realm. Miracles are most often used to authenticate the gospel message. People with this gift speak truth with confidence and have it authenticated.

TONGUES

There are three types of tongues. One is a private prayer language (1 Corinthians 14:14–15). Another is the ability to speak out a divine message in a new language in order for the body of Christ to be built up. The third is an entire language as a gift, which is to be used for missionary work.

PASTORING

Pastors are those who guide, counsel, protect, and disciple a group of believers. Many times this gift is joined with the gift of teaching. People with this gift are great leaders and have a heart for discipleship.

KNOWLEDGE

Knowledge is the ability to understand the Word and make it relevant to the church or specific situations. This gift includes supernatural words of knowledge that are to be used in serving others. People with this gift are able to seek out truth in the Bible and typically have unusual insight into situations or a person's life.

HEALING

Healing is the ability to be used as a vessel by God in order to cure sickness and restore health. People with this gift are able to demonstrate the power of God through prayer, the laying on of hands, or a spoken word.

DISCERNMENT (DISTINGUISHING OF SPIRITS)

Discernment is the ability to perceive what is from God through the recognition of good and evil spirits. People with this gift can easily tell what is from God and what is counterfeit.

INTERPRETING OF TONGUES

Interpreting of tongues is the ability to translate a foreign language that the hearer doesn't know, whether it is an earthly language or a heavenly language.

▶ Which denomination do you associate yourself with?

▶ Have you ever given up on someone in hopes that they will learn on their own? If so, did they?

▶ What do you know about spiritual gifts?

▶ Which view on spiritual gifts do you hold? Why?

▶ Describe a time when you feel God used you, whether you knew it involved your spiritual gift or not.

▶ What is the purpose of spiritual gifts (1 Peter 4:10–11)?

► Can you think of a way to exercise your gift(s) to grow in it (them)?

► How could you show love to those around you through your gifts?

2 CORINTHIANS

REASON
Second Corinthians was written by Paul as a defense of himself in response to the group of apostles challenging his authority and ministry. He wanted to encourage the church in their offering for Jerusalem and to remind them of their victory in Christ.

THEME
Victory in Christ.

KEY VERSE
"But thanks be to God, who in Christ always leads us in triumphal procession, and through us spreads the fragrance of the knowledge of him everywhere" (2 Corinthians 2:14).

SECTIONS
Paul's defense of himself (ch. 1–7), the poor in Jerusalem (ch. 8–9), Paul's attack on others (ch. 10–13).

KEY WORDS
Comfort, affliction, confidence, weakness

STORY OVERVIEW

While the first letter to the Corinthians dealt with practical issues within the church, the second letter deals with personal insults that forced Paul to stand up for himself. We know that a group of apostles came into Corinth once Paul left, and they tried to take over by building themselves up and pushing Paul down. We don't know who they were exactly, but the content suggests they were Jewish.

Some of the attacks on Paul's character were that he wasn't bold enough, that he didn't care for the Corinthians since he was in a different city, that he wasn't a good speaker, and that he wasn't qualified to be teaching them. The antagonistic apostles knew that if they successfully attacked Paul, his message would be thrown out as well. Paul does a good job of handling himself in such a crazy situation. He begins the letter in a sincere way and encourages them in their walk.

Around chapter 9 he gets a little upset, though, and starts to attack them for going against his teaching. Sometimes a little heat is necessary. Right in the middle of his encouragement and defense, Paul includes a large section on collecting money to give to the poor in Jerusalem. It's a quick pivot that is worth mentioning. We know from the past that Paul has a major heart for the poor, so that makes sense, but it does seem a little random. However, the Corinthians knew the importance of love, considering the whole chapter on it in his previous letter to them. It was a part of the gospel and therefore a part of their life.

These apostles at Corinth weren't teaching love. They were attacking Paul and focusing on the negative. Paul knew that if he focused on loving others through donating to the poor, they would turn toward the truth. And this approach worked because Paul's third visit to Corinth was a joyous one. Second Corinthians encourages believers to embrace the transformed life that values generosity and humility. ∎

gifted saints

▶ Describe a time when you had someone attack your character:

▶ How did you handle it?

▶ What are some ways you can better serve the poor?

AUTHOR
The letter to the Galatians was written by the apostle Paul. He is the perfect person to write on the topic of freedom from the Law because of his past as a fully devoted Jew and a Pharisee. He knew about freedom in Christ alone more than anyone.

DATE
The dating of Galatians is highly debated. Some people believe that it was written early on, as the first book in the New Testament, around AD 48, while others put the writing at around AD 55.

If Paul was writing to northern Galatia from Ephesus, the later date would make the most sense. On the other hand, if Paul was writing to southern Galatia from Antioch, the earlier date, before the Jerusalem Council, would fit better.

AUDIENCE
Whether you believe Galatians was written to the northern or southern part, we can agree that it was written to the churches of Galatia.

REASON
Paul was teaching the Galatians to be free from the Law because there were Judaizers and false teachers telling them otherwise.

THEME
Freedom through Christ alone.

KEY VERSE
"For freedom Christ has set us free; stand firm therefore, and do not submit again to a yoke of slavery" (Galatians 5:1).

SECTIONS
Personal (ch. 1–2), doctrinal (ch. 3–4), practical (ch. 5–6).

KEY WORDS
Christ, freedom, circumcision, Law

GALATIANS

STORY OVERVIEW

The vibe of Galatians is much more negative compared with most of Paul's other letters because of how serious he is about being set free from the Law. Freedom is everything. The Jewish people were strangling themselves with the Law. There was no way to fulfill it, but they still did their best to gain God's approval.

The most important ritual for a Jewish male was circumcision. It was mandatory back then, and in Jewish culture, still is today. It is a commandment from God! Paul is showing the Jews they no longer need to be circumcised to be saved, because Jesus's blood was the fulfillment of the circumcision covenant. Paul focuses on telling the Jewish people there is truly nothing they can do physically to become saved. It's all about grace.

They didn't get it, though, because for their entire lives, the idea of having to work for their salvation had been drilled into their heads. So the main issue that we are dealing with here is whether salvation is received by faith or works. Paul says that it is by faith alone. A love like that was incomprehensible to the Jews. Quite frankly, it's incomprehensible to most believers today, many of whom still believe that going to heaven is about being a good person. That's a risky subject, if you ask me. Because then I would have to ask this: How good do you have to be to go to heaven? What's the measurement?

The gospel is truly scandalous. God's love doesn't make sense to the normal individual, but once you understand the gift is freely given, it makes it easier to accept. Galatians 2:20 says, "I have been crucified with Christ. It is no longer I who live, but Christ who lives in me. And the life I now live in the flesh I live by faith in the Son of God, who loved me and gave himself for me."

I've learned that people crave simple plans. They want a checklist of things to follow to ensure their reward will come, which happens to be the mindset in many churches today. They want to know what they can and cannot do to one day go to heaven. Guess what, it's not all about one day getting to heaven. When you become a new creation, the focus of your life should shift to bringing heaven here, now. But for some reason, many denominations struggle with that understanding and provide the consumer with their simple plan instead.

Following rules to get into heaven is a great business model; it's just far from the truth because in that model, an actual relationship with Christ is put on the back burner or is never even taught in the first place. Instead of getting so caught up in what we should and shouldn't do, I believe that we need to redirect our attention to our identity in Christ and who God says we are. Galatians 4:6–7 says, "And because you are sons, God has sent the Spirit of his Son into our hearts, crying, 'Abba! Father!' So you are no longer a slave, but a son, and if a son, then an heir through God."

Because of what Jesus did, you are an heir to the throne and have received the same inheritance Jesus received. This. Is. HUGE. That means God blesses YOU the same way He blessed His Son, JESUS. With salvation, providing for our needs, understanding the

YOU
ARE AN
HEIR
TO THE
THRONE.

Father's heart, joy, gifts, communication with God, answered prayers, etc. Our inheritance was already paid for, so God is just waiting for you to accept it. He gets joy out of blessing you. So take it in!

Some people may be wondering what it means to accept the blessing of the Father. It's as simple as asking Him for it and accepting your new identity. You are royalty. You are a son or daughter of the living God. LEGALLY. No ifs, ands, or buts. So look at yourself that way. Maybe you need to tell yourself that every day while looking in the mirror until it sticks. Seriously, DO IT. Your Father loves you and wants to bless you. New identity brings new fruit.

In chapter 5, Paul shares with us that God calls humanity to interact with others while bearing what he calls the fruit of the Holy Spirit. The fruit is produced by nine characteristics that empower an individual to live a strong Christian life, displaying the love of Christ in every relationship. The parts of the fruit are love, joy, peace, patience, kindness, goodness, faithfulness, gentleness, and self-control.

Notice that it isn't nine different fruits that Paul talks about. A lot of people make that mistake. It's one fruit; nine characteristics. They are all needed to bear the fruit of the Holy Spirit. Reflecting on your life and looking at how the Holy Spirit is working through you is a great way to see your spiritual growth. You will know you are on the right track when all characteristics of the fruit are present in your life. Whereas society tells us that our identity is based on the way that we look physically, God's focus is always on the internal and the work of the Holy Spirit. You are now an heir through God and have been set free from religion. Your new position calls for a relationship instead. So take advantage of that!

Remember, Galatians 2:16 says, "We know that a person is not justified by works of the law but through faith in Jesus Christ, so we also have believed in Christ Jesus, in order to be justified by faith in Christ and not by works of the law, because by works of the law no one will be justified." ∎

QUESTIONS

▶ Historically, why are Jews circumcised (Genesis 17:10–14)?

▶ Do you remember what happened in the Jerusalem Council (Acts 15)?

▶ What do you think Paul meant when he said it was no longer he who lived, but rather Christ who lived in him? How can you apply that to your own life?

▶ What was the purpose of the Mosaic Law that Moses received from God in Exodus and Leviticus?

▶ What rules do you see Christians placing on themselves today?

▶ How have you seen God's blessing on your life?

▶ What are the nine characteristics of the fruit of the Holy Spirit (Galatians 5:22–23)?

▶ What areas of the fruit do you need to improve in? What can you do to become better?

▶ Read Galatians 2:16. How does this influence the way you live?

EPHESIANS

AUTHOR
The letter to the Ephesians was written by the apostle Paul.

DATE
Paul likely wrote Ephesians around AD 60 to 62, during his Roman imprisonment. It can be assumed that Paul wrote from there because he was on house arrest while in Rome, which meant he had the freedom to preach, and his friends were still able to visit him.

AUDIENCE
Paul wrote this letter to the church at Ephesus in Asia Minor, and it was probably to be used as a circulatory letter to all the churches in the area.

Ephesus was a rough city. It was saturated with idol worship and the people there would do anything to acquire salvation. Even so, the Ephesian church had a strong foundation.

REASON
Paul wrote this letter to teach the Ephesians about identity and to show them how to stand firm by loving one another in their current culture.

THEME
Walking in your new identity.

KEY VERSE
"For we are his workmanship, created in Christ Jesus for good works, which God prepared beforehand, that we should walk in them" (Ephesians 2:10).

SECTIONS
Identity in Christ (ch. 1–3), walking it out (ch. 4–6).

KEY WORDS / PHRASES
In Christ, *walk*, *body*, *armor*

CITIZENSHIP
CITIZENSHIP
CITIZENSHIP
CITIZENSHIP
CITIZENSHIP
CITIZENSHIP
CITIZENSHIP

KINGDOM

HEAVENLY
PLACES

EARTH

STORY OVERVIEW

After his greeting, Paul begins Ephesians with, "Long before he laid down earth's foundations, he had us in mind, had settled on us as the focus of his love, to be made whole and holy by his love. Long, long ago he decided to adopt us into his family through Jesus Christ. . . . He wanted us to enter into the celebration of his lavish gift-giving by the hand of his beloved Son" (Ephesians 1:3–6 MSG).

There is so much about our new identity in this little section alone! We have been adopted. We are to be made whole and holy. God's desire is to bless us. Those are all amazing things! Paul also uses the word *predestination*, which is a highly debated concept today. To predestine means to "determine an outcome or course of events in advance by divine will or fate."*

There are two main views on predestination: Calvinism and Arminianism.

Calvinism is the belief that we were chosen for salvation. God chooses who He wants to be in the kingdom, and all of life is worked out in order for His plan to come to fruition. Calvinists preach largely that everything in life happens for a reason.

In Arminianism or Wesleyanism, on the other hand, the belief is that we were chosen to be in God's kingdom. In this view, your faith is conditioned upon that, and your future destiny is based on your actions now. Those in this school of thought believe in free will but hold that once you have chosen to follow Him,

God has a predestined plan for your life. You can find out more about each view and make up your mind.

Paul says in 2:6 that when we were saved, God "raised us up with him and seated us with him in the heavenly places in Christ Jesus." That means we are seated up there with Him right now. We have dual citizenship in heaven and earth. Having a heavenly perspective should change the way you go about your day. It's now about bringing the kingdom into each of our situations. That means we can be confident, whatever comes our way, because we are already victorious with Christ.

Ephesians 2:10 says, "For we are his workmanship, created in Christ Jesus for good works, which God prepared beforehand, that we should walk in them." Yes, we are saved by grace through faith, but that also means that we were created for good works. Faith results in works. They go together. God expects us to bless those around us, to make disciples, to pray for our friends, to lay hands on the sick, to cast out demons, and to walk in love constantly.

Paul tells us to be imitators of God in chapter 5. In other words, our lives should reflect Jesus. That means it is our job to bring the kingdom of God into our everyday life. Some people have such a hard time trying to figure out what the will of God is. I believe the overarching will of God, after we receive His Son, is to bring heaven to earth and to ruin the works of the devil every day (1 John 3:8). That's it!

In chapter 6, Paul goes into this cool section described as the armor of God and teaches us the keys to success in spiritual warfare. The battle we

---

*"predestine," *The Oxford Pocket Dictionary of Current English*, Encyclopedia.com, May 27, 2023, https://www.encyclopedia.com /humanities/dictionaries-thesauruses-pictures-and-press-releases /predestine.

are fighting is not in the natural realm but the spiritual. We can fight in confidence though, because we are already victorious in Christ. Since we have been given the Holy Spirit and spiritual armor, we have everything we need to fight. But the question is whether we know how to use it.

Paul compares the outfit of the Roman soldier to what we need in the spiritual realm.

The belt of truth: The belt of the Roman uniform was used to hold everything together. Therefore, seeking out truth is what holds your life together. Jesus said, "I am the Way, and the TRUTH, and the life" (John 14:6, emphasis added). If you seek after Jesus, you will know how to dodge Satan, the father of lies.

The breastplate of righteousness: A soldier's breastplate protected his heart and organs. Righteousness is a gift attached to our new identity in Christ, and we must be confident that we are righteous in Christ to stop Satan's lies from entering our hearts.

The shoes of the gospel of peace: As believers in Jesus, we have peace with God and are to walk in peace with others everywhere we go.

The shield of faith: Roman shields were made out of damp wood covered in leather to extinguish flaming darts of the enemy. They were very large so that a soldier could protect his entire body by hiding behind it. We must hide behind our faith and believe the promises of God.

The helmet of salvation: The helmet protected the head, but more importantly, the mind. Our salvation should give us confidence to block out false teachings and to live from our new nature instead of our old, sinful ways.

The sword of the Spirit: Our spiritual sword is the Word of God, the most powerful piece of weaponry available. When Jesus was tempted in the desert for forty days, His every response to Satan was to declare Scripture and hold true to it. We must do the same. But this doesn't come naturally. We have to be trained in how to use the sword and then practice, practice, practice. That's why I'm so proud of you for going on this journey through the Word with me.

One thing to notice when looking at our armor is that there isn't a piece of armor for your back. That means you must never turn your back on the enemy in retreat. You are fighting from a place of victory!

Paul also says that we must continue praying in the Spirit. You need protection, but you also need prayer. Prayer helps us stand firm against the enemy's attacks.

So, the full armor of God consists of truth, righteousness, the gospel of peace, faith, salvation, the Word of God, and prayer. Every one of those pieces of armor are necessary in living a victorious Christian life. Remember, you are fighting a spiritual battle, not a physical one. You have the power of Christ inside of you, and there is no problem too big for Him to handle. So fight in God's strength! Fight with confidence! Fight from a place of victory!

I challenge you to read Ephesians 6:10–20 every morning for one week straight. Then write out how you feel at the end of the week, sharing stories of breakthrough, newfound joy, or assurance of the power that lies within you. ■

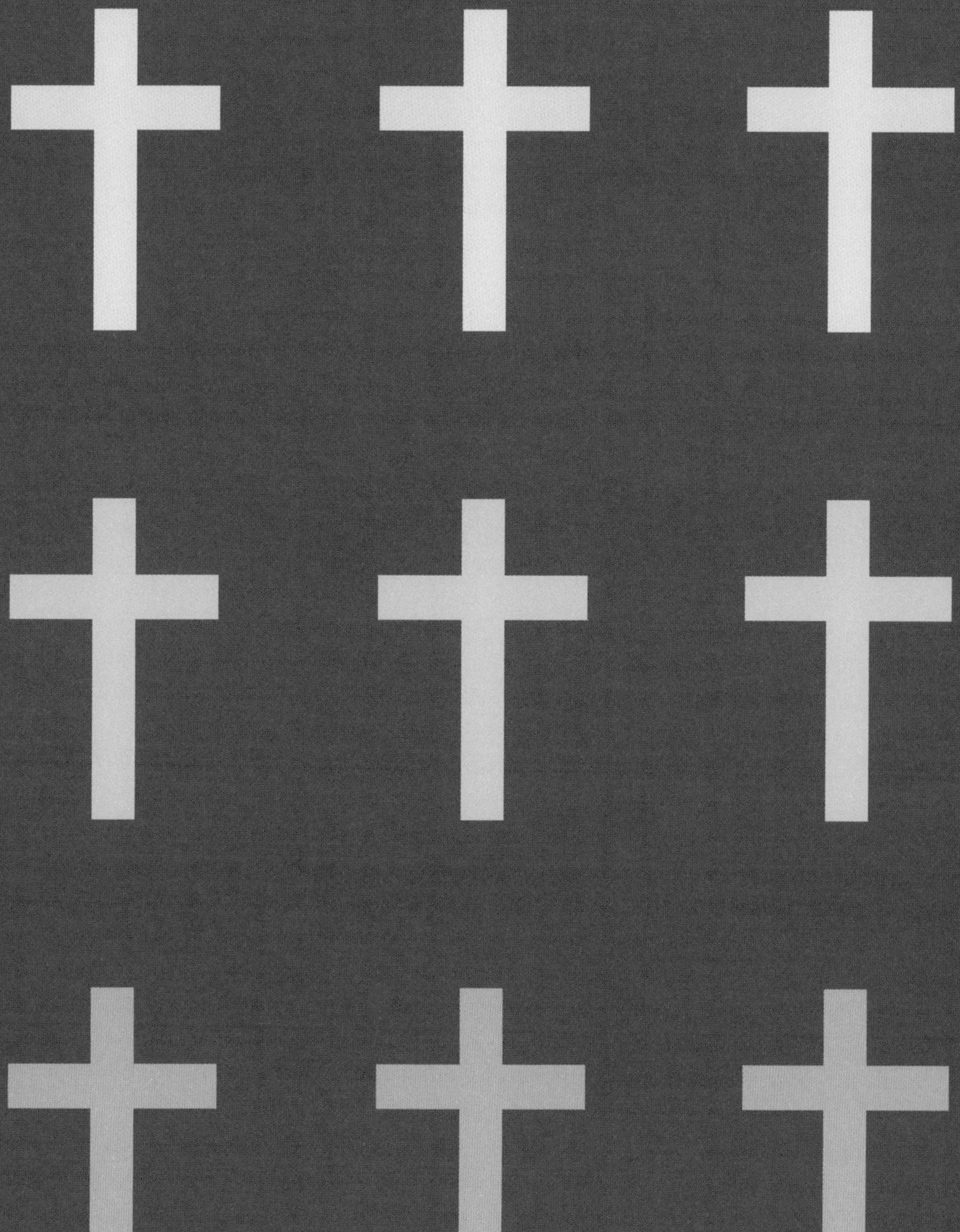

▶ What does it mean to be adopted into the kingdom?

▶ What does it mean to be made whole and holy?

▶ Do you understand that God wants to bless you with gifts just because you are an heir to the throne? You don't have to do anything; it's just part of His character. Spend a few minutes meditating on this, then write down what you sense God saying to you:

▶ Do you have any thoughts on predestination? Would you say you are more Calvinist or Arminian in nature?

▶ Which place of citizenship do you tend to view life from? A heavenly one? Or earthly? What are some things you can do to have more of a heavenly perspective?

▶ What are some ways you can bless those around you?

▶ Have you ever been aware of dealing with spiritual warfare? How can you ruin the works of the devil in your daily life?

▶ List the armor of God below:

1.

2.

3.

4.

5.

6.

▶ Which pieces of armor do you need to begin putting on or taking up daily? Put together a plan for doing so:

PHILIPPIANS

AUTHOR
The letter to the Philippians was written by the apostle Paul.

DATE
Philippians was likely written around AD 61–62, toward the end of Paul's Roman imprisonment.

AUDIENCE
Paul was writing to the church in Philippi, which consisted mainly of Gentiles.

REASON
Paul warned the Philippians about false teachings that were creeping into the church and encouraged them to remain joyful in the Lord.

THEME
Joy in the Lord.

KEY VERSE
"Rejoice in the Lord always; again I will say, rejoice" (Philippians 4:4).

SECTIONS
Meaning of true life (ch. 1), example of true life (ch. 2), goal of true life (ch. 3), walking out of true life (ch. 4).

KEY WORDS
Gospel, Christ, joy, think

STORY OVERVIEW ———————————————————

When looking at the Bible as a whole, the letter to the Philippians can be put in the category of *prison epistles*, alongside Ephesians, Colossians, and Philemon. Philippians was written after those three, as Paul was ending his stint under Roman house arrest.

Paul had been told of issues among the Philippians by a gentleman named Epaphroditus, who was sent to Paul as somewhat of a housekeeper. This letter was a response to those issues and a promise that Epaphroditus would be sent home soon.

Early on in Paul's letter we get the famous quote "For to me to live is Christ, and to die is gain" (1:21). Paul is eager to go to heaven, but he's willing to stay because he loves people that much. Obviously, God wants him to stick around, since he came so close to death on his journeys but never ended up dying. The biggest problem the Philippians were dealing with was disunity within the church. Pride and jealousy were seeping in regarding blessings and spiritual gifts. Some people were becoming jealous because they weren't receiving the same spiritual gifts as others, which caused resentment among the group.

In reality, the body of Christ, the church, is one. So when one person receives a gift, we all receive that gift because we are in the same body. We should rejoice over every blessing our brothers and sisters receive, not become jealous. And besides, who says God wouldn't give that gift again? Remember, it's the Spirit who apportions to each one individually as He wills.

In the letter, Paul tells them to "join in imitating me" (3:17) because he was so like Christ. He's not being cocky, as we might assume after reading that; he's just confident in who he is. He's imitating Christ, so that's what the Philippians should be doing. He's their tangible evidence of someone following Christ and properly walking in their new identity.

Verses 2:5–8 are kind of the climax of the book. Paul looks at Christ's choice to empty himself to be like us so that He could save us. That does not mean Jesus was no longer fully God. He was both fully God and fully man the entire time. He gave up His power, not His nature, to be an example for us regarding what is possible with the Holy Spirit dwelling inside us.

In chapter 4, Paul begins to fire off a bunch of commands to the Philippians. It seems that they were last-minute thoughts he had to get on the page before the letter was sent off. This is also where we see the key verse, "Rejoice in the Lord always; again I will say, rejoice." That's a huge command if you really think about it, and most of us struggle with fulfilling it every day. Finding joy can be difficult in many situations, especially considering the way the world is heading.

Another tough task is remaining peaceful in a world where there is so much disagreement and disunity. Paul says that the peace of God will guard your heart and mind if you control your thoughts and remain thankful. Focusing on the positive in every situation allows us to be more joyful. If we are to restore our minds to fullness, we must begin with our thought

ONE BODY

ONE BODY

ONE MIND

ONE CHURCH

ONE GOD

ONE GOD

ONE MIND

ONE CHURCH

ONE BODY

ONE MIND

ONE CHURCH

ONE GOD

ONE BODY

ONE MIND

ONE BODY

ONE CHURCH

ONE GOD

ONE GOD

ONE MIND

ONE CHURCH

ONE BODY

ONE MIND

ONE CHURCH

ONE GOD

life. Paul makes it clear that joy and peace are dependent on what we choose to think about.

I love being joyful and peaceful, so I try to remain focused on everything listed in verse 4:8 that we are to think about. To think about anything else is actually going against our new nature. Every day we have the choice to renew our mind through Scripture, to be transformed and to have a kingdom mentality instead of an earthly one. I truly believe that you can have a good day every day. Many people think I'm crazy for believing that. Maybe it's just some hippy mindset I have, but really, I believe it's possible.

As you know, Paul spent a lot of time in jail. People weren't too keen on his causing a scene in their city by talking about Jesus and disrupting business, so they would just send him off in shackles. Wouldn't you think that after the first or second time, he'd quiet down a bit? He didn't. He just brushed off his shoulder and kept on going. If it weren't for his prison sentences, we wouldn't have the prison epistles, so I'm alright with it.

Honestly, what else would you do while in prison but write motivational letters to churches, telling them to keep doing the same thing you're currently in jail for? Duh. It's wild, though, because this letter is filled with Paul being in constant joy, and he mentions a ton of times that believers should rejoice because life is wonderful.

Paul believed that no matter what happened in his life, it would all be used for a higher purpose. If he was in jail, he could work with it. If he was having the worst day ever, he could work with it. Paul was joyous no matter what happened because he knew God was always looking out for him. So that's where I'm at. You want to know how I can have a good day every day, no matter what I'm put through? It's because my joy comes from knowing Jesus. That's it. Nothing more, nothing less. ■

▶ What does the statement "to live is Christ" mean? How can you go about doing that?

▶ In what way can you imitate Paul today?

▶ When it says that Jesus "emptied" himself, what do you think that means?

▶ What does it mean to rejoice always? How is that even possible?

▶ In which areas of your life do you struggle with remaining joyful?

▶ What does Paul tell us to think about in verse 4:8? How can you obey that personally?

▶ Do you typically tend to look at the positives or negatives in situations? What are some ways you can turn negative situations into positive ones?

▶ In what ways can changing your outlook on life help you navigate your current circumstances?

COLOSSIANS

AUTHOR
The letter to the Colossians was written by the apostle Paul.

DATE
Paul wrote Colossians at the same time as Ephesians and Philemon, around AD 60–61, during the beginning of his Roman imprisonment.

AUDIENCE
This letter was written to the church at Colossae, which was made up of mostly Gentiles.

REASON
Paul wrote to correct some false teachings that were distorting the Colossians' view of Jesus, to show them the full deity of Christ, and to show their fullness in Christ.

THEME
Fullness in Christ.

KEY VERSES
"For in him all the fullness of Deity dwells in bodily form, and in Him you have been made complete, and He is the Head over all rule and authority" (Colossians 2:9–10 NASB).

SECTIONS
Fullness of Christ (ch. 1–2), new life in Christ (ch. 3–4).

KEY WORDS
Fullness, wisdom, knowledge, faith

STORY OVERVIEW

As we learned when looking at Ephesians and Philemon, Paul was under Roman house arrest at the time of this writing. While under house arrest, he could have visitors and live somewhat freely, all the while chained to a Roman soldier.

A man named Epaphras, who was part of the church in Colossae, reported to Paul that things were going badly. Paul had no real authority over the Colossians, but he did his best to redirect their focus to better understand their new identity in Christ. A large portion of Colossians matches the content in Ephesians, so we don't have many new topics to look at in this book. It also helps that Paul writes to them in a very straightforward way so they understand it.

False teachings were arising among the church in Colossae because they felt there was no way Christianity could be so simple. So they made it hard. They added rules and regulations to their doctrine, which took away the simplicity of the gospel and formed a religion instead. In reality, Jesus came to save us from religion. The true gospel is Jesus plus nothing. But people made countless additions.

That's what makes Colossians so relevant to us today. When we spend our time adding tasks to the gospel, Jesus loses His authority. He is really the be-all and end-all. He is all we need. God is looking for people who will live in the simplicity of the gospel and let the work of Jesus reign supreme in their lives. He wants to work with you on creating wholeness in your every situation and relationship. He desires a relationship, not religion.

One distinct characteristic of Colossians is that it is a great example of Christology, the study of Christ. Paul gives an in-depth analysis of who Christ is, and how He relates to us. We have looked at it multiple times, but when we come into Christ, we become a completely new creation. Our old self is gone, and our new self has taken over. The past has LITERALLY been forgotten because God loves you SO MUCH. There is no need to dwell in the old anymore. Christ is now living inside us, and He wants to influence the lives of everyone around us.

Sharing God's love and the good news about Jesus are our main purpose now. You may be the only Christian the people around you come in contact with today, and Jesus loves them just as much as He loves you. So share it. ■

JESUS + NOTHING
JESUS + NOTHING
JESUS + NOTHING
JESUS + NOTHING
JESUS + NOTHING

QUESTIONS

▶ What do you add to your faith out of habit or from church pressure that may distract you from your relationship with Jesus?

▶ By turning Christianity into a religion, what do you miss out on? Intimacy with Jesus? Powerful time in prayer? The Spirit moving in your life?

▶ What are some characteristics of Christ that stood out to you while reading Colossians?

▶ What are your favorite ways of sharing the love of Christ?

▶ To go along with this new understanding of putting on your new self, we are going to draw it out in order to visualize it. First off, write out words inside of the "old self" outline below that you would have used to describe your old self.

THE OLD SELF IS GONE

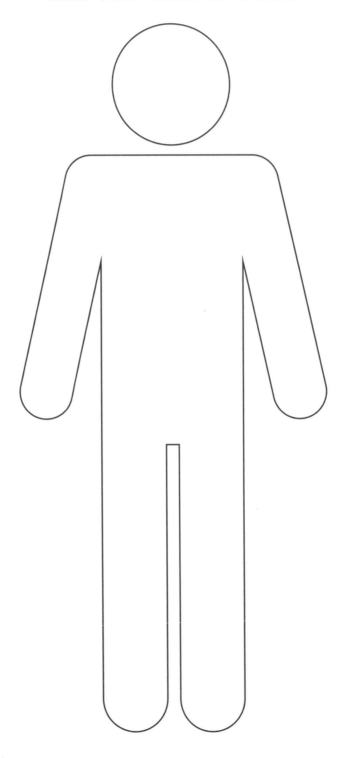

▶ Next, go back to your "old self" and color in the body with a black marker because all of those titles are no longer relevant. Now on the blank body below, write out all of the things that God says you are after having put on your new self. This is your true identity (see Ephesians 1 for starters).

THE NEW SELF IS PUT ON.
THIS IS WHO I REALLY AM.

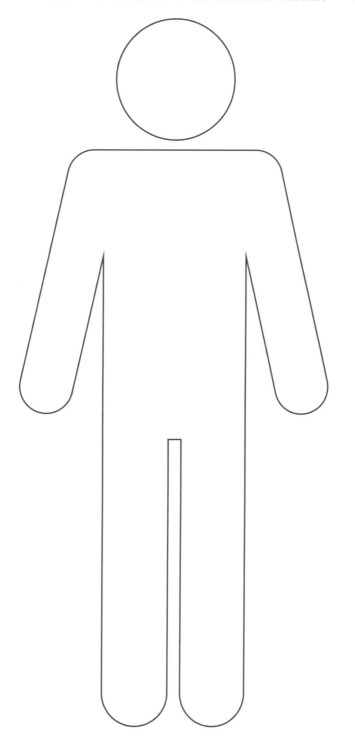

1 THESSALONIANS

AUTHOR
The two letters to the Thessalonians were written by the apostle Paul. Silas and Timothy were present during the writing, but the doctrine was all Paul's.

DATE
Paul wrote the first letter to the Thessalonians around AD 50–51 while in Corinth, and the second letter was sent just a few months later.

AUDIENCE
The Thessalonians were a group of new believers who didn't get much formal training from Paul. They were likely predominantly Gentile and had been brought up under pagan worship. They were already being persecuted for their faith and were being sent false letters that claimed to be from Paul in order to sway them from the truth.

Thessalonica was at the northernmost part of the Aegean Sea, and it was along the Egnatian Way on land. It was in one of the best spots possible for starting a church in hopes of its message being spread all over the Greco-Roman world. Business flourished there. It was definitely the place to be.

Paul visited Thessalonica on his second journey after being led there by the Holy Spirit. We read in Acts about when the Holy Spirit blocked Paul and his companions from going to Asia, but Paul saw a man in his dream who urged him to go to Macedonia. Thessalonica was the capital city of Macedonia during the Roman empire.

A little while after establishing the church in Thessalonica, Paul was working in Corinth and received a support letter from the Thessalonians. This first letter to the Thessalonians is in response to their gift.

REASON
Paul wrote to encourage the Thessalonians to press on in their faith, to not listen to the false accusations against him, and to keep working hard until the Second Coming.

THEME
In expectation of Christ.

KEY VERSE
"Now may the God of peace himself sanctify you completely, and may your whole spirit and soul and body be kept blameless at the coming of our Lord Jesus Christ" (1 Thessalonians 5:23).

SECTIONS
Praise (ch. 1–3), encouragement (ch. 4–5).

KEY WORDS / PHRASES
Gospel, faith, hope, day of the Lord

STORY OVERVIEW

Paul starts off by commending them for living out their faith so well. You can tell he is happy with the way they have been doing things. Paul tends to be a professional motivator. He knows just what to say to get people to progress in their faith. And it works almost every time because they know he truly cares about them and does it from a place of love. Paul also focused more on their holiness than on themselves.

The Thessalonians are taught to excel in love toward one another and to work hard so that they wouldn't be in need of anything. He writes in verses 4:10–12, "We urge you, brothers, to do this more and more, and to aspire to live quietly, and to mind your own affairs, and to work with your hands, as we instructed you, so that you may walk properly before outsiders and be dependent on no one." Yikes. For some reason, work is a topic rarely discussed within the church today. In Genesis 3, God says that, because of the Fall, we will be forced to work and it won't be fun.

Paul is continuing with the same statement here. He is saying that if you are able to work, you should be making your own money and taking care of your responsibilities, not expecting to live off of others' money.

One of the best ways to share the love of Jesus to those around us is through encouragement and speaking truth into their lives. As Paul writes in verse 5:11, "Therefore encourage one another and build one another up, just as you are doing." The sanctification process is bringing your heart more in line with the Father's heart every day. That means you will be able to see people the way God sees them and share how He feels about them. That's amazing!

We can partner with God in building up people that He loves. That goes for believers and unbelievers alike. Encouraging each other's gifts increases our confidence in what God gave us. It can also allow us to push boundaries and grow in our spiritual life.

Chapter 5 is packed with a bunch of unrelated goodies Paul wanted to tell them before closing out the letter. He says that it is God's will for us to rejoice, pray, and be thankful at all times (vv. 16–18). Then, he says not to quench the Spirit (v. 19) and not to despise prophetic utterances, but to examine them carefully (vv. 20–21). Both are very important.

Many times we can be extra skeptical toward prophecies, especially in the US, because they aren't a commonly taught subject. But the New Testament consistently shows that prophecy is a major part of the Christian life. That sure is something to pray about. Let God speak to you about His heart on this subject. ■

YOU GOT THIS
DON'T GIVE UP
KEEP GOING
I BELIEVE IN YOU
GOD'S GOT YOU

YOU GOT THIS
DON'T GIVE UP
KEEP GOING
I BELIEVE IN YOU
GOD'S GOT YOU

QUESTIONS

▶ Who is the most motivating person that you know? What is it about them that motivates you?

▶ What are your views on work-ministry-life balance?

▶ Would you consider yourself a hard worker? Do you view work as if you're working for the Lord?

▶ Some people believe in the rapture based on 1 Thessalonians 4:13–18; do you have any views about the rapture? Do you think God would remove believers from earth before bringing judgment?

▶ Who are some people you want to encourage? How will you do this?

▶ Paul says it is God's will for us to rejoice, pray, and be thankful at all times (1 Thessalonians 5:16–18). How good a job are you doing with those three commands? How can you improve?

▶ Paul also talks about quenching the Spirit. Think of a few ways we tend to quench the Spirit in our lives:

2 THESSALONIANS

REASON
Paul wrote to comfort the Thessalonians in affliction and combat false teaching regarding the Second Coming.

THEME
Comfort until the Second Coming.

KEY VERSES
"Since indeed God considers it just to repay with affliction those who afflict you, and to grant relief to you who are afflicted as well as to us, when the Lord Jesus is revealed from heaven with his mighty angels" (2 Thessalonians 1:6–7).

SECTIONS
Perseverance (ch. 1), the future (ch. 2–3).

KEY WORDS / PHRASES
Coming of Christ, affliction, man of lawlessness, faith, day of the Lord

STORY OVERVIEW

Second Thessalonians is far different from Paul's first letter to the Thessalonians, even though they were written only a few months apart. Paul now seems to be very distant from them and upset over something reported to him shortly after the first letter was sent.

He starts off by complimenting them, but quickly gets into the heavy stuff. The Thessalonians had received a false letter that claimed to be from Paul saying that the Second Coming was just around the corner so there is no need to work or press on in their faith. The sad thing is that many people believed it.

Paul goes on to say that it couldn't be close because the man of lawlessness had yet to make himself known. Paul continues on with his thoughts on work from the first letter and encourages the Thessalonians again to keep at it. He goes so far as to tell them not to give Christians food if they aren't willing to work (3:10).

A lot of the Thessalonians were being lazy. I see that a lot today as well, not necessarily in the area of work, but definitely in the areas of evangelism and prayer. This is not a time to slow down! We should be ramping up our evangelism and prayer lives more than ever if we truly believe the Second Coming is approaching.

God created us to work alongside Him. But we aren't His robots. He desires us to be creative with Him and co-labor throughout the day, whatever that looks like for our situation—it's different for everyone. It's such a privilege to work with our Father every day.

It's interesting to note that what are likely the first two letters written in the New Testament are about the Second Coming. There has been a lot of talk about the topic lately, and many people are wondering if it will happen during their lifetime. That would obviously be a GREAT thing for us, but a TERRIBLE thing for those around us who have yet to be saved. It's our responsibility to share the gospel with them. ■

Rejoice

Pray

~~Complain~~

Be thankful

QUESTIONS

▶ What are some other names for the Antichrist? What do we know about him (Psalms 10:2–4, 53:3, 74:8–10; Isaiah 10:5–12, 14:2; Daniel 7:8, 9:27; Ezekiel 28:12; Jeremiah 4:6–7; Revelation 9:11; 2 Thessalonians 2:3; Zechariah 11:16–17)?

▶ Do you think the antichrist will rise up during your lifetime? Why or why not?

▶ This should be a time when we focus more on evangelism and prayer more than ever before. What are some things you can be praying for? Who could you share the good news of Jesus with?

▶ Do you have a good enough understanding of hell to make you want to evangelize? Or are you fine knowing some of the people around you will go there?

▶ How can you bring the kingdom of God into your workplace?

▶ Since God has the answer to all business solutions, drama, cures, etc., what kind of answers can you be praying for in your line of work?

▶ List three people you want to evangelize this year and outline a short plan for encouraging each of them:

AUTHOR
The two letters to Timothy were written by the apostle Paul.

DATE
First Timothy was written around AD 64–66, likely from Macedonia.

AUDIENCE
Paul wrote this letter to Timothy, whom he loved so much that he considered him his own son. He trusted Timothy immensely and encouraged him to press on through his timidity.

REASON
Paul wrote to encourage Timothy amid opposition from false teachers and to instruct him on leadership within the church.

THEME
Leadership roles in the church.

KEY VERSES
"I hope to come to you soon, but I am writing these things to you so that, if I delay, you may know how one ought to behave in the household of God, which is the church of the living God, a pillar and buttress of the truth" (1 Timothy 3:14–15).

SECTIONS
Order in the church (ch. 1–3), behavior in the church (ch. 4–6).

KEY WORDS
Teach, sound, faith, doctrine

1 TIMOTHY

2 TIMOTHY

DATE
The apostle Paul wrote this second letter to Timothy around AD 67, just before Paul's martyrdom. Paul was back in prison in Rome at the time.

AUDIENCE
Timothy, Paul's "beloved child" (2 Timothy 1:2), was still in Ephesus and was dealing with false teachers.

REASON
This is Paul's final epistle, in which he hands over the ministry responsibilities to Timothy. Paul encourages him to have sound doctrine and to stand strong against opposition that will come his way.

THEME
Finish strong, Timothy!

KEY VERSE
"As for you, always be sober-minded, endure suffering, do the work of an evangelist, fulfill your ministry" (2 Timothy 4:5).

SECTIONS
Timothy's faith (ch. 1), stand strong and be sound (ch. 2), fighting false teachers (ch. 3), Paul's death in view (ch. 4).

KEY WORDS / PHRASES
Endure, faith, abide, sound, doctrine

STORY OVERVIEW ———————————————————

First Timothy, Second Timothy, and Titus were all written by Paul between his final missionary journey and the beginning of his second Roman imprisonment. They are known as the *pastoral epistles* because Timothy and Titus were in pastoral positions in different cities, and Paul is teaching them how to get their people in line. He knew how important order in the church was for effective evangelism. And we all know Paul's thoughts on evangelism: It was everything.

Even though they are called the pastoral epistles, it was neither Timothy's nor Titus's job to remain in each location as pastor. Paul sent them to set things straight, but the main desire of his heart was for them to meet him in Rome before he was martyred.

Timothy was sent to deal with the leadership in Ephesus, but we know that he was a very timid man, meaning the task was far outside his comfort zone. Titus, on the other hand, was sent to Crete to deal with the church as a whole (elders and members), but he was strong and self-sufficient, which made Paul's job much easier. Not only were these letters used as motivation and direction, but Paul knew they would also be used as credentials to prove the authority of Timothy and Titus.

From these letters and also from the book of Acts, we know that Timothy had a Greek father and a Jewish mother. His father may not have been around much, so Timothy had a Jewish upbringing by his mom and grandma. In Acts 16, Paul urged Timothy to get circumcised, not for religious reasons, but to be allowed into the synagogue for evangelism.

Paul sent Timothy to sort out the issues in Ephesus that could not be handled through a letter. Not only were things bad in Ephesus, but Christians in Rome were facing an alarming level of persecution by Nero.

Paul was in prison, and he knew his martyrdom was right around the corner. Therefore, it was time to hand things over to Timothy. That's why Paul is so adamant about Timothy continuing in the faith and persevering until his mission is complete.

Time and again, Paul had seen people backtrack in their faith when persecution began to heat up. Timothy was not going to be one of them, not if Paul had anything to do with it. Paul's advice was to keep pressing on, no matter what happened. He knew it would all be worth it in the end, even though Timothy was beginning to lose hope.

The biggest issue Timothy was dealing with in Ephesus was poor leadership within the church. Paul told him to replace the bad elders with good ones, otherwise the church was going to fall apart. Calling people out for their wrongdoing must have been one of the hardest things for timid Timothy to do. But the gospel was far more important than Timothy's comfort.

Paul knew that if the leaders within the church were doing their job well, the congregation would follow suit and model their lives after them. This repeats a theme of many of Paul's letters: foundation. A solid foundation is mandatory for spiritual growth—then and now.

fear

Love.
Power.
Sound Mind.

In 1 Timothy chapter 3, Paul breaks the leadership down to elders and deacons, with requirements attached. He doesn't stop at whether or not they are qualified, but he makes sure Timothy looks at their character too. If you don't display a lifestyle of holiness outside the church, what makes you think you can reflect holiness inside it? Paul was looking for people who were solid in every aspect of their life. If the bad leaders remained in office for too long, the doctrine of the church might be compromised.

The most important thing for leaders to do today, I believe, is to make sure their doctrine is completely scriptural. That doesn't mean pulling one verse out of context and creating a new doctrine out of it either. All teaching must be in line with the Father's heart and confirmed in multiple places throughout the Bible.

You have a responsibility to know the Word and call out leaders who are straying from the truth. Being grounded in Scripture protects the body from crumbling through false teaching. Knowing what God says to us and about us is the greatest thing we can ever focus our minds on.

Timothy was timid, but his calling overpowered what people said about him. The same thing goes for you today. Typically, your calling is something impossible in the eyes of society but is always in line with God's will. Good thing for you that our God is the God of the impossible, and He almost always calls the unqualified.

Just as Paul is telling Timothy to press on through the impossibilities, he is telling us the same thing. God likes to show off through our lives. But in so many cases, we fail to recognize that because we have a worldly mindset. If you keep your eyes on God and acknowledge that He wants to use you for His divine tasks, you will soon realize what a privilege it is to work for your Father every day. ∎

HOLD FIRMLY TO THE TRUTH

HOLD FIRMLY TO THE TRUTH

▶ Based on our study of Ephesians, do you remember what was happening in Ephesus at the time?

▶ Do you know anybody who was a strong believer but ended up leaving their faith? What were their reasons?

▶ How do you stay strong when times get tough?

▶ Who do you model your life after? Why?

▶ What characteristics do you think good leaders have?

▶ Do you sense God calling you to do something impossible by human standards? What is it? What is stopping you?

AUTHOR
The apostle Paul wrote this letter to Titus.

DATE
Paul wrote to Titus at the same time as he wrote First Timothy, around AD 64–66 while in Macedonia.

AUDIENCE
Titus was Paul's representative, and he didn't need to have his hand held. He was strong and followed directions well, always finding a way to accomplish the given task. Paul had sent him to the island of Crete to get the members of the church there in line. Unlike Timothy, Titus was fully Greek and an uncircumcised believer.

REASON
Paul quickly touches on leadership, then instructs Titus how to teach godly living among members of the church in Crete.

THEME
Sound doctrine is everything.

KEY VERSE
"Therefore rebuke them sharply, that they may be sound in the faith" (Titus 1:13).

SECTIONS
Church order (ch. 1), sound doctrine (ch. 2), godly living (ch. 3).

KEY WORDS / PHRASES
Be sound, good deeds, grace, doctrine

STORY OVERVIEW ────────────────────────

Notice how different the tone is in the letters to Timothy and Titus. Whereas Timothy was timid, Titus was strong and self-sufficient. Paul knew that he could send Titus to perform a task and be assured he would find a way of getting it done. Titus didn't need his hand held and Paul knew it. He dropped Titus off on the island of Crete and had him get to work.

Crete was a bad place. It was similar to parts of Las Vegas today. Immorality at its worst. Titus was put in the thick of it, and although he was kind of in over his head, that didn't stop him from giving it a shot.

Paul wrote to encourage Titus and help him to deal with the immorality all around him. As he did with Timothy, Paul told Titus what to do regarding the leadership, but his main focus was on the people, since false teachings were beginning to creep into the Cretan's doctrine. Paul teaches the members how to act to keep the entire church in line. He focuses on two things: character and truth, both of which must be present in all members. He emphasizes having a good character outside the church and having a solid foundation in Scripture.

Paul says that we are to adorn the gospel. We should look good to unbelievers and show them that what we have is better than what they have. We have the Creator of the universe available 24/7, and therefore we have the answers to life's problems. I believe the church really needs to improve in this area. We have separated ourselves so far from society that we often have no idea what would draw unbelievers in. Society portrays us as prudish, boring, and hypocritical. Paul says that we must live up to what is

good in society's eye and take that one step further. Our goodness and love should draw unbelievers in.

In 2:14, Paul commands the Cretans to be zealous for good works, meaning we should pursue good works with enthusiasm. Good deeds affect the world around us, and we can share the love of Jesus through them.

You may be thinking, *Wait a second, I thought I was saved by grace not by works?* Our salvation should now result IN good works every day, not result FROM them. Paul teaches Titus that his disciples MUST be producing fruit. All real believers produce fruit. That is part of the sanctification process. We get better over time, and God becomes more and more noticeable in our actions. If you aren't producing fruit and becoming godlier, then there is something wrong in your spiritual life.

The pastoral epistles all focus on fighting for truth to reign supreme in the church. Paul knew that if the foundation was strong, the building wouldn't collapse. There are many teachings infiltrating the church today that are NOT biblical. We must fight for truth. Our lives should reflect the gospel, and it should be our desire to bring the kingdom everywhere we step. In my own life, I hit a point in my life where I was fed up with Christians around me. Really, I was fed up with my hypocritical self. I grew up in the church. I spent a ton of time at Christian camps, even working at one for a summer. I went to a Christian university. But when it came down to it, I didn't really know what I believed. Yeah, I knew the basics, but that was it.

good fruit

One night I was sitting in my basement, contemplating life and whether or not I could consider myself a Christian still. I thought about other religions and how seriously those believers take their faith. Jewish boys in Israel are required to have the entire Torah memorized by the time they are TWELVE. And what do we do? Take some confirmation classes for a season and we're good? I couldn't have told you what 90 percent of the books in the Bible are about at that point. Yet I claimed to believe it with all my heart. It was ridiculous. So that's when I departed on my journey to Australia to spend 70 hours a week in the Bible for nine months. Studying. Praying. Crying. Worshiping. Falling in love in a way I didn't know was possible. The foundation I built was as solid as concrete. And nothing can shake me now. I'm in too deep.

As we saw in Timothy and Titus, having a strong foundation is the most important thing we can do, as false teaching continues to infiltrate the church. We have to know our stuff. ■

▶ What do you think it means to adorn the gospel? In what ways can you do this?

▶ What virtues does our culture associate with "good people"? How can we live those out?

▶ Ask God to point out anything in your life that might be holding you back from maturity, and then write it below:

▶ Now put together a plan of attack for how to deal with those roadblocks:

▶ In what ways can you build a firmer foundation in your faith?

PHILEMON

AUTHOR
The author of this letter to Philemon was the apostle Paul.

DATE
Paul wrote to Philemon at the same time he penned the letters to the Ephesians and Colossians, around AD 60–61, during his Roman imprisonment.

AUDIENCE
The letter was written to Philemon, but Paul also includes Apphia, Archippus, and their house church in Colossae, possibly to hold Philemon accountable for the content of the letter.

REASON
Paul wrote as an appeal for Philemon to forgive Onesimus for running away and to show that Onesimus was now useful in sharing the gospel.

THEME
Forgiveness, equality, and reconciliation in Christ.

KEY VERSE
"I appeal to you for my child, Onesimus, whose father I became in my imprisonment" (Philemon 10).

SECTIONS
Introduction (vv. 1–3), praise for Philemon (vv. 4–7), plea for Onesimus (vv. 8–20), encouragement (vv. 21–25).

KEY WORDS
Slave, receive, appeal, love

STORY OVERVIEW ————————————————————

Philemon is the only personal letter of recommen-dation in the Bible. So what is going on here that makes this book part of Scripture? Well, back in the day, slavery was much different from what it is today and has been in the more recent past. Whereas our views regarding modern slavery are all about dehumanization and brutality, being a slave in the Greco-Roman world could be a decent profession. Neither the conditions nor the wages were neces-sarily bad, and some scholars contend there were more slaves than there were free people. So here we have a man named Onesimus who was a slave of a man named Philemon. Onesimus had run away, most likely while he was out running an errand for the wealthy Philemon.

We don't know exactly what happened—some sur-mise he stole from his master, though Scripture does not say that—but we do know the penalty for running away was death. Onesimus ran so far away that he wouldn't be found by Philemon. While he was in Rome he was introduced to Paul, who was under house arrest.

During their time together, Onesimus gave his life to Christ. Before Onesimus could go any further, Paul made him go back home and ask Philemon for forgiveness. Yikes.

When you enter into life with Christ, it doesn't mean that you can run from your past. Yes, you are for-given and have been made clean, but you also have the opportunity to make your past right by bringing wholeness to your relationships or situations.

I have a buddy who got into some serious trouble with the law before he became a Christian. The judge, at his parents' request, allowed him to go into a Christian sobriety program for a year to reduce his sentence. My friend agreed and now he is really on fire for the Lord. That doesn't change the fact that he still has to do some time in a state workhouse after the program. But the situation changes when your mindset changes. In my view, he's being taken care of by the government to share the gospel with other guys who did some bad stuff too. It's all about the way you look at it.

Like Onesimus, my buddy has to deal with his past before he can get rolling on the Lord's work for the rest of his life. The good thing about Onesimus's situation was that Paul knew Philemon, so he could send a letter to him and intervene. But that didn't mean Onesimus was off the hook. His life was still in the hands of Philemon.

On top of that, Paul was making Onesimus hand-deliver the letter. He had to walk nearly 1,200 miles

I FORGIVE YOU.

without knowing the outcome. This letter was literally life or death for him.

One of the coolest things about this story is that the name Onesimus means useful. By sending the slave back with this letter, Paul is saying that he will now live up to his name and be useful to Philemon, as he has been to Paul. He's a new creation and has a purpose. But first things first, he needs to get his relationships right. We assume that Philemon handled it well because we still have the letter today.

Forgiveness isn't an easy thing, but it can be the one thing that changes your life. God has forgiven you of your past and has given purpose to your formerly useless life, just as we see here with Onesimus.

If you have hurt someone in the past or been hurt by someone, you may need to take an Onesimus journey of your own to make things right with them—even if it's difficult. A challenging application for this week: Spend some time thinking about whether you need to make that journey or not. If you do, reach out and either ask for forgiveness or forgive someone. If you don't, that decision could hold you back from a life of blessings. ■

▶ Did you need to reconcile any relationships once you became a Christian? How did it go?

▶ What do you think was going through Onesimus's mind on his journey back to Philemon?

▶ What do you think happened when Philemon opened the door to see Onesimus standing there? Do you think Onesimus threw the letter at him and ran away until he had read it?

▶ If you needed to make an Onesimus journey of your own, share the story below:

journey

HEBREWS

AUTHOR
Nobody really knows who the author of Hebrews is, and there are several possibilities: Luke, Paul, Barnabas, Apollos—even Priscilla and Aquila have been proposed. Understanding the content of the book is not based on your view of the authorship, so do not get hung up on trying to figure it out.

DATE
The book of Hebrews was most likely written around AD 64–65. The temple had yet to be destroyed, and Nero was just beginning his persecution of Christians.

AUDIENCE
The author of Hebrews directed his attention toward Hebrew believers who were turning their focus back to the religious nature of Judaism.

REASON
Hebrews was written to show how Jesus and the New Covenant are superior to Judaism and the Law. The author also encouraged Hebrew believers in their faith journey as they dealt with a new wave of persecution.

THEME
Jesus is better than Judaism.

KEY VERSE
"But in fact the ministry Jesus has received is as superior to theirs as the covenant of which he is mediator is superior to the old one, since the new covenant is established on better promises" (Hebrews 8:6 NIV).

SECTIONS
Jesus is better than angels (ch. 1–2), Jesus is better than Moses and Joshua (ch. 3–4), Jesus is better than the Aaronic priesthood (ch. 5–7), Jesus is better than the Old Covenant (ch. 8–10), faith and perseverance are key (ch. 11–12), conclusion (ch. 13).

KEY WORDS
Better, covenant, perfect, faith

STORY OVERVIEW

Hebrews is not an easy book for many Gentile readers to get through because of their lack of Old Testament knowledge. As I have said, it is *crucial* to put yourself in the shoes of the reader as best you can, otherwise your understanding of the context will fall short.

In chapter 1 the author displays Jesus as being perfect. He lists seven reasons why He is better from the get-go (vv. 2–4), and we know that the number seven symbolizes divine perfection. In a further listing of Jesus's superiority, the writer's first main point is that Jesus is better than angels. What does that mean? It means Jesus is a much better messenger between God and man than anything people had experienced in the past. Jews relied heavily on interaction with angels to know the heart of the Father. But we have the heart of the Father in human form, Jesus, giving us the opportunity to align our hearts with His. Also, as much as some angels may want to be as great as God himself—remember Satan—angels are not and will never be like God.

Then the author looks at Jesus as being better than Moses and Joshua (chapters 3 and 4), with the main focus on Moses. Moses was the be-all and end-all in Judaism. Jews look to him as the definition of holiness and the image to strive after. Moses was sometimes viewed as being interchangeable with the Law because he was the one that received it from God.

We also learn that Jesus is better than the Aaronic priesthood. The Old Testament is great at showing what types of leadership did and did not work for the Israelites. When it came down to it, none of the types of leadership the people desired ended up working well. They tried the leadership of prophets, kings, and priests individually, but what they really needed was someone who could fill all three of these roles.

The Aaronic priesthood was birthed out of the holiness required under the Law. The Law was something to measure holiness against and, in reality, showed the people that a holy life was impossible without a savior. The Israelites' hope was to remain in their future Messiah. And until the Messiah came, life was going to be very difficult. The coming of Christ erased the need for the priesthood because, whereas the Law brought death, Christ brought life and life abundantly. Hallelujah!

Then we see in chapters 8 through 10 that Jesus is better than the Old Covenant, which was inferior because it was not God's original intention. People couldn't live up to the 613 laws they were called to obey. They wanted to live a life that mimicked the surrounding societies, and peer pressure had a major influence. Time after time, God gave them what they wanted, but it was never enough. The Law and God's involvement wasn't the issue. It was the people's selfish desires and pride that made them stumble. They needed a foolproof way to be right with God.

JESUS IS BETTER

They needed Him to perform something miraculous. They needed a new covenant and a new nature.

Hebrews addresses the importance of perseverance in chapters 11 and 12. Chapter 11 is an unbelievable chapter that displays what many call the "Hall of Faith." It's an overview of the most faithful people in Israel's history, including Abraham, Sarah, Jacob, Moses, Rahab, and others. These people set the bar, and we should look up to them as believers. Having great faith doesn't come easily. We can believe all day long, but acting upon our beliefs—stepping out in faith—can be much more difficult.

As believers, we should daily strive to live by faith. It isn't easy, because the devil does a great job of scaring us out of it. But let me tell you, walking by faith is FAR more enjoyable than living in fear. We serve a powerful God who chose to make His home inside of us. The least we can do is let Him work through us.

The author of Hebrews makes it clear that focusing on religion will get you nowhere, but accepting the redemptive work of Jesus will give you eternal life and an abundant life here and now. Our job is to act in faith in response to what God calls us to do. ■

▶ From the beginning of this book, the author lists seven reasons Jesus is perfect. List those seven things:

1. Hebrews 1:2b

2. Hebrews 1:2c

3. Hebrews 1:3a

4. Hebrews 1:3b

5. Hebrews 1:3c

6. Hebrews 1:4a

7. Hebrews 1:4b

▶ List everything the author says Jesus is better than:

1. Chapters 1–2

2. Chapters 3–4

3. Chapters 5–7

4. Chapters 8–10

▶ What characteristics make Jesus better than angels (Hebrews 2:9–18)?

▶ Describe Moses in five words:

1.

2.

3.

4.

5.

▶ How else is Jesus better than Moses?

▶ Read Hebrews 3:7–19. How would you define unbelief? What are some ways Christians can help each other to continue believing?

▶ Melchizedek is known as a type of Christ. What/who are other types of Christ in the Old Testament?

▶ In what ways is Jesus better than the Aaronic priesthood?

▶ How were people under the Old Covenant judged and saved vs. those under the New Covenant?

▶ Who is your role model in Hebrews 11? What can you pull from their life as motivation to grow in your faith?

▶ On a scale of one to ten, where would you put your faith (with one being "I am a realist and don't think that God can use me to do the impossible" and ten being "If God says 'Jump,' I JUMP")?

1   2   3   4   5   6   7   8   9   10

▶ What's holding you back from having greater faith?

▶ Make a plan of attack for how you can better walk out your faith:

AUTHOR

The author of this epistle is James, the brother of Jesus.

DATE

There are two highly disputed timeframes for when the book of James was written.

The early view holds that James was written around AD 47–48, before the Jerusalem Council took place. Hence the reason for not using any of the content from the Jerusalem Council when disputing such relevant topics.

According to the late view, however, James was written around AD 60–62, after the Jerusalem Council. This view would be taken if James was clarifying various misinterpretations of Paul's word.

AUDIENCE

James wrote to all the Jews scattered in the Dispersion that followed Stephen's death in Acts 8. It was a circulatory letter (meaning it was to be circulated among the churches), not addressed to a specific location.

REASON

James wrote to explain what fruit should be produced when we live an obedient Christian life and also stressed the need for wisdom from above.

THEME

Faith, works, and wisdom.

KEY VERSES

"So also faith by itself, if it does not have works, is dead. But someone will say, 'You have faith and I have works.' Show me your faith apart from your works, and I will show you my faith by my works" (James 2:17–18).

SECTIONS

Trials and testing (ch. 1), faith and works (ch. 2), the tongue and wisdom (ch. 3), worldliness (ch. 4), wealth and patience (ch. 5).

KEY WORDS

Faith, works, law, wisdom

STORY OVERVIEW

The book of James could definitely be called the Proverbs of the New Testament. It's called *wisdom literature*, which means it is packed with content on how to live your life as a Christian. It's the least doctrinal type of writing, but it is the most practical for day-to-day living.

The five main topics that James looks into are:

- Trials
- Faith and works
- The tongue
- Wisdom
- Wealth

Wisdom literature doesn't typically follow an outline. James goes back and forth between topics with no obvious reasoning behind it. We are going to touch on the five main topics and see how they can each apply to today.

Trials

Christians know a lot about trials. As we have looked at before, and will continue to see, being a new creation means you are no longer worldly. You now belong to the kingdom of heaven instead of the earth. Spiritual warfare tends to ramp up heavily when you begin walking in your new identity as a child of God, which creates trials and tribulations in your day-to-day life. A great description many believers use is that we are "in the world, but not of it," based on Jesus's words in John 15:19 and 17:14–16.

Our true home is in heaven now, making this earthly sod just a pit stop on the way there. One thing to realize when dealing with trials, spiritual warfare, or persecution is that God may test you, but it is always Satan who tempts you. Testing is a way for you to grow in your faith, while tempting is done in hopes of making you fail. As you read in 1 Corinthians 10:13, "No temptation has overtaken you that is not common to man. God is faithful, and he will not let you be tempted beyond your ability, but with the temptation he will also provide the way of escape, that you may be able to endure it." In the Old Testament, God allowed Satan to TEST Job's faith in Him because He knew Job was a faithful servant. Job was not given more than he could handle. So no matter what trial or tribulation you are put through, always keep your focus on Christ and allow Him to make you stronger in your faith.

Faith and Works

James approaches the topic of faith and works in a way we do not see anywhere else in the Bible. Paul taught that salvation is through grace alone, not works, but he was talking about works from the Law, not good deeds. It is true that works do not create salvation, but it is also true that faith should result in good works. The Christian faith isn't just about saying that you believe in God, as many churches claim today. The Christian faith is about growth. It's about transformation. It's about sharing the love of Jesus through our actions.

SPEAK LIFE
SPEAK LIFE
SPEAK LIFE
SPEAK LIFE
SPEAK LIFE
SPEAK LIFE
SPEAK LIFE
SPEAK LIFE
SPEAK LIFE
SPEAK LIFE
SPEAK LIFE

SPEAK LIFE

The Tongue

The tongue is the most powerful part of your entire body. Because of that, it is also the most difficult to control. Our tongues have influence. Probably way more influence than we would like them to have. So small yet so potent. In *The Message* translation, James 3:6 reads, "By our speech we can ruin the world, turn harmony to chaos, throw mud on a reputation, send the whole world up in smoke and go up in smoke with it, smoke right from the pit of hell." You don't hear much biblical teaching today on the tongue or the power of words, yet so many people struggle in this area.

I struggled with it for a long time. Before going to Australia, words didn't really mean much to me. I would tell everyone that they were the "best," and I was sarcastic in my humor. I was eventually confronted about it, and God changed my entire perspective on the power of words. "Death and life are in the power of the tongue," as Proverbs 18:21 says so clearly. James was upset that his audience was using the same tongue to bless the Lord and curse people. We should be people who are speaking truth into other people's lives through encouragement and holding strongly to what the Word says about us. Gossip and negativity toward others should never be attached to us.

When the Holy Spirit began convicting me about all of this, there were a few people in my life who bugged me like crazy. I could just hear their name and instantly think something negative about them. So every time I started to think something bad about them, I would thank God for something about them instead. It changed everything. I would definitely suggest giving it a try if you struggle in that area.

What would it look like if you focused on living out what James is saying here? What if we were known as people who never talk badly about others? If we spoke words of thankfulness instead of disgust? Love instead of gossip? Let's be the generation that destroys the stigma of Christians being judgmental and hypocritical. Let's share the goodness of Christ in our actions and words every day. Changing your words can change your life.

Wisdom

Next up, James shows that there are two different kinds of wisdom. One is earthly wisdom; the other is heavenly wisdom. As we have seen while looking into other books of the Bible, it is important as believers to maintain a heavenly mindset in every situation, even when it is difficult. Having wisdom from above means you understand the Father's heart and act accordingly. It means that you are focused on prayer and hearing the Lord's perspective on situations. It's all about relationship—not religion. We approach situations with earthly wisdom when we rely on our own experience. Every one of us comes from a different background that has informed our way of thinking. For example, some of us are street smart while others are book smart.

James shows that the goal is not to make decisions the same way our peers do, but to reach for wisdom from above, the ultimate wisdom.

Wealth

The last topic James covers is wealth and the negative impact it can have on us and on the poor. Thanks to social media and the entertainment industry, we are constantly being told what is cool, right, and sexy. Every ad tries to show us what kind of lifestyle we could be living if we just had their product. Ads try to make us feel we are missing out if we don't buy the advertised product. But once we buy it, there is always something bigger and better coming along that we will want. It's a never-ending cycle. Citizens of the United States have a lot of money. As a whole, we are very wealthy. And yet we have a LOT of problems.

The audience that James was writing to also had a lot of problems, many of which revolved around money. They were ignoring the poor and were com-pletely self-centered—two things that should not characterize us as believers in Jesus. James's audience needed to redirect their money mindset and share the love of Christ with everyone around them, rich or poor. One thing that I must state is that money is never the problem. I know many believers who are loaded. It's the *love of money* that is at the root of all kinds of evil (see 1 Timothy 6:10). It's a heart issue.

So trials, faith and works, the tongue, wisdom, and wealth—those are the five areas James breaks down throughout this book. ◼

▶ What are some ways you can be a light in this dark world?

▶ Can you remember any times of great testing in your life? What about tempting?

▶ After you became a believer, did you notice any change in your actions? If so, what specifically happened?

▶ What type of good deeds could you do tomorrow to bless those around you?

▶ Can you think of a time when you wish you would have either spoken up or kept your mouth shut? If so, what happened?

▶ What are some ways you can teach yourself to speak words of life instead of death?

▶ Do you typically use wisdom from above or from below? Are you alright with that?

▶ How do you think we can be heavenly minded during difficult times?

▶ Out of the five themes we just looked at in the book of James, which would you like to improve on? Why? What are some things you can do today to begin the improvement process?

AUTHOR
The author of 1 Peter is the apostle Peter, the leader of the twelve disciples. Peter was one of Jesus's favorite disciples, even though he denied Jesus three times.

DATE
Peter likely wrote this first letter around AD 64 near the beginning of Nero's persecution of Christians. So who was Nero and what was his deal?

Nero was the Roman Emperor that reigned from AD 54–68. He was an average emperor at the beginning of his reign, but things took a turn for the worse around AD 64 during the Great Fire of Rome. Rome's citizens blamed him for starting the fire because they knew he had grand plans for the city. Nero, however, blamed the fire on the Christians. From then on, persecution of Christians ramped up in disgusting ways, as Nero did anything to gain popularity. He would torture Christians by crucifying them, using them as entertainment in fights against lions, and most horrifically, soaking them in oil and impaling them on poles in his garden to be burned as torchlights for his dinner parties.

Rome was anything but a pretty sight for Christians. Word was getting out among churches all over the Greco-Roman world, so Peter wrote to them in preparation for what was to come. He knew he would be crucified eventually, so this was one of his last forms of contact with them.

AUDIENCE
Peter wrote this letter to the Twelve Tribes of the Dispersion spread out around Asia Minor. Remember, Paul was the missionary to the Gentiles, while Peter was the missionary to the Jews.

REASON
Peter was writing to encourage believers to remain holy in their suffering and to submit to authority in hopes of sharing love and peace.

THEME
Suffer now and be taken care of later.

KEY VERSE
"And after you have suffered a little while, the God of all grace, who has called you to his eternal glory in Christ, will himself restore, confirm, strengthen, and establish you" (1 Peter 5:10).

SECTIONS
Our salvation (1:1–12), called to holiness (1:13–2:12), submission (2:13–3:7), our suffering (3:8–4:11), the urge for change (4:12–5:14).

KEY WORDS
Suffering, glory, hope, salvation

STORY OVERVIEW

First Peter is a book about persecution and warning for what was to come in the near future. As things get crazier in our world every day and Christians are persecuted more and more, this book is very relevant for us. As we saw in the Gospels, Jesus said there would be persecution and suffering for those who believed in Him. Jesus is worth more than the cost of any persecution we might suffer, and we can hold on to that promise until we meet Him.

Though persecution may come, Peter also teaches that we have been born into a royal priesthood. We are princes and princesses—*royalty*. So many times we fail to act like it because we don't want to appear conceited. That's garbage. God is saying you and I are royalty, so we need to believe what He says about us! We are a special group, a holy nation. Transforming our minds to accept this truth is crucial in understanding our identity.

Peter brings up the fact that we are the temple of God (see 1 Peter 2:5). We are His dwelling place on earth. That means He can now be anywhere that we are. Because God dwells within His children, we should be cautious about how we treat our bodies. Believers should be fit, joyful, peaceful, and walking in His strength and power.

Peter makes it clear that suffering is to be expected. It's part of the Christian life. But if your foundation is built on Jesus Christ, you will press on and be rewarded greatly later. Perseverance in our Christian walk is crucial, especially when society is doing everything that it can to veer us away from the cross.

Learning how to submit to authority is one way we can persevere. We are to pray for our governmental leaders whether we agree with their decisions or not. We should, however, stand up against their decisions when they go against Scripture. It can be tough to pray for people we don't agree with, but it is also one of the most humbling things we can do.

Throughout this letter, Peter makes it clear we are to suffer as Christ suffered. Think about the way Christ suffered and remember, no matter what kind of suffering you may experience now, you will be greatly rewarded in heaven for all eternity. The best is yet to come!

Remember what we learned in Ephesians? We are in a battle every day, so of course the enemy is going to attack us. But we are *victorious* in Christ. Put on the armor of God daily so you can stand firm and fight back with God's weapons such as prayer, faith, love, God's Word, and the Holy Spirit. As relevant as 1 Peter is to this time and place, we are told that it is only going to become more and more relevant as time moves forward. ■

▶ In what ways have you experienced physical, spiritual, or mental persecution?

▶ Why do you think Christians are more likely to deal with persecution?

▶ How can your life reflect your title as royalty?

▶ How can we honor our government leaders even when we don't agree with some of their choices?

▶ Pick one person you know who is not a believer. Write out a prayer plan for them and how you want to see God move in their life:

▶ What did you learn from Peter that will help you the next time you deal with persecution?

"YOU ARE A CHOSEN RACE,
A ROYAL PRIESTHOOD,
A HOLY NATION, A PEOPLE
FOR HIS OWN POSSESSION."

1 PETER 2:9

2 PETER

AUTHOR
The second letter of Peter was also written by the apostle Peter.

DATE
Peter knew his death was right around the corner because of how bad the persecution of Christians had gotten in Rome. He likely penned this last letter around AD 66.

AUDIENCE
Peter is writing this letter to the same people his first letter was written to, the churches in Asia Minor.

REASON
Peter wrote this second letter because false teaching was at an all-time high, and their doctrine was becoming blurred. He is encouraging them to stick to the truth.

THEME
Watch out for false teachers.

KEY VERSES
"Therefore, dear friends, since you have been forewarned, be on your guard so that you may not be carried away by the error of the lawless and fall from your secure position. But grow in the grace and knowledge of our Lord and Savior Jesus Christ. To him be glory both now and forever! Amen" (2 Peter 3:17–18 NIV).

SECTIONS
Growth in truth (ch. 1), false prophets and teachers (ch. 2), the coming of judgment (ch. 3).

KEY WORDS / PHRASES
False teachers, truth, godliness, knowledge

STORY OVERVIEW

Second Peter has a layout similar to that of 1 Peter, in the sense that it focuses on salvation, warnings, and how to deal with what is ahead. Both letters focus on having a strong foundation so we will not be shaken.

Through God's promises, Peter writes, we can "become partakers of the divine nature" (1:4). Peter doesn't say that we become God, as Buddhism or New Age beliefs may suggest, but we are going from glory to glory, becoming more like Christ every day, as we read in 2 Corinthians 3:18.

Verses 1:5–7 list qualities that produce more fruit in our lives and more like-mindedness with Christ. They are virtue (moral excellence), knowledge, self-control, steadfastness (perseverance), godliness, brotherly kindness, and love. We should be striving to practice these qualities every single day.

When we get to Jude later on, you will realize that 2 Peter 2 is almost the same as Jude. Whereas the mockers are present in Jude, 2 Peter shows that they are in the future, so Peter most likely wrote first. It can be assumed that Jude and Peter were friends, since Jude was Jesus's brother. The same problems were present in both of their churches. Peter and Jude knew that if there was false teaching in the church, it would crumble from the inside out. That's why Peter is again emphasizing the importance of a strong foundation. If the people have a scriptural understanding of salvation, they will be able to discern between what is true and what is of the enemy.

For some odd reason, many churches today fail to acknowledge the Second Coming in their teachings. But that should be our hope for the future! Peter says that Jesus hasn't come back yet because He is allowing people more time to be saved. It isn't a bad thing at all. He wants as many people as possible in the kingdom, but He is giving them the choice. That way their love for Him will be pure.

In the New Testament epistles, there is a sense of urgency in gaining believers that has been lost in much of Christianity today. It all comes down to whether we have an eternal view of life.

When I studied 2 Peter for the first time, I thought it was a book I couldn't really relate to. When Peter talked about false teachers, that didn't click with me because I didn't think it was an issue in the church today—at all. Then I began to study some of the beliefs of various denominations and was shocked to realize there is false teaching going on EVERY-WHERE. I am blown away by how unbiblical some teachings are, yet people believe them because they don't know the Bible for themselves.

SUNSHINE

Well guess what:

- The belief that you must repent through another person is NOT biblical.
- The belief that miracles no longer happen is NOT biblical.
- The belief that the Holy Spirit is no longer relevant is NOT biblical.
- The belief that child baptism covers you for life is NOT biblical.

There are many things taught in some churches today that are flat-out lies, but you wouldn't know that unless you knew the truth. That's why I am so proud of you for taking the time to dive into the Word this year and learn for yourself what is and what is not of God.

We have the two greatest gifts in the world available 24/7: the Holy Spirit and the Bible. Don't let a day slip away without taking advantage of each of them. Spend some time in prayer this week thanking God for providing you with the desire to study His Word. Also, ask Him to open your eyes to see what is from Him and what is a lie that has masqueraded as truth in your life. ▪

▶ Read 2 Peter 1:5–7. What can you do today to increase in each of those qualities? Make a list of what you need to improve on:

▶ How can you respond to people who make fun of your beliefs or mock you?

▶ What are some things you can do to have more of an eternal mindset in your day-to-day life?

AUTHOR

The apostle John wrote all three letters at the end of his 30-year residence in Ephesus.

DATE

These three letters were written before John's death in AD 98 and after he wrote his Gospel, making it around AD 90–95.

AUDIENCE

John's first letter was written to the churches in Asia Minor, surrounding where he lived in Ephesus. He had an amazing relationship with all the churches after being there for thirty years, and they were all in true fellowship with one another.

REASON

John wrote this first letter to focus even more on fellowship within their communities, to teach them more about sin, to confirm their salvation, and to discredit any false teaching that was infiltrating the area.

THEME

Security in eternal life.

KEY VERSE

"I write these things to you who believe in the name of the Son of God, that you may know that you have eternal life" (1 John 5:13).

SECTIONS

Walk out light (ch. 1–2), walk out love (ch. 3–4), walk out confidence (ch. 5).

KEY WORDS

Fellowship, sin, light, love, truth

1 JOHN (LETTERS OF JOHN)

STORY OVERVIEW

As is apparent in this letter, John sees things in a very black-and-white manner. Everything in life falls into one of two categories: It's either good or evil. You are influenced by both and can choose which one you want to focus on. As we saw in the Gospel of John and will see in Revelation, John always writes in sevens. He knows the divine importance of the number and follows that structure throughout his main points.

In this letter, he looks at seven main contrasts:

- Light and darkness
- Truth and lies
- Loving the Father and loving the world
- Life and death
- Children of God and children of the devil
- Love and hate
- Good works and bad works

What happens to darkness when you flip on a light? It disappears. It is the same with Christ. We know that He IS light and since He is inside us then we also are light. That is a profound revelation. That means whenever we go into a dark area, it is no longer dark because Christ in us dispels the darkness. Having that realization should develop confidence for the next time you are in a place that lacks the presence of God. We can overpower any tactic the enemy uses against us, based on Jesus's shed blood and who we are in Christ. That's amazing stuff right there.

John goes on to tell the reader to love the Father and not the world, meaning the world system. The world is full of lust, pride, greed, and unrighteous-ness, while the kingdom of the Father is full of life, light, love, joy, peace, goodness, etc. We are given the choice to decide which we will follow. The right answer for us is to walk in our true citizenship of heaven. When we walk in the way of our Father instead of the world, that is when heaven really comes to earth. It isn't easy, though. The opposition from this world is strong, but we can be confident and bold because Christ is in us and goes with us.

John then dives into a topic that is highly debated and seems to contradict many teachings in the church today; 1 John 3:9 says, "No one born of God makes a practice of sinning, for God's seed abides in him; and he cannot keep on sinning, because he has been born of God." I don't know about you, but I can definitely still sin. The issue here is about living in sin and continuing to practice sin even when you know it's wrong.

The life of a Christian is about the process called sanctification we explored in Galatians. It's the work the Holy Spirit does in our lives internally. When I decided to start pursuing Christ with all of my heart, He had some serious cleaning up to do. I felt like a punching bag, getting swung left and right to change my thoughts and desires personally, professionally, and relationally. I admit that I still struggle with changing, but the intensity of the battle has decreased as I have become more and more like Jesus. That's what John is getting at. The closer you get to Christ, the less sin will impact your day.

Our desire should be to become more Christlike. If you are truly pursuing Him, then there should be visible signs of progress. As a new creation walking by the Spirit, it is not natural for us to sin anymore. The seed of God inside us contradicts the influence of the devil on the outside of us. Sin is no joke, and God doesn't take it lightly. We must redirect our focus to allow Him to do work inside of us and be used for His greater purpose.

Verse 3:8 says, "The reason the Son of God appeared was to destroy the works of the devil." With Christ in us, that is one of our purposes today. On our job. At our school. In our love life. We are called to destroy the works of the devil. Everything in life for a believer comes down to four letters: L-O-V-E. Love for God and love for others. That should be the motive behind everything we do. Paul also preached heavily on this love in 1 Corinthians 13.

John says that we are to love in "deed and truth," not in "word or talk," in verse 3:18. And in verse 4:8 he states that "God is love." I actually have that tattooed on my forearm, but I didn't really understand what it meant until a year after I got it. John doesn't say "God loves," he says that God IS love. God can only BE love. He is the Father, Son, and Holy Spirit, all in one. In perfect harmony. In loving nature. There is no judgment between them, no jealousy, no pride. The Trinity moves in the essence of love. God thought this love so good He wanted to share it with others, because He is selfless. That's why we were created. So humanity could share in the love of God. And when you know the true love of the Father, you understand why He wanted to share it. That's what John is telling us to do: share it.

John wants us to have confidence in our new nature. We are living on the opposite end of the spectrum from what we used to know. Life really might be just as black and white as John makes it out to be. There's good and evil. Pick a side. ▪

LIGHT
TRUTH
GOOD
LOVE FATHER
GOOD WORKS
SPIRIT
LOVE

▶ What does it mean to be a citizen of heaven while here on earth?

▶ Read 1 John 3:9. What are your thoughts on this statement?

▶ What has the Holy Spirit called you to give up during your sanctification process?

▶ In what ways can you destroy the works of the devil?

▶ What are some ways to love in deed and truth?

▶ What do you think "God is love" means?

AUDIENCE

The audience of 2 John is widely debated because he does not specify who the "elect lady and her children" in the greeting are. That leaves it up to you to decide between three main options:

First, John could be writing to an unknown woman who has her own house church, most likely in Ephesus.

Second, John could be writing to a church as a whole and its members. The "elect lady" would be the church itself, her "children" could be the members, and her "sister" could be another church.

Third, which is rarely taught but makes the most sense to me, is that John was writing to Mary, the mother of Jesus. Mary would have been known as an "elect lady" considering she was the mother of Jesus Christ. We know she had other children and a sister. Also, John was told by Jesus to look after her, which would be in line with the topic of this letter.

But we don't know for sure, and it isn't that important.

REASON

John writes as a warning against showing hospitality to false teachers.

THEME

Hospitality.

KEY VERSE

"If anyone comes to you and does not bring this teaching, do not receive him into your house or give him any greeting" (2 John 10).

SECTIONS

Love others (vv. 1–6), be cautious (vv. 7–13).

KEY WORDS

Love, abide, antichrist, teaching

(LETTERS OF JOHN)
2 JOHN

3 JOHN

(LETTERS OF JOHN)

AUDIENCE
John wrote his third letter to a man named Gaius who had a house church somewhere in Asia Minor.

REASON
John wrote to encourage Gaius in his love for hospitality, to deal with the pride of Diotrephes, and to tell them to accept the teaching of Demetrius.

THEME
Be accepting of other believers.

KEY VERSE
"Therefore we ought to support people like these, that we may be fellow workers for the truth" (3 John 8).

SECTIONS
To Gaius (vv. 1–8), about Diotrephes (vv. 9–10), about Demetrius, and final greetings (vv. 11–15).

KEY WORDS
Truth, testimony, good, evil

STORY OVERVIEW

Second and Third John are small, nearly identical letters that are written to a woman and a man. Each needed to be written from a different angle, considering the different ways men and women think. The main issue for both was hospitality.

In Second John, the key verse is 10, which says, "If anyone comes to you and does not bring this teaching, do not receive him into your house or give him any greeting."

John writes to the elect lady as a warning against showing hospitality to false teachers. That's about it for this letter.

In Third John, the key verse is 8, which says, "Therefore we ought to support people like these, that we may be fellow workers for the truth."

John is telling the recipients of his second and third letters how to be better at showing hospitality. The woman needed to be more cautious, and the man needed to be more open. There were many missionaries traveling the Greco-Roman world, and they were dependent on the hospitality of other believers. That situation allowed for false teaching to spread because oftentimes anybody who was a "believer" was accepted.

In the third letter, John calls out Diotrephes for being too prideful about accepting authority and for not showing hospitality to anybody who came to his door. Diotrephes's lack of hospitality meant the church was missing out on great truths and testimony. One good testimony was that of Demetrius, so John charges them to pay attention to him. ■

God is Love.

▶ Who is the most hospitable person that you know? Why?

▶ How can you be more hospitable to other believers?

▶ Pick an area you would like to grow in most from those we looked at in these three books: being light, loving the Father, not practicing sin, loving others, or being hospitable. Now put together a POA (plan of attack) for how you will grow over the next month or two.

You can follow this example:

I want to focus on becoming more holy (not practicing sin). In order to do so

- I am going to spend thirty minutes in a quiet time every morning, praying and meditating on Scripture.
- One of my prayers will be, "Lord, make me holy as you are holy. Whatever that looks like on my part. Sanctify me."
- Every time I deliberately sin, I am going to align my heart with the Father's immediately, to raise my awareness of sinning in the first place.

JUDE

AUTHOR
The author of Jude is "Jude, a servant of Jesus Christ and brother of James" (1:1). That would make both Jude and James half-brothers of Jesus.

DATE
Jude was written shortly before or after 2 Peter, but before the destruction of the temple in AD 70, likely making it between AD 67 and 69.

AUDIENCE
Jude most likely wrote to believers from the Dispersion who were possibly located in Antioch, since it was a hub and easily accessible for false teachers.

REASON
Jude wrote because false teachers were influencing the church and causing believers to stray. Jude is encouraging them to stay strong and fight for their faith.

THEME
Contend for the faith.

KEY VERSE
"Beloved, although I was very eager to write to you about our common salvation, I found it necessary to write appealing to you to contend for the faith that was once for all delivered to the saints" (Jude 3).

SECTIONS
Denouncing false teachers (vv. 1–16), the proper response (vv. 17–25).

KEY WORDS / PHRASES
Contend, false teachers, ungodly, godliness, judgment

STORY OVERVIEW

Jude is a book that many people skip over because they don't understand the importance of it. Honestly, it is a pretty strange one. If you compare it to 2 Peter 2, it's almost the same letter. Jude addresses a few problems the audience is facing, which began with a group of false teachers who were teaching that you could abuse grace, saying that once you were saved you could sin all you wanted and it didn't matter. That's not the Father's heart at all.

Yes, grace covers us when we mess up, but our lifestyle should no longer reflect a life of sin. We are new creations and have the power inside us to live righteously, to go from glory to glory.

The false teachers were teaching that Jesus was not the ONLY way to heaven, but just ONE of the ways. I don't need to explain that one. You know Jesus is the only way.

Jude compares what is happening in these churches to Israel with the golden calf in the wilderness, the Nephilim, and Sodom and Gomorrah.

Jude also likens the false teachers to Cain, Balaam, and Korah. He's pretty savage, actually. The situation was crumbling, and Jude makes it clear the people need to reject these false teachers and change their ways quickly, otherwise they will crash and burn. Jude truly cared about their salvation and knew what would happen to them if they didn't stick to the truth.

The sole focus needs to be on following Scripture and modeling the Father's heart toward those who have been deceived. That means approaching the situation in a loving yet firm manner. We need to make the truth known, but our actions must flow from a heart of love.

Jude begins characterizing the false teachers as "ungodly." He actually uses that word four times in two verses to describe them. Their godlessness was a mockery of godliness. Talk about a fitting topic! The church today is constantly being mocked in our culture. We have become the brunt of society's jokes. God tells us in His Word that this would happen, though, so we can't be too surprised or get too upset when it does.

One thing Jude makes clear is that we are to contend for the gospel. We must fight and stand up for the truth. Jesus is the way, the truth, and the life; nobody comes to the Father except through Him (see John 14:6). No matter what your peers say, if you remain focused on your relationship with Jesus, then you will always be on solid ground.

As things get crazier and crazier in the world, we must be prepared to stand up for the truth no matter what comes at us. One way to contend for the faith is by memorizing Scripture, holding on to those truths, and sharing them with others. Knowing what God says about himself and about you will serve as great support when things begin to heat up. ▓

▶ Which Scriptures would you use to combat the false teachings we see here?

▶ Jude compares what is happening with these churches to Israel with the golden calf in the wilderness, the Nephilim, and Sodom and Gomorrah. Can you recall what happened in all of those instances?

Golden calf (Exodus 32):

Nephilim (Genesis 6:4):

Sodom and Gomorrah (Genesis 19):

▶ Jude likens the false teachers to Cain, Balaam, and Korah as examples. Do you remember what those three people did?

Cain (Genesis 4):

Balaam (Numbers 22; 2 Peter 2:15):

Korah (Numbers 16):

▶ How would you deal with false teachers in your church today?

REVELATION

AUTHOR
The author of Revelation is the apostle John, who also wrote the Gospel of John and three epistles.

DATE
Revelation was written toward the end of John's life and after his other writings, putting it sometime in the mid-90s AD.

AUDIENCE
According to Revelation 1:11, John is writing this book "to the seven churches, to Ephesus and to Smyrna and to Pergamum and to Thyatira and to Sardis and to Philadelphia and to Laodicea."

REASON
John wrote the book of Revelation to show the completion of God's plan.

THEME
The current church and its future.

KEY VERSE
"Write therefore the things that you have seen, those that are and those that are to take place after this" (Revelation 1:19).

SECTIONS
Past (ch. 1), present (ch. 2–3), future (ch. 4–22).

KEY WORDS
Church, Jesus, judgment, Satan, nations

STORY OVERVIEW

After reading Revelation, it wasn't as daunting a task as people make it seem, was it?

Revelation has a strange stigma attached to it that causes many people to steer clear of attempting to read it. Yet it is the only book in the Bible that promises a blessing upon the reader, which is super interesting to me.

Yes, some of the visions may seem weird to us because they aren't the type of thing we see every day in the natural realm. That's because Revelation is what we call *apocalyptic* writing. It looks into the future from the spiritual realm instead of the natural. It's the future as God sees it.

Revelation completes the story of redemption. We can hold on to the hope for a better tomorrow based on what God's Word says about the future. This is His promise of what will one day be our reality.

Before we look at the text more closely, let's do a quick eschatology overview. The two major views of eschatology are *amillennialism* and *premillennialism*.

Amillennialism is a symbolic interpretation of the millennium; the amillennialist doesn't believe that Jesus will have a literal thousand-year earthly reign or that there will be a rapture.

Premillennialism is a literal interpretation and holds that Jesus will have an earthly reign with a rapture of Christians.

Speaking of the rapture, there are three major views on that as well: *pre-tribulation, mid-tribulation, and post-tribulation*.

Pre-tribulation: There will be a rapture of Christians sometime before the time of tribulation.

Mid-tribulation: The rapture will take place halfway through the tribulation when the Antichrist breaks the peace treaty with Israel.

Post-tribulation: Christians will live through the tribulation period and be taken away right at the end of the world.

And that's all if you believe there will be a specific time of tribulation.

On top of that, there are four main views on how to interpret Revelation: *preterist, historicist, futurist, and idealist*. Many in the church in America for the last hundred years have believed the futurist view, which is what the *Left Behind* series was born out of. But a lot of the early church and church fathers held more of an idealist view. I've been studying both lately, and everyone has a different opinion on what is to come. I'm learning just like you are learning.

I encourage you to research all these views more in depth, instead of just thinking about the *Left Behind* series and what your church may teach on the subject. My views on all of it have changed over time, and the truth of the matter is that some things in Scripture we won't know until they actually happen. There are great arguments on all sides and it's okay to disagree with other people's views. At the end of the day, one view may be right and one view may be wrong, but it shouldn't influence our salvation. We should all be sharing our testimonies and preaching the gospel no matter what happens. So

definitely do some research, look at what the early church believed, review different commentaries, and have fun with it.

Now, we saw that the key verse, 1:19, gives an overview of the entire book. John is told to "Write therefore the things that you have seen, those that are and those that are to take place after this."

Chapter 1 is that which he has seen, chapters 2 and 3 are the seven churches, which were currently there, and chapters 4–22 are what is to come after the time of the churches.

In chapters 2 and 3, John is told what to tell the seven main churches in Asia Minor at the time. Not only were the churches dealing with their own particular issues, but all the churches showed evidence of spiritual issues that the church as a whole has dealt with throughout history. Some scholars believe that each of the churches mentioned in Revelation represents a different period in church history, which would most likely place us in the seventh and final church, Laodicea, which deals with lukewarm faith.

> The church of Ephesus had left their first love behind.
> The church of Smyrna was on the verge of suffering great persecution.
> The church of Pergamum was dealing with the influence of false teaching and pagan idolatry.
> The church of Thyatira was being led astray by a Jezebel spirit inside the church.
> The church of Sardis had become deadened to their faith.
> The church of Philadelphia had persevered and held tightly to God's promises.
> And the church of Laodicea was lukewarm, neither cold nor hot.

John is told to critique each of the churches in order to build them up into the holy church they were created to be, not to discourage them. We can apply that today. For example, I used to get offended when people would critique my work or thinking, but they were really just trying to make me a better, holier person.

When we get to chapter 4, John is now in heaven with all seven of the churches and everyone is in full-on worship mode. John gives us a great description of what was happening in the throne room and who was present. He introduces us to a group of twenty-four elders who are ruling alongside Christ. There are also the four creatures we saw both in Ezekiel and Isaiah, who have different faces and six wings, and are full of eyes. And everyone is worshiping. Praising the King of Kings.

Next up, a scroll with seven seals is given to the Lamb that was slain, representing Christ as the ultimate sacrifice. The angels, creatures, and elders all exalted the Lamb with praise because the time had finally come to jump-start the beginning of the end—the seal, trumpet, and bowl judgments from chapters 6 through 16. Those chapters are very difficult to interpret because it is unclear when each of them will take place. But what we do know is that the judgments get worse as time moves on.

If you condense each judgment and look at them sequentially, it is easier to grasp what John says will happen during the end times.

First, The Seven Seals:

> The first seal brought forth the white horse with the Antichrist coming forth.
>
> Second seal: the red horse brought major wars.
>
> Third seal: black horse brought famine.
>
> Fourth seal: pale horse brought death.
>
> Fifth seal: displayed all of the martyrs during this time.
>
> Sixth seal: earthquake that caused terror throughout the world.
>
> Seventh seal: called for silence in heaven for thirty minutes, followed by the seven trumpet judgments.

Then we see the seven trumpets, which are part of the seventh seal:

1. Fire and hail mixed with blood. A third of the earth and trees were burned up, along with all of the grass.
2. A massive, flaming rock hurled into the sea. A third of the sea became blood; a third of the creatures died and a third of the ships were destroyed.
3. Star fell from heaven, hitting the earth's rivers and springs of water, turning the water bitter. Many men died as a result.
4. The sun, moon, and stars were all darkened, and daylight was decreased by a third.
5. Demons unleashed to torment unbelievers for five months.

6. A demonic army of 200 million horsemen were released to kill a third of humanity.
7. The kingdom of God reigns supreme after a major earthquake and hailstorm, introducing the seven bowl judgments.

Are you sticking with me? This is why it's confusing.

Later, we see the seven bowl judgments.

1. Sores appear on the flesh of unbelievers.
2. Every living thing in the sea dies.
3. Rivers and springs of water become blood.
4. The sun's heat is turned up, and scorches humanity.
5. The kingdom of Satan becomes darker, and the first bowl is intensified.
6. Water from the Euphrates is dried up, and the kings of the world assemble at Armageddon.
7. There is a major earthquake and a hailstorm.

As terrible as all of these things are, it is crucial to remember that God is just in all His judgments and ways. This judgment period will be the final chance for people to repent of their sins, be forgiven, and receive eternal life in Christ.

There is a pause in the story in chapters 10 and 11, between the sixth and seventh trumpets. John is asked to measure the temple, not including the outer court because that will be handed over to the Gentiles for forty-two months. He is also told about the two witnesses who will preach throughout the earth and be given authority from God for 1,260 days (aka 42 months or three and a half years). The authority

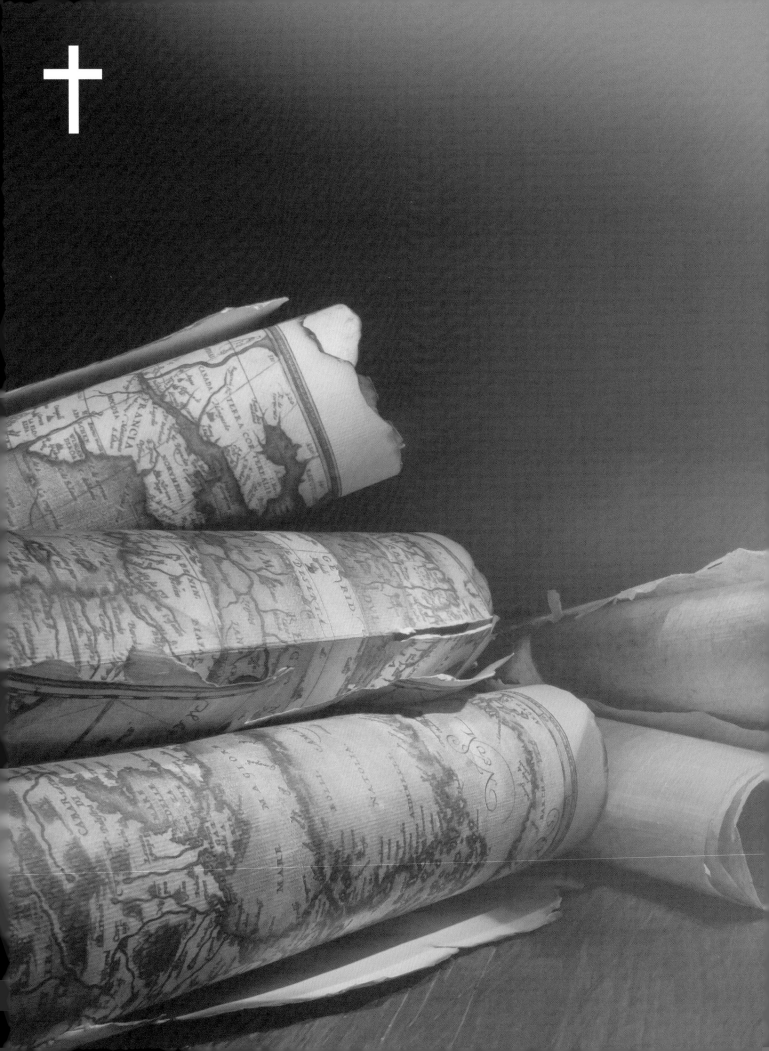

new

the witnesses have been given allows them to pour fire from their mouths, to shut up the sky so that it doesn't rain, to turn the water into blood, and to strike the earth with various plagues. After they preach for forty-two months, the Antichrist will finally be given permission to kill the two witnesses. After doing so, he leaves their bodies in the street so everyone in the world can see his "power over God." Three and a half days later they rise from the dead and ascend into heaven, giving every witness of this miracle another reason to repent.

This is such a great picture of the Father's heart. He truly does want every person to surrender themselves to Him and accept His salvation.

In chapter 12, John is given a strange vision of a woman who has a male child, and a dragon is trying to eat the child. What?!

Let's break it down a little bit:

> The woman is an image of Israel, the people of God.
> The male child is Jesus.
> The dragon is Satan.

Now that we have that understanding, the story makes a lot more sense.

It is an entire summary of God's plan of redemption for His people, and it includes the enemy trying to thwart God's plan. It is a vision of the past as well as a prophecy for the future.

During the time of persecution of the woman, the dragon calls on two beasts to take over: one from the sea and one from the earth.

Both are influenced by Satan for forty-two months.

They are what are commonly called the Antichrist and the False Prophet. A large amount of deception will come from these two leaders because they will portray themselves as peaceful people. The False Prophet will even be able to perform miracles, tricking many people into believing he is the Messiah. These two will convince people to receive the "mark of the beast," which is a pledge of allegiance to their cause. If you do not have the mark, you will not be able to buy or sell anything.

Next up is the famous Battle of Armageddon that people have been talking about for ages. It is a time when the kings of the south, north, and west all go into battle with each other, only to be attacked by the kings of the east and eventually defeated by Jesus himself. Remember the big earthquakes we saw in the seventh seal, trumpet, and bowl judgments? Chapters 17–18 are about that time. It's the final destruction of Babylon. The entire Bible has been a tale of two cities: Jerusalem and Babylon.

We saw the woman who represented Israel in chapter 12, and now we see the mother of the harlots, which is Babylon. One issue that we see today is that Babylon is no longer a major city.

In chapter 17, the woman is shown riding a beast that has seven heads and ten horns. In comparison to the prophecies in Daniel, we know that the horns represent governments or political figures. The beast is clearly empowered by Satan and will do what is necessary to wipe out Christians and Jews alike. It's the age-old battle of good versus evil. God verses Satan.

When interpreting this section, things may become clearer if you look at who wants to destroy Christians and Jews. The battle between good and evil will NOT last forever.

Jesus will come down for the second time and take over completely, which also brings up a very controversial part of Scripture: the millennium and whether or not there will be a physical thousand-year earthly reign of Christ.

According to Scripture, Jesus will come down and reign on earth for a thousand years, from His temple in Jerusalem. After this thousand years, the devil will be released for a short time and will try to convert more people to his side. But he will be defeated again in the final battle and sent to hell for eternity. Scripture shows us that the millennial reign will be a time of abundant harvest for everyone, that the Lord will be physically present with us, that sin will still be present, and that people will have a choice as to who they want to follow.

After the millennium, every unbeliever will be judged for their sin, and every believer will be rewarded for their works. Each will go their separate ways for the rest of eternity.

Then it is out with the old and in with the new. God will put the new heaven and the new earth in place and set everything back to His original intent. We will be in communion with God 24/7. Free from sin. Covered in goodness. The events that take place during the church age in Revelation are not ones to be taken lightly. They are God's judgment on humanity. We can waste time debating what is going to happen and when it will happen, or we can see this book as a warning and as our hope.

We know there are ups and there are downs. There is back-and-forth. Satan wants to win. But so does God. And in the end, He will.

Seven is the number of perfection. It shows completeness. So it only seems right that to have the perfect ending, the events leading up to it take place in sevens—seven seals, seven trumpets, and seven bowls.

Many would state that God's judgment in Revelation is torture for those who didn't follow Him. That is a blatantly false assumption. God's judgment is an act of love. It's a second chance. Amidst judgment, God's granting more time for repentance. For people to fall on their knees before Christ and receive Him as Savior and Lord. God's wrath shows His true heart.

God doesn't want us to spend eternity in hell. He eagerly desires for every person to spend eternity in the new heaven and the new earth. This was His plan all along—it wasn't for people to suffer eternally. But God loves us and gives us a choice. We can choose Him or not. He didn't create us to be robots. But rather He desires a relationship with us. He loves us that much—just look at the cross. ■

▶ How did you feel about Revelation before reading it vs. after reading it? Why do you think so many people choose not to study it?

▶ Do you believe this book is meant to be studied literally or symbolically?

▶ Do you subscribe to any specific view of the end times?

▶ In chapter 1 alone there are twenty-four titles or descriptions of Jesus Christ. In all of Scripture there are more than 200. What titles of Jesus can you think of?

▶ How do you handle criticism? Can you relate to any of the seven churches? If so, what does John suggest you do regarding a negative trait?

► Everyone is worshiping, praising the King of Kings in heaven. How does worship currently influence your life?

► Now that you have studied the entire Bible, how do you justify God's wrath during the end times, even though He is a God of love?

► What do you think the mark of the beast will be? Why do you think it is placed on your right hand or forehead?

► What do you think the new earth will be like? What will we eat? What will we do?

CONCLUSION

THE BIBLE STUDY

THE BIBLE STUDY

Congratulations!

You made it! You just accomplished something that most believers have never done—studied the entire Bible, front to back. But YOU did. I am so proud of you, and I know that God is too.

Before we say our goodbyes, there is one final thing I would like you to do—use the next page to explain the Gospel message in an easy-to-understand way that you can use for evangelism.

Matthew 28:19 says, "Go therefore and make disciples of all nations, baptizing them in the name of the Father and of the Son and of the Holy Spirit." Now that you know the Word better, go and share it! Make disciples! Spread the LOVE of our Father!

May God bless you all.

—Z

How to Share the Gospel

Sharing your faith with others can be awkward. We get that. So we broke it down into three easy steps to help you start sharing the gospel today.

> **Step 1: Understand the gospel.** Why is it called "good news"? And why should it be shared?
>
> **Step 2: Listen before you speak.** What does your friend currently believe?
>
> **Step 3: Live it out.** Does your life reflect the message you want to share?

Step 1: Understand the gospel. Why is it called Good News? And why should it be shared?

As we learned earlier in this study, when we read the word *gospel* in the New Testament, it means good news. The New Testament was originally written in Greek. So this word *gospel* is in Greek *euangelion*. It's where we get the word *evangelist*. But our focus here is the Good News.

So why is the gospel Good News? Well, you have to start by looking at the bad news. As a reminder, in the Old Testament, we learn about a man named Moses. Now in Moses's day, the nation of Israel, God's chosen people, were in slavery in Egypt. God ends up using Moses to set the people free from slavery through a bunch of miracles.

Once the people were free, God gave them what we know as the Law. Yes, the Law was a bunch of rules to follow, but that was because of our sin nature at the time, and God wanted us to live to higher standards. So it was more of a manual on how to live a holy life. The Law stated that the only way to be fully cleansed from sin was through the sacrifice of an innocent life. To us that sounds crazy, but at the time, that was part of the culture. Eventually the nation of Israel fell away and lost sight of the Law.

Then we get into the New Testament, and Jesus enters the scene, announcing that the kingdom of God is here and that God's reign over Israel was being restored. And it was going to be through Him. This was the Good News.

But the political people at the time didn't like Jesus's message because it threatened their status. Jesus was saying that God's kingdom was going to take over. So they killed Him. Little did they know that this sacrifice of an innocent, sinless life is exactly what needed to happen to cover the sins of anyone who believed in Jesus and the message He preached. But He didn't remain dead. Three days later He rose from the dead, proving that He was the true King and that God's kingdom reigned supreme.

And the best news of all is that Jesus offers to share this victory with us. We are no longer held down by the Law, but we can be free and can live for eternity in heaven and eventually a new earth. We can't earn our salvation; it's a free gift. That's the best news ever. That's the gospel. And it's our responsibility to continue spreading it.

Step 2: Listen before you speak. What does your friend currently believe?

Sharing your faith cannot be done without understanding where the other person sits. What are their views on God? Life? Religion? Have they had any good or bad experiences with other Christians?

Too often, Christians attempt to share their faith through passionately talking at people, but not with them. Sharing your faith begins with a healthy dialogue, which happens when you listen. But listening requires patience, empathy, discernment, and wisdom. When listening is done well, it results in the other person being heard. This is so important. Their responses should help equip you with what to say and what not to say. Don't force anything; keep it natural. It's okay if they don't believe right away—it could take years. Just stay patient and keep the conversation going.

Step 3: Live it out. Does your life reflect the message you want to share?

The most effective way you can share the gospel is by living it out. Let the Good News of your life be your witness. People notice when you live with a greater sense of hope, peace, joy, and patience. And we know that comes from our relationship with Jesus.

People love to see things in action, and sharing the gospel is no different. When your life aligns with your message, that's when people begin to listen. And living out the gospel is simple. Follow the lead of Jesus and let love be your guide. Remember that it's a marathon, not a sprint. Some people will take a long time just to understand why you believe what you believe, and others may never understand. Some will want exactly what you have. Your sole responsibility in following Jesus is to keep going and let God do the rest. You've got this, and the best is yet to come!

FAITH SAYS

HOLD ON

———

WHEN DOUBT SAYS

LET GO

NO OTHER NAME

JESUS

Shout-Outs

Gisela Windahl for teaching me what it means to love like Jesus.

Pete and T. Windahl for always inspiring me to chase my dreams, spending countless hours helping with this study, and for being my voice of reason.

Caleb Brose, Bree Graham, and Valentina Martinez for believing in our projects enough to keep pushing them forward with such passion.

Katlyn Hovland for making all our products look way cooler than I ever could.

Scott and Kelly McClintock, Jesse Roberson, Justin Satterberg, and Alex Kruse for testing out the content and allowing me to bounce my crazy ideas off of you.

Bryan Hunsberger, the staff, and all the students from my time in Australia. Each and every one of you impacted my life more than you will ever know and for that I am forever grateful.

And finally, shout-out to YOU for helping make this dream a reality.

About the Author

ZACH WINDAHL is a digital entrepreneur and author with a passion for creating
resources and products that help others
grow in their faith. He is the founder of The
Brand Sunday. Marrying his passion for
entrepreneurship and making faith simple
and attainable has landed Zach in a unique
place in the Christian landscape, where he
reaches hundreds of thousands of followers
on social media and thinks outside the cyni-
cal box that is so common in people today.
Zach lives in Orlando with his wife, Gisela,
and their mini bernedoodle, Nyla. Learn more
at ZachWindahl.com.